D0934336

THE AMERICAN ESTABLISHMENTS SERIES

EDWIN M. SCHUR, *general editor*

Each book in the AMERICAN ESTABLISHMENTS series examines a single, broadly defined "vested interest" in our society. The volumes focus on power and resistance to change in these American institutions, providing a radical reassessment of their future influence.

Pamela Roby, editor of this book, is currently an associate professor of sociology and community studies at the University of California, Santa Cruz. She is the co-author of The Future of Inequality and has edited Child Care—Who cares? Foreign and Domestic Infant and Early Childhood Development Policies.

THE POVERTY ESTABLISHMENT

edited by PAMELA ROBY

A SPECTRUM BOOK

PRENTICE-HALL, INC., *Englewood Cliffs, New Jersey*

Library of Congress Cataloging in Publication Data

ROBY, PAMELA A comp.
  The poverty establishment.

  (American establishment series)
  Includes bibliographical references.
  1. Poor—United States—Addresses, essays,
lectures. 2. Poverty—Addresses, essays, lectures.
3. Economic assistance, Domestic—United States—
Addresses, essays, lectures. I. Title.
HC110.P6R63   301.44′1   74–7422
ISBN 0–13–693705–5
ISBN 0–13–693697–0 (pbk.)

I wish to thank James P. Mulherin
for critically reading the first chapter of this volume
and for his helpful criticisms and suggestions
for the rest of the book.
I am also indebted to Fred L. Block, G. William Domhoff,
Matthew Edel, Richard England, Frances Fox Piven,
and Howard Wachtel for their assistance.
In addition, I wish to thank S. M. Miller,
the Union of Radical Political Economists,
and Edwin Schur for the various roles they played
in leading me to edit this book.

10 9 8 7 6 5 4 3 2 1

Printed in the United States of America

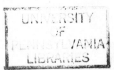

Contents

The poverty establishment

PAMELA ROBY

The poor have been researched so often that many are now demanding that social researchers leave them alone. Their caretakers—welfare workers and low-level poverty program officials—have also been studied, although not so frequently. But until very recently, the actual power structure that controls both the poor and their caretakers has been totally ignored by social scientists, journalists, and others. *The Poverty Establishment* brings together in one volume recent articles (two of which are previously unpublished) on the power structure that not only creates and maintains poverty programs to regulate the poor, but also preserves inequality by continuously generating schemes to increase the profits and power of the rich.

The Poverty Establishment is part of a series that includes *The Education Establishment, The Crime Establishment,* and *The TV Establishment,* among others. Articles pertaining to the poverty establishment may be found in other volumes of the series. Especially recommended is "Unequal Education and the Reproduction of the Social Division of Labor" by Samuel Bowles in *The Education Establishment.*

The processes that these chapters describe relate to processes occurring throughout the world, for today *multi*national rather than national corporations are the basic unit of our capitalist economy. The imperialist actions of these corporations exacerbate poverty and inequality among people and nations around the world much as they do in the United States.

The Poverty Establishment will show how wealth and poverty are intricately related. More specifically, it will describe how in the United States the wealthiest class has quietly created a billion-dollar establishment and social welfare state for itself while loudly advertising the few dollars it and the public (average- and low-income workers) donate to the poor.

The first section of *The Poverty Establishment* examines the maintenance of poverty and wealth in America from a long-term historical perspective. The second part surveys current government subsidization of the well-to-do through farm subsidies, tax allowances, and corporate subsidies, and explores the impact of governmental actions on corporate profits and individual wages. Part three investigates governmental programs that regulate the poor. The exploitation of poverty programs and the poor by large holding companies, and attempts by the poor to make their way by working within the corporate system are explored in part four. The articles in section five examine the causes of poverty within our affluent society. The final section analyzes the role social scientists have played in legitimating establishment poverty programs and other actions affecting the poor, and concludes with recommendations for steps social scientists and others could take to actually reduce poverty and inequality.

WHO IS THE ESTABLISHMENT?

How is the fate of the poor determined in the United States? The lives of the poor are shaped less by much-heralded poverty programs than by those factors in the U.S. economy that cause some to be poor and others to be rich in the first place. The features of our capitalist-social welfare state economy that have generated and continue to generate great inequalities in the distribution of resources in the United States will be discussed below in greater detail. First, however, it is worth noting that the 1972 mean per capita, before-tax income in America was $4,478.[1] For a family of four this came to an income of $17,912 or almost *$18,000*. In other words, *if income were distributed equally or even nearly equally in the United States, not one family or individual would be poor* (e.g., no family would have an income falling below the 1972 Social Security Administration's poverty line of $4,334 for a nonfarm family of four). Furthermore, the incomes of *eighty to ninety percent* of American families, which now fall below the $17,912 mean, would be increased.

Poverty programs are one means by which questioning of this grossly unequal distribution of resources is prevented. The chapters in this book reveal that the outlines of these programs are generally drawn by the upper echelon of the poverty establishment. In addition, local, state, and federal administrators of poverty programs and legislators—the lower echelon of the poverty establishment—are ultimately answerable to the upper echelon. The upper echelon consists of those who play a large role in shaping the distribution of income and the lives of the poor and others in this society—the multinational corporate

---

[1] Social and Economic Statistics Administration, Department of Commerce, Press Release BEA73-33, "Total and Per Capita Personal Income by States, 1972," May 1973. The high level of mean income in the United States was brought to my attention by an article by Bertram Gross, "A Closer Look At Income Distribution," *Social Policy* 3, no. 1 (May, 1972): 60.

elite. This elite circulates freely between the public and private sector, and sits not only on the boards of the multinationals but of foundations, hospitals, universities, and social service groups such as the Committee for Economic Development, the President's Income Maintenance Commission, the Urban Coalition, and Common Cause. This elite, which comprises the upper portion of the poverty establishment, also comprises the upper portion of the power structures of virtually all the other establishments discussed in this series.

Much has yet to be learned about this elite—top level managers, executives and members of the board of directors of major corporations who are among the wealthiest one or two percent of our population.[2] They are not easy to study. Unike the poor, they are guarded from the inquisitive by secretaries, lawyers, and the police. Furthermore, foundations and governments are not inclined to give funds for the study of the upper class. Despite the barriers, some work is currently being undertaken (in addition to the preliminary work cited or included in this volume on the power of the elite) to better understand interrelationships among,[3] and the patterns of influence of the elites.[4] Hopefully more will be forthcoming.

[2] In 1967, when the median annual income of families was $7,974, the average annual income of the top executives of the top 1,271 companies in six major types of business (manufacturing; retail trade; gas and electric utilities; life insurance; fire, marine, and causualty insurance; and commercial banking) was $110,000. In addition, most of these executives received executive bonus awards, executive stock options, deferred compensation, and executive pension benefits. U.S. Bureau of the Census, Department of Commerce, "Consumer Income," *Current Population Reports*, Series P-60, no. 75, December 14, 1970, table 9, p. 25; National Industrial Conference Board, *Top Executive Compensation* (New York: National Industrial Conference Board, 1969), p. 1.

[3] Joel H. Levine is undertaking an ongoing study of the interlocking directorates of major companies and banks. Cf. Joel H. Levine, "The Sphere of Influence," *American Sociological Review* 37 (February, 1972): 14–27. A Bureau of Applied Social Research Group has undertaken a survey of 546 "American leaders." The interview with each of the "leaders" included extensive data on their "involvement in the national issue he or she chose to discuss—including activities related to that issue, sources of information, perceptions of obstacles to the issue's solution, attempts to influence others. Whom he or she talked to and perceived as influential related to that issue—as well as opinion and background data." Among the preliminary findings are: 1) "influence among U.S. leaders . . . seems to include a rather narrow range of individuals and an even narrower range of institutions for a nation as the United States;" 2) the federal government is the focal point of both influence and discussion in attempts to alleviate a wide variety of national problems; no institution in or outside of the political sectors sees itself as able to deal with major societal problems without the resources of the federal government; the executive branch is more often credited with influence, while legislature is apparently more active in interaction." Gwen Moore Bellisfeld, "Preliminary Notes on the Influence Structure of American Leaders" (stencil, New York University, 1973), pp. 4, 37; cf. Allen H. Barton, "Sampling and Field Work for the American Leader-

The lower echelon of the poverty establishment includes persons in local, state, and federal legislatures; the U.S. Office of Economic Opportunity, the U.S. Departments of Labor, Agriculture, Housing and Urban Development, and Health, Education and Welfare; and foundations and voluntary associations that work on issues relating to the poor. They work under the elite described above. As administrators, members of the lower echelon of the poverty establishment have limited resources and limited decision-making or implementational power. Should they exceed the limits of the power granted to them, they are generally asked to resign or, as in the case of those in the U.S. Office of Economic Opportunity, find that their whole organization is "out of business." As legislators, they are daily bombarded by lobbyists who not only explain in detail the positions of corporate interests but offer to write congressional speeches and bills. Occasionally they find that corporate interest groups stage demonstration projects to illustrate proposed programs that they would like the government to fund.[5] Should legislators refuse these corporate services, which by virtue of corporate wealth far exceed the services and information that can be provided by representatives of poor and average citizens, they will be reminded of their actions when opposed in future elections by well-funded corporate candidates.

Administrators of local and federal poverty programs work, sometimes willingly and sometimes unwillingly, for the "Fortune 500" corporate elite.[6] Not all the members of the elite choose to actively shape policy; perhaps they don't need to as long as others of the upper class do. But most of those who do shape social policies in a major way are members of the elite.

---

ship Study" (unpublished paper, Bureau of Applied Social Research, Columbia University, August, 1972).

4 Cf. Judith P. Carter and Reginald K. Carter, "The Corporate Elite: Managers or Technicians?" New York City: The 68th Annual Meeting of the American Sociological Association, August 28, 1973.

5 For excellent analyses in addition to those included in this book on the influence of the elite on government social programs for the poor see Gabriel Kolko, *The Triumph of Conservatism* (Chicago: Quadrangle Books, 1963); James Weinstein, *The Corporate Ideal in the Liberal State 1900–1918* (Boston: Beacon Press, 1968); Martin J. Sklar, "Woodrow Wilson and the Political Economy of Modern United States Liberalism," in James Weinstein and David W. Eakins, eds., *For A New America: Essays in History and Politics* (New York: Random House, 1970); Anthony M. Platt, *The Child Savers, The Invention of Delinquency* (Chicago: University of Chicago Press, 1969); G. William Domhoff, "Chapter Six: How the Power Elite Shape Social Legislation," *The Higher Circles: The Governing Class in America* (New York: Random House, 1970); and G. William Domhoff, *Who Rules America?* (Englewood Cliffs, N.J.: Prentice-Hall, Inc., 1967).

6 See Linda Grant Martin, Sydney Ladensohn Stern, and Lenore Schiff, "The Fortune 500 Directory of the 500 Largest Industrial Corporations," *Fortune, Vol. 87,* no. 5, May 1973, pp. 220–247.

Their principles, ideologies, and actions generally resemble one another. This is not because of a conspiracy among them, although often they do discuss matters together, but because they have developed similar consciousnesses as a result of being similarly socialized and similarly positioned in the social and economic structure.[7] Occasionally, the wishes of this elite, the upper echelon of the poverty establishment, are thwarted; occasionally, they must pay more of their profits than they would like in order to keep the poor quiet and in their place. But to date, this elite has been extremely successful in maintaining inequalities and preserving its own supreme place. Their success will be documented in the following section on Inequality in America.

INEQUALITY IN AMERICA

Few statistics reveal as much about the operation of an economy as do those on income distribution. Although the levels of living that are possible in any society are prescribed by the size of the national product, a given output can be distributed in many different ways. It can provide palaces for live kings and pyramids for dead ones, but hovels and hunger for the mass of mankind; or it can be widely distributed and provide reasonably uniform levels for all.[8]

One would expect that Who gets what in the United States? would be a question of interest to nearly every American. Nevertheless, the distribution of income and wealth are seldom mentioned by major television networks and newspapers. The distribution of resources, although overlooked by the media, cannot be overlooked by persons concerned with poverty or with American society as a whole.

As noted above, if American incomes were distributed equally or nearly equally, America would have neither poverty nor a poverty establishment. Our unequal distribution of resources rather than a lack of resources has maintained poverty.

How is national income distributed among our nation's population when the population is ranked according to income?[9] How has this distribution changed over time? If income were distributed equally,

---

[7] Cf. Domhoff, *Higher Circles,* op. cit.

[8] U.S. Bureau of the Census. *Income Distribution in the United States,* 1969 Census Monograph prepared by Herman P. Miller (Washington, D.C.: Government Printing Office, 1966), p. 1.

[9] Today, these measurements of pretax income comprise the best single indicator of living standards in the United States. A more accurate approximation of well-being in the nation would involve, as Miller and Roby have pointed out, not only assessment of posttax incomes but also measurement of "assets, basic services, self-respect, opportunities for education and social mobility, and participation in many forms of decision-making." S. M. Miller and Pamela Roby, *The Future of Inequality* (New York: Basic Books, 1970), chapter 1.

each twenty percent of the people would get twenty percent of all income. Instead, in the U.S., the richest twenty percent of all families received *forty-two* percent of the income and the poorest twenty percent of all families only *five and one-half* percent of the income in 1971 (see chart 1). Looked at another way, we find that *the richest fifth enjoyed well over twice as much income as the combined income of the bottom two fifths of the family population.* Among unrelated individuals in the United States, the richest fifth get slightly more income (50.4 percent) than the combined income of the bottom four-fifths of the population (49.6 percent—see chart 1).

Looking back in history, one might have expected the distribution of income to have been equalized substantially during the period of post-World War II prosperity and during the War on Poverty of the sixties. It was not. Chart 2 illustrates that over the twenty-four year period from 1947 (the first year for which comparable census data are available) to 1971, a period of increasing economic sophistication, the share of income going to the poorest fifth of our nation's families never fluctuated more than one percentage point. In 1971, it was only one-half of one percentage point higher than in 1947. Throughout the period, the share of income going to the richest fifth was over *seven times* that going to the poorest fifth of our family population. The discrepancy between the share of national income going to the poorest and richest fifths of the population (and that between the middle and richest fifths) is likely to have grown during 1972 and 1973 as a result of inflation coupled with the administration's heavy controls on wages and welfare (the chief sources of income of the bottom four-fifths) and lack of control over profits (the chief source of income of the richest fifth).

The inequalities described above in the distribution of pretax income are often dismissed on the grounds that federal tax and spending patterns are highly redistributive. The actual distributive impact of federal policies needs to be researched much more thoroughly than it has been to date. Nevertheless, enough research has already been conducted for us to conclude that federal policies are not significantly progressive (they do not redistribute income downward) and that combined federal-state-and-local tax and spending policies may actually be regressive (they may redistribute income upward).[10] Economists

10 Because of the inadequacy of the data on the overall distribution of federal, state, and local taxes, opinion is divided concerning the redistributive effect of taxes in the United States. For 1961, the Tax Foundation reported: "For all taxes (federal, state and local), the cumulative distribution closely resembles the distribution of income, reflecting the essential proportionality of the total tax burden up to $10,000 income level." George Bishop, *Tax Burdens and Benefits of Government Expenditures by Income-Class, 1961 and 1965* (New York: Tax Foundation, 1967), p. 27. Cf. Richard A. Musgrave, *The Theory of Public Finance* (New York: McGraw-Hill, 1958); U.S. Congress, House, Committee on Ways and Means "How Progressive

Howard M. Wachtel and Larry Sawers have made the most comprehensive and current examination of the distributive impact of federal taxation and expenditure practices (see chapter three of this book).

Before we leave the question of how resources are distributed in America, it is important for us to ask who owns the nation's wealth—its corporate stock real estate, cash and bonds. Wealth has many useful attributes. It may provide its owner with considerable income without requiring him/her to expend labor or thought. Wealth, if consumed, will not continue to provide labor-free income, but will enhance its owner's well-being. Finally, wealth is an important source of power. It may be utilized to control corporate actions, to finance political campaigns to "sell" Presidents, to lobby national and local governments, and to influence the public through mass-media advertising and other techniques.

Wealth is more unequally distributed than income in the United States. Wall Street proponents often advertise that millions own the giant corporations by owning corporate stock. Indeed, in 1972, 32.5 million or slightly under one-fifth of the U.S. population owned corporate stock.[11] However, most stock is not owned by this seventeen percent of the population (itself not a terribly large proportion) but by a very small fraction of the population. The wealthiest *one* percent of the U.S. population owned *sixty-one* percent of all corporate stock in 1962. The University of Michigan Survey Research Center study by Dorothy Projector and Gertrude Weiss, which revealed this statistic, also showed that the wealthiest *one* percent of all U.S. consumer units (families and unrelated individuals) owned *thirty-one* percent of *all* U.S. wealth including corporate stock, real estate, cash, bonds, insurance, equity, pension fund reserves, and personal trusts. Most of the poor, in contrast, owed more than they owned. Unfortunately, the Projector-Weiss study has not been repeated since 1962 (again, studying the wealth of the wealthy is not a popular thing to do.)[12] Economist James

---

Is the Individual Income Tax?" *Tax Revision Compendium* 3 (Washington, D.C.: Government Printing Office, 1959); Joseph A. Pechman, *Federal Tax Policy* (Washington, D.C.: Brookings Institution, 1966); Henry Aaron and Martin C. McGuire, "Benefits and Burdens of Government Expenditures," mimeographed (Washington, D.C.: Brookings Institution, 1968); Robert Lampman, "How Much Does the American System of Transfers Benefit the Poor?" in Leonard H. Goodman, ed., *Economic Progress and Social Welfare* (New York: Columbia University Press, 1966); Robert Lampman, "Transfer and Redistribution as Social Process," mimeographed (Madison: University of Wisconsin, 1968); Lee Soltow, ed., *Six Papers on the Size-Distribution of Wealth and Income* (New York: National Bureau of Economic Research, 1969).

11 "Census of Shareholders," reported in *The Associated Press Almanac*, 1973, p. 584.

12 Dorothy Projector and Gertrude Weiss, *Survey of Financial Characteristics of Consumers* (Washington, D.C.: Federal Reserve System, 1966), pp. 110–14, 151. Cf.

CHART 1: PERCENTAGE SHARE OF AGGREGATE U.S. INCOME IN 1971
RECEIVED BY EACH FIFTH OF FAMILIES AND UNRELATED INDIVIDUALS,
RANKED BY INCOME

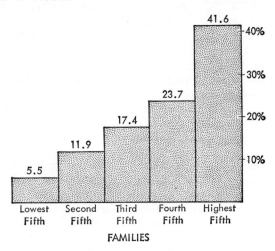

FAMILIES

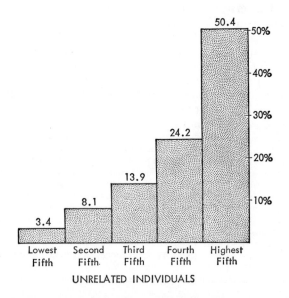

UNRELATED INDIVIDUALS

Source: U.S. Department of Commerce, Bureau of the Census, *Current Population Reports,
Consumer Income,* P-60, no. 85, December 1972, p. 38, table 14.

CHART 2: PERCENTAGE SHARE OF AGGREGATE U.S. INCOME IN 1947 TO 1971 RECEIVED BY LOWEST AND HIGHEST FIFTHS OF FAMILIES RANKED BY INCOME

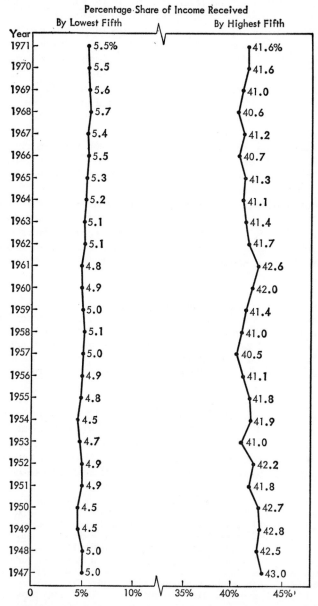

Percentage Share of Income Received

By Lowest Fifth — By Highest Fifth

Year	By Lowest Fifth	By Highest Fifth
1971	5.5%	41.6%
1970	5.5	41.6
1969	5.6	41.0
1968	5.7	40.6
1967	5.4	41.2
1966	5.5	40.7
1965	5.3	41.3
1964	5.2	41.1
1963	5.1	41.4
1962	5.1	41.7
1961	4.8	42.6
1960	4.9	42.0
1959	5.0	41.4
1958	5.1	41.0
1957	5.0	40.5
1956	4.9	41.1
1955	4.8	41.8
1954	4.5	41.9
1953	4.7	41.0
1952	4.9	42.2
1951	4.9	41.8
1950	4.5	42.7
1949	4.5	42.8
1948	5.0	42.5
1947	5.0	43.0

0   5%   10%   35%   40%   45%

Source: U.S. Department of Commerce, Bureau of the Census, *Current Population Reports, Consumer Income,* P-60, no. 85, December 1972, p. 38, table 14; and U.S. Bureau of the Census, *Trends in the Income of Families and Persons in the United States: 1947 to 1960,* Technical Paper No. 8 (Washington, D.C.: U.S. Government Printing Office, 1963), table 1, pp. 36–43.

D. Smith has estimated, however, that today we would be unlikely to find wealth any more equally distributed than in 1962.[13]

In addition to being an important source of power, wealth is also the *most* important source of *income* for people with high incomes. Although most people earn their livings through the expenditure of their labor and brainpower, the wealthy get *most* of their income by creaming off profits from the efforts of others. In 1970, for example, table 1 shows that 95.5 percent of the adjusted gross income of those with under $20,000 incomes (the vast majority of Americans) came from wages, salaries, and small business profits. In the same year, 56.9 percent of the income of those with over $100,000 incomes came from dividends, the sale of capital assets, and interest—e.g., pure "capitalist income," the result of simply investing inherited or otherwise previously accumulated money.

The inequalities portrayed in table 1 are striking. Nonetheless, the data in the table vastly understate the amount of inequality that actually exists. Although the Internal Revenue Service statistics reported in the table are the best available data on the source of income of people in different economic classes in the United States, we know these data exclude:

1) most income associated with business expenses including much travel and many dinners, parties and trips to the theatre (see table 1, footnote 2 for the definition of "adjusted gross income"), 2) one-half of some dividends and of all long-term capital gains (these are excluded because they are not taxable —a nice benefit to the wealthy), and 3) data on people whose incomes were beneath the amount requiring them to file an income tax return.

The 1969 Tax Reform Act which raised the income level at which a tax return had to be filed, alone resulted in 1,554,557 *fewer* returns being filed in 1970 than in 1969 (in 1970 the income level at which a tax return had to be filed was increased to $1,700 for a single person and $2,300 for a married couple entitled to file a joint return or a single person age 65 or over). The exclusion of millions of low-income

---

Robert Lampman, *The Share of Top Wealth—Holders in National Wealth 1922–1956* (Princeton, N.J.: Princeton University Press, 1962). In addition to personal wealth, wealth is held by foundations and pension funds. Foundations generally are established by and serve the interests of the wealthy (see chapter by Horowitz and Kolodney). In 1969, total pension fund assets amounted to $238 billion or less than ten percent of national wealth. Frank Ackerman, Howard Birnbaum, James Wetzer and Andrew Zimbalist, "Income Distribution in the Unitel States," *Review of Radical Political Economics* 3, no. 3 (Summer, 1971), p. 26.

13 James D. Smith, quoted in "Who Has the Wealth in America," *Business Week*, August 5, 1972, p. 55.

TABLE 1: SOURCES OF INCOME BY INCOME CLASS OF ADJUSTED GROSS INCOME REPORTED IN U.S. INCOME TAX RETURNS, 1970: DOLLAR AMOUNTS AND PERCENTAGE DISTRIBUTION*

| Size of Adjusted Gross Income:** | Number of Tax Returns | Sources of Income | | | |
		All Types	Wage & Salary	Small Business***	Capital Assets****
		Dollar Amounts (Billions of Dollars)			
Total all sizes	74,279,831	$631.7	$531.9	$53.9	$45.9
Under $20,000	70,255,573	497.0	448.6	26.5	21.9
$20,000–$50,000	3,595,590	97.2	69.8	17.0	10.4
$50,000–$100,000	350,978	23.1	9.9	7.7	5.5
Over $100,000	77,690	14.4	3.6	2.7	8.1
		Percentage Distribution			
Total all sizes		100.0%	84.1%	8.5%	7.4%
Under $20,000		100.0	90.2	5.3	4.5
$20,000–$50,000		100.0	71.7	17.4	10.9
$50,000–$100,000		100.0	42.9	33.1	24.0
Over $100,000		100.0	24.7	18.4	56.9

* *Source:* Calculated from U.S. Internal Revenue Service, Department of the Treasury, *Statistics of Income, 1970: Individual Income Tax Returns* (Washington, D.C.: U.S. Government Printing Office, 1972), table 4, pp. 14–16.

** Adjusted gross income is gross income minus all income subject to tax deductions such as the following: "ordinary and necessary expenses of operating a trade or business; employee business and moving expenses; expense deductions attributable to rents and royalties; expenses of outside salesmen attributable to earning a salary, commission or other compensation; depreciation and depletion allowed life tenants and income beneficiaries of property held in trust; exclusion of allowable sick pay if the sick pay was included in gross salary; deductible losses from sales of capital assets and other property; deductible half of the excess of net long-term capital gain over net short-term capital loss; business net operating loss carryover; and contributions to a retirement fund by the self-employed." Ibid., p. 278.

*** As calculated in this table, "small business" income included the following Internal Revenue Service categories of income: "business or profession," "farm," "partnership," "small business corporations," and "taxable portion of pensions and annuities." "Business or profession" comprised 4.8 percent, "farm" 0.4 percent, "partnership" 1.7 percent, small business corporations 0.2 percent and taxable portion of pensions and annuities 1.2 percent of total adjusted gross income.

**** As calculated in this table, "capital assets" included the following Internal Revenue Service sources of income: "sales of capital assets" (1.4 percent of total adjusted gross income), "dividends" (2.5 percent of total adjusted gross income), "interest" (3.4 percent of total adjusted gross income), "ordinary gain from sales of depreciable property (less than 0.1 percent of total adjusted gross income), "sales of property other than capital assets" (less than 0.1 percent of total adjusted gross income), "rents" (0.3 percent of adjusted gross income), "royalties" (less than 0.1 percent of adjusted gross income), "estates and trusts" (0.2 percent of adjusted gross income), and "other sources" (0.3 percent of total adjusted gross income).

individuals from our data distorts our distributional statistics by over-representing the percentage of our population with high incomes and vastly underestimating those with low income. These exclusions are straightforward and result in our underestimating the proportion of capitalist income of the wealthy. In addition, of course, no one can accurately estimate the extent to which those who file tax returns underreport their incomes.

In the paragraphs above, we have examined the distribution of income and wealth in America, and have found them to be highly unequal. Why is this so? Why are a few Americans so very wealthy, many very poor, and the majority just managing?

Generally and perhaps not accidently the *attributes* of the poor—inadequate education, old age, poor health, and so forth—have been incorrectly viewed as the *causes* of poverty. Throughout American history, the poor have been blamed for their own poverty in ways succinctly summarized by William Ryan in chapter nine. To correctly understand the causes of poverty, one must examine society, something which the rich and those to whom they give funds are naturally reluctant to do. When one begins to examine American society as Howard Wachtel has done in chapter ten, one finds that "poverty and inequality are the result of the normal functioning of the principal institutions of capitalism—labor markets, social class divisions and the state." In sum, Wachtel points out, an individual's wage—whether he or she is poor or middle class—depends on four types of variables, few of which are within his or her control:

1. Individual characteristics over which the individual exercises no control—age, race, sex, family class status, and region of socialization.

2. Individual characteristics over which the individual exercises some degree of control—education, skill level, health, region of employment, and personal motivation.

3. Characteristics of the industry in which the individual is employed—profit rates, technology, product market concentration, the relation of industry to government, and unionization.

4. Characteristics of the local labor market—structure of labor demand, unemployment rates, and rate of growth.

The importance of many of these variables in the determination of wages derives from the nature of our political economy. Health is one example. Ten percent of persons of working age with incomes below the poverty line did not work in 1971 because they were too ill or disabled to do so.[14] If the United States had health programs for its people similar to those of Israel or Sweden, its population would be healthier and many of its citizens who are now too sick to work would be able to do so.[15] Furthermore, economic status need not be linked to health and the ability to produce. A nation with the resources of the United States could assure all its people a decent living whether they are sick or healthy, regardless of their past or current contribution to the labor force.

The relation of industry to government is another example of the impact of our political economy on the distribution of wages. Barry Bluestone carefully examines the importance of government subsidization of industries to the wages of those industries in chapter eleven. He shows that when one holds individual characteristics of workers, the characteristics of their work and of their industry constant, government subsidies to the industry (or the lack of subsidies) significantly affect workers' wages.

Finally, many unemployed poor would like to work but cannot find adequate work, and many full-time workers in the United States have poverty-level wages. Twenty-five percent of all persons aged fourteen to sixty-four whose incomes were beneath the poverty line were employed full-time, year round in 1971; over fifty-one percent of black male family heads whose family income was below the poverty line were so employed. Thus, over three million people in the United States were poor despite working full-time, year round. Another fifteen percent of the poor did not work because they were in school. These people "earned" their poverty. Within our political and economic structure there was little else they could do to obtain a decent living.[16]

Individuals have no more control over nonwage than wage sources of income. The purely capitalist sources of income—dividends, capital gains and interest—accrue to individuals either through inheritances, a matter which they hardly control, or through the accumulation of savings from large wages stemming from the variables discussed above. Finally, many individuals gain small amounts of money and a few

[14] U.S. Bureau of the Census, Department of Commerce, "Consumer Income Characteristics of the Low Income Population, 1971," *Current Population Reports* P-60, no. 86, December 1972, table F, p. 6.

[15] For a discussion of Israeli and Swedish health programs, see Pamela Roby, ed., *Child Care—Who Cares? Foreign and Domestic Infant and Early Childhood Development Policies* (New York: Basic Books, 1973), chapters 19 and 26.

[16] U.S. Bureau of the Census, *Current Population Reports*, P-60, no. 86, op. cit.; Cf. David M. Gordon, *Theories of Poverty and Underemployment: Orthodox, Radical and Dual Labor Market Perspectives* (Lexington, Mass.: Heath-Lexington Books, Inc., 1972).

gain large amounts of money through government transfer payments. Low welfare payments and high federal subsidies to wealthy land-owners to not farm land that they never intended to farm, are deter-mined by many variables, most of which are political.[17] And in politics having wealth to begin with is a major asset.

INEQUALITY AND IDEOLOGY

WHY THE WELFARE STATE?

Viewing the poverty establishment as part and parcel of the overall capitalist system's establishment's effort to protect the holdings and in-crease the profits of a few rather than to alleviate inequality reduces the puzzlement that normally arises when one actually looks at the activities of poverty programs in the United States. American poverty programs have traditionally done nothing to reduce inequality. Edu-cation has been treated as a panacea for poverty although most of the poor are too old to benefit from school and although those who are of school age are taught in school only how to be obedient in low-wage, poverty-level jobs.[17] Housing programs for the poor are primarily concerned with not interfering with the housing industry and usually end up benefiting construction companies and contractors more than the poor. The occasional government and foundation programs that have appeared to actually benefit the poor have been miniscule and short-lived compared with those to benefit the rich.

The programs that have actually enhanced the well-being of the poor—swimming pools in low-income areas of New York, summer jobs that put money in the pockets of ghetto teenagers, and Head-Start, which gave low-income preschoolers better health and some fun; as opposed to useless-if-harmless programs—e.g., training programs for jobs that do not exist, community-action boards that have power to do nothing have been created only as a result of hard-won struggles by the poor. War on Poverty program proposals, which stressed the goals of keeping the streets cool and preventing revolution rather than shar-

17 John Hanrahan, "Wealthy Get Tax Breaks, Subsidies on 'Farmland'," *The Washington Post*, March 1, 1971, p. A1.

18 Cf. S. M. Miller and Pamela Roby, "Education: The Answer to Poverty?" *Dissent* 17, no. 2 (March, 1970): 177–82; Samuel Bowles, "Unequal Education and the Reproduction of the Hierarchical Division of Labor," in Richard C. Edwards, Michael Reich, and Thomas E. Weisskopf, eds., *The Capitalist System* (Englewood Cliffs, N.J.: Prentice-Hall, 1972); Colin Greer, *The Great School Legend: A Revisionist Interpretation of American Public Education* (New York: Basic Books, 1972); Michael B. Katz, *The Irony of Early School Reform: Educational Innovation in Mid-Nineteenth Century Massachusetts* (Boston: Beacon Press, 1970).

ing America's wealth were not a new phenomenon. Piven and Cloward in chapter one of this volume, and in their book, *Regulating the Poor,* demonstrate historically that since the existence of capitalism, relief-giving has been initiated or increased when there has been the need to stem political disorder, and decreased when there has been the need to enforce low-wage work during periods of economic and political stability. The latter type of period is illustrated by the early 1970s. Once large scale riots had subsided at the end of the sixties, one poverty program after another experienced severe cuts or was dissolved. These cutbacks in Head-Start, legal services, health care, community action, and many other programs were made at a time when rising unemployment and inflation were cutting ever deeper into the meager budgets of the poor.

In addition to keeping the poor quiet with minimal expenditures, America's patchwork welfare state enables upper middle-income and wealthy groups who have a genuine sense of *noblisse oblige* to live with themselves. It also, intentionally or unintentionally, tends to separate lower middle-income and working-class groups from the poor by making the former believe, often justifiably, that their own families are suffering as a result of being made to hand over some of their already small incomes to the poor. This feeling leads to hatred and battles between two economic groups that might logically be united in fighting for a larger share of the pie.

America's welfare state has failed to reduce inequalities and to eliminate poverty not because its programs are too small or inefficient. Nor is the problem that individual welfare workers or poverty program administrators—the lower echelon of the poverty establishment—do not try hard enough. Certainly, a sweet, hard-working welfare worker will be preferred by a low-income mother over a nasty, lazy one—but in either case, as Sol Stern describes in chapter five, both the worker and the client are caught in the capitalist wage system, and it is the workings of this system that often turn dedicated and energetic welfare workers into lazy, cynical ones. It is also this system that precludes programs that would actually eliminate poverty.

Although most poor would probably prefer the Johnson programs to the Nixon cutbacks, the former came far from providing a decent level of living for those on the lower end of our income distribution. Even during the War on Poverty years, many poor were excluded from minimal welfare state benefits; and few, if any, were comprehensively covered. None were guaranteed all of the following: adequate housing, good health and child care, secure income adequate to provide for food, clothing, and other familial needs; and a future toward which each child might look forward. Instead, a few received a little better health or child care but no improvement in their jobs, while others received slightly better jobs but experienced no improvement in social services.

Although America's welfare state programs have improved slightly the lot of the poor, they have failed to significantly reduce inequalities or poverty. Those in power never meant them to do so. The preservation of a capitalist political and economic system has been, to date, the primary goal of the establishment. Because the preservation of this system is the establishment's number one priority, the reduction of poverty is important only when poverty threatens the system; and the elimination of inequality is considered out of the realm of possibility, for inequality is intrinsic to the system.

INEQUALITY AND IDEOLOGY IN EVERYDAY LIFE

Today many ideological justifications, rationalizations, and appeasements buttress the inequalities described above. Textbooks', Independence Day Orators', and the media's emphasis on equality of opportunity, coupled with the existence of a little social mobility in our society, motivate some Americans to gamble that by working hard within the system they will "make it big." Patriotic rhetoric neither notes how slim their chances are of doing so,[19] nor questions whether "making it" is worth the effort and other human costs. Poverty is rationalized, as Ryan usefully shows in chapter nine, by "blaming the victims": they do not work hard enough, they have too many babies, they have low I.Q.s or bad genes, or are caught in a "culture of poverty."[20]

For the capitalist system not to collapse, workers must be motivated to work. Because many are not motivated by their work itself, posters at work and evening television ads continuously remind them that they will be happier with higher incomes and more goods. Both factors are, of course, tied to their production within the wage system. Higher incomes and rising levels of living for all groups in the U.S., no matter how low they are on the totem pole, have generally been made possible

[19] For the most extensive study of social mobility in the United States see Peter M. Blau and Otis Dudley Duncan, *The American Occupational Structure* (New York: John Wiley and Sons, 1966).

[20] For critiques of certain of these allegations see chapter ten of "Blaming the Victim" by William Ryan; and Samuel Bowles and Herbert Gintis, "I.Q. in the U.S. Class Structure," *Social Policy* 3, no. 4 (February 1973): 65–96; S. M. Miller and Frank Riessman, "The 'Culture of Poverty': A Critique," in *Social Class and Social Policy* (New York: Basic Books, 1968); S. M. Miller, Arthur Seagull, and Frank Riessman, "The Deferred Gratification Pattern: A Critical Appraisal," in Louis Ferman, Joyce Kornbluh, and Alan Haber, eds., *Poverty in America* (Ann Arbor: University of Michigan Press, 1965); Charles A. Valentine, *Culture and Poverty: Critique and Counter Proposals* (Chicago: The University of Chicago Press, 1968).

by economic growth. The rising standards allow people to feel that they are making progress, and that their work and loyalty has been worth it.

The system gains the loyalty of some through these methods. But many, perhaps most, see through them. The hours of labor they give to and their cooperation with the system are gained less because they believe the myths of the system than because they see few alternatives for the survival of themselves and their families. Huber, Form, and Pease found this to be especially true of low-income and working-class people. They asked a sample of 350 Muskegan, Michigan residents about why people are poor, rich, or on welfare; about how educational and occupational opportunities are distributed; and about how power is distributed in the United States. They found that the rich much more than the poor, especially the black poor, viewed poverty as the result of unfavorable attributes, principally that the poor don't work as hard as other people and that they don't really want to get ahead.[21] Conversely, low-income persons were much more likely than the more affluent to take a sociological perspective of mobility. They perceived the influence of social structure on income much more readily than those who were getting high rewards.[22] Beliefs about power distribution appeared more affected by years of education than by income. Of the respondents with a high school or college education, seventy-three percent believed that the pluralist and eight percent believed that the Marxist description of power best portrayed American society; of those with less than eight years of schooling, forty percent believed that the Marxist and thirty-three percent believed that the pluralist description of American society was most accurate.[23]

21 Joan Huber, William H. Form, and John Pease, "Income and Ideology: General and Situated Beliefs about the American Opportunity Structure" (Paper presented at the American Sociological Association Meetings, Boston, 1968), p. 11; cf. Huber, Form and Pease, "Income and Stratification Ideology," *American Journal of Sociology* 75, no. 4, part 2, (January, 1970): 703–16.

22 Ibid, p. 14. Two Gallup polls supported these findings. They showed a marked division of opinion by income level and more especially by race on issues relating to the redistribution of wealth and income. American Institute of Public Opinion, *The Gallup Report,* June 16, 1968 and January 5, 1969.

23 The pluralist model abstracted from David Riessman's *The Lonely Crowd* stated: "No one group really runs the government in this country. Instead important decision about national policy are made by a lot of different groups such as labor, business, religious, and educational groups, and so on. These groups influence both political parties, but no single group can dictate to the others, and each group is strong enough to protect its own interests." The statement abstracted from C. Wright Mills' *The Power Elite* and chosen by twenty-six percent of those with less than eight years of schooling and twenty percent of those with sixteen percent or more years, read as follows: "A small group of men at the top really run the government in this country. These are the heads of the biggest business corporations, the highest officers in the Army, Navy and Air Force, and a few important senators,

WHY WE NEED EQUALITY

This book is about poverty and the poverty establishment. But poverty is part of inequality. The examination of, and attempt to grapple with, poverty during the sixties led many to recognize that not only poverty, with its historic connotation of rags and starvation, but also inequality, as depicted by Gabriel Kolko's *Wealth and Power in America,* is at issue in high-income industrial nations.[24]

Absolute increases in living standards are important to the very poor. They affect individuals' physical health as well as their satisfaction. But individuals judge their level of living not only in comparison with what they had ten, twenty, or thirty years ago, but also in comparison with the standard of living of others around them. The sting of being poor in the United States is one's comparative lower standard. America's poor are well-to-do in comparison with those of many other nations, but they are defined as poor in America because their level of living lags so far behind that enjoyed by other United States citizens.[25]

Why do we need equality? First, as noted above, inequality involves human pain. Second, it appears, as the Swedish sociologist Sten Johannsen has suggested, that the greater degree of inequality that a highly educated, highly industrialized nation has in times of relative peace, the greater the degree of social mobility and economic growth the nation requires in order to maintain political stability.[26] Both have their damaging aspects.

Social mobility is required in nations with a high degree of inequality to pacify a large segment of the population for a considerable portion of their lives, and to make them into cooperative workers by encouraging them to believe that by working hard they will eventually have a satisfying, well-paying position, e.g., they will "make it," a fact that Blau and Duncan's data on U.S. occupational mobility show that very few ever achieve.[27]

---

congressmen and federal officials in Washington. These men dominate both the Republican and Democratic Parties." The Marxian statement abstracted from Lewis Feuer's *Marx and Engles* said: "Big businessmen really run the government in this country. The heads of the large corporations dominate both the Republican and Democratic Parties. This means that things in Washington go pretty much the way big businessmen want them to." William H. Form and Joan Huber, "Ideological Beliefs on the Distribution of Power in the United States," *American Sociological Review* 34, no. 1 (February, 1969), p. 22.

24 Gabriel Kolko, *Wealth and Power in America* (New York: Frederick A. Praeger, 1962).

25 For further discussion supporting the interpretation of poverty in terms of inequality in high-income nations, see S. M. Miller and Pamela Roby *The Future of Inequality* (New York: Basic Books, 1970), chapters 1 and 2.

26 Sten Johannsen, International Sociological Association Meetings, Session on Povery and Inequality, seminar discussion, Varna, Bulgaria, September, 1970.

27 Ely Chinoy, *Automobile Workers and the American Dream* (Garden City, N.Y.: Doubleday and Company, 1955); Blau and Duncan, op. cit.

In societies with a high degree of inequality, *economic growth* pacifies those who are not socially mobile by allowing them to at least look back on their own past with a feeling of accomplishment, for economic growth (when at least a portion of the new resources go to poorer groups) allows all in the nation to have more real take-home pay—bigger houses and better refrigerators—without structural change or reductions in inequalities between the rich and poor.

Although both social mobility and economic growth were considered desirable goals to strive for in the past, we are taking another view of them today. Students and others are questioning the value of life dedicated to continuous competition. Douvan, Adelson, and other social psychologists' findings have supported the feelings of these youth. They have shown that a social system characterized by a high degree of social mobility not only involves psychological defeat and often material deprivation for static and downwardly mobile individuals but also involves much personal anguish in terms of broken social ties for the upwardly mobile.[28] Furthermore, as Milner has suggested, even the "chosen"—the upper and upper middle classes—become weary from the years of schooling they must pass through just to maintain their elite positions within a system of inequality rationalized by pseudo-meritocratic principles. Within this system, he notes, there is constant "status inflation," the "social process through which the status value of any absolute amount of individual resources decreases as the average level of these resources increases." This erosion of the *status quo* "leads to more striving by the individual. When a large percentage of the population so strives," Milner observes, "the result is additional status inflation and the process begins again." Status inflation follows from equality of opportunity amidst significant inequality because everyone can lose as well as gain status. This possibility produces status insecurity or anxiety among most individuals and encourages status seeking which leads to status inflation. The treadmill it produces is tiring.[29]

In terms of ecology and pollution, America can no longer afford continued high economic growth. Attempts to maintain present rates of economic growth will not only endanger our health and perhaps our lives, but will also require us to continue consuming an increasingly disproportionate share of the world's natural resources.[30]

28 Elizabeth Douvan, "Social Status and Success Strivings," *Journal of Abnormal and Social Psychology* 56 (1958); Douvan and Joseph Adelson, "The Psychodynamics of Social Mobility in Adolescent Boys," *Journal of Abnormal and Social Psychology* 56 (1958).

29 Murray Milner, Jr., *The Illusion of Equality: The Effect of Education on Opportunity, Equality and Social Conflict* (San Francisco, Jossey-Bass, Inc., 1972), pp. 2, 8, 24.

30 Matthew Edel aptly summarizes recent information and arguments concerning the effects of economic growth on the environment. Matthew Edel, *Economics and the Environment* (Englewood Cliffs, N.J.: Prentice-Hall, Inc., 1973), chapter 4, "Growth, Pollution and Social Cost."

A third reason for concern about inequality is that a high degree of inequality seemingly leads to much economic loss, for it generates rage that is often released by persons' destroying material goods, the work of others. In 1972, for example, millions of dollars worth of damage was done to school buildings alone. In addition, if, as numerous leaders of the left argued in 1945 and the postwar years, economic growth in the absence of redistribution of domestic resources requires the United States to become an international imperialist, forever expanding its markets whether welcomed by the host nations or not, then the United States must accept the cost of wars—of Korean, Vietnamese and Cambodian conflicts—as part of the cost of economic growth coupled with domestic inequality.[31]

Fourth, in his brilliant book on equality, Tawney stresses subtle forms of alienation that are generated by inequality—the lack of community and human relationships among men.[32] Similarly, the Alva Myrdal report states:

> Greater equality in conditions of living is not merely a goal in itself. Great disparities in standards and influence complicate and poison relationships and communication between individuals and groups. Socialism should be seen as a freedom movement, in which freedom from the pressure of external circumstances, class divisions and insecurity is considered a *prerequisite* for new human relationships marked more by cooperation and community and less by self-assertion, competition and conflict among various groups in society. Equalizing conditions of life then becomes a means of changing human relationships and of creating a better social climate.[33]

Fifth, equality in the distribution of resources would allow for a more efficient use of human resources than is currently possible. Today, the talents of many low-income children are lost because they are deprived of adequate nutrition and a good education. America has the resources, if they are distributed equitably, for all children to have adequate nutrition and good educations. The development of their talents would be a great social and economic gain as well as a great gain for the individual human beings.

Sixth, as the Alva Myrdal report points out, greater equality would

---

[31] These leaders did stress that economic growth could alternatively be achieved at much lower cost through the redistribution of domestic resources and the growth of domestic markets. The tension between these two alternatives is described in David W. Eakins, "Business Planners and America's Post War Expansion," in David Horowitz, ed., *Corporations and The Cold War* (New York: Monthly Review Press, 1969).

[32] R. H. Tawney, *Equality* (New York: Capricorn Books), 1931.

[33] Working Group on Equality of the Swedish Social Democratic Party and the Swedish Confederation of Trade Unions, *Towards Equality: The Alva Myrdal Report* (Stockholm: Socialdemokraterna, 1971), p. 15.

lead to greater diversity. Full equality would give each individual the freedom of choice to shape his or her future. Each person would develop "their own unique character," cultivate "their personal interests, their particular way of life and generally" create "variation and diversity in society." The report notes further that "it is inequality, class distinctions, which pigeonhole people and limit their opportunities to shape their lives freely. A more equal distribution of resources, influence and opportunities for choice increases variety in society and in the life of the individual." [34]

Finally, Frank Ackerman and other members of the Union of Radical Political Economists have observed that meaningful democracy is impossible in a society where the bases of power, such as wealth, are unequally distributed. In the United States, a nation in which many, perhaps most people prize democracy, this consideration should be of special concern.[35]

CONCLUSION:

This chapter has described the poverty establishment and has outlined the inequalities that pervade our society. The chapters to follow examine carefully the workings and beneficiaries of various parts of the poverty establishment. Each chapter gives many insights that lead to new questions concerning the operation of American society. These questions need to be researched, reported, and acted upon.

This book is primarily a critique. Other volumes are sorely needed to create models of the good world and to suggest how to get there. Toward this end, this chapter has suggested reasons for and possible consequences of equality, and the final chapter by Piven recommends how social scientists and others might better utilize their resources and expertise for achieving social change.

As we live, we should remember that there *are* alternatives to current forms of resource distribution. Resources may be distributed not only on the basis of previously established power distributions or on the basis of individual productivity, but also on the basis of equal shares for all, the basis of chance, or on some combination of these. Within the foreseeable future the system may not be changed, but if it is not, we all—rich, middle income, and poor alike—will be the losers.

34 *The Alva Myrdal Report*, op. cit., pp. 15–16.
35 Frank Ackerman, Howard Birnbaum, James Wetzler, and Andrew Zimbalist, "Income Distribution in the United States," *Review of Radical Political Economic*, 3, no. 3 (Summer, 1971): 20.

I

How the establishment keeps the poor poor, and the rich rich

> . . . among a free people every excess of capital must in time be repaid by the excessive demands of those who have not the capital . . . if the capitalists are wise, they will aid us in the effort to prevent injustice.
>
> JUSTICE LOUIS D. BRANDEIS*

> And so, my fellow Americans, ask not what your country can do for you —ask what you can do for your country.
>
> JOHN F. KENNEDY**

> The people who advocate the welfare ethic spend their time discussing how to cut up the pie we have—but those who believe in the work ethic want to bake a bigger pie, and I am for baking a bigger pie. . . . The work ethic tells us there is really no such thing as something for nothing and that everything valuable in life requires some striving and some sacrifice. The work ethic holds that it is wrong to expect instant gratification of all our desires and it is right to expect hard work to earn a just reward. . . . The welfare ethic, on the other hand, suggests that there is an easier way. It says that the good life can be made available to everyone right now, and that this can be done by the government.
>
> RICHARD M. NIXON***

In this section, Frances Fox Piven and Richard Cloward describe historically the expansion and contraction of relief-giving and argue that the chief function of relief is to regulate labor rather than to meet the varying economic needs of the poor. The expansion of relief, they maintain, occurs in response to uprisings or potential threats to the system. When the threat sub-

---

* Quoted in Alpheus T. Mason, *Brandeis: A Free Man's Life* (New York: Viking, 1946), pp. 141, 149.
** Inaugural Address, January 20, 1961.
*** Labor Day Message, September 3, 1972.

sides, relief is cut back and many or most of the poor are forced
to return to low-paid work and to thereby fatten the profits of
industry. Piven and Cloward trace the rise and fall of relief
from its early capitalist European origins through the most
recent relief expansion in the late 1960s. Since 1970 their thesis
has been further supported. With the decline in the turmoil of
the sixties, "workfare" rather than welfare has been the subject
of numerous political orations, and many individuals have been
forced off the rolls into jobs paying poverty-level wages.

David Horowitz and David Kolodney describe another side
of "charity" in their chapter. The great foundations—Rockefeller, Ford and Carnegie—have often been heralded as the epit-
omy of the *noblisse oblige* ethic of America's rich. Horowitz and
Kolodney show that the charity of the rich has resulted more
from their kind heartedness toward themselves than toward
others. The authors document that threats of antitrust actions
and heavy income and inheritance taxes to family fortunes led
to the creation of each of the big foundations. Furthermore,
they demonstrate in fine detail that the foundations have operated carefully and intentionally to not only preserve family
power but to extend the realm of the capitalist system from
which America's wealthiest families so obviously benefit. The
foundations have, through educational giving programs that far
outstrip those in many low-income areas of the United States,
created in many developing nations a capitalist middle class to
look out for the interests of American corporations. They have
initiated and financed research institutes to shape social legislation protective of business and affecting every realm of American life.

Read together, chapters one and two give clues to how sophisticated leaders of America's largest corporations and financial
institutions generally are able to use government for their own
ends. When these leaders have pressed for minimal reforms, they
have done so in order to stem the pressure of the have-nots which
has threatened them with the creation of larger, more significant
reform. These leaders have not supported *laissez-faire* principles.
Rather, they believe in and are active participants in social engineering to protect and further their own ends.[1]

---

1 Readers who, after completing this book, are interested in learning more about
corporate social engineering are referred to James Weinstein, *The Corporate Ideal
in the Liberal State* (Boston: Beacon Press, 1968); and Gabriel Kolko, *The Triumph
of Conservatism* (Chicago: Quadrangle Books, 1963).

chapter 1

Regulating the pier

FRANCES FOX PIVEN AND RICHARD A. CLOWARD

Aid to Families with Dependent Children (AFDC) is our major relief program. It has lately become the source of a major public controversy, owing to a large and precipitous expansion of the rolls. Between 1950 and 1960, only 110,000 families were added to the rolls, yielding a rise of 17 percent. In the 1960s, however, the rolls exploded, rising by more than 225 percent. At the beginning of the decade, 745,000 families were receiving aid; by 1970, some 2,500,000 families were on the rolls. Still, this is not the first, the largest or the longest relief explosion. Since the inauguration of relief in Western Europe three centuries ago, the rolls have risen and fallen in response to economic and political forces. An examination of these forces should help to illuminate the meaning of the current explosion, as well as the meaning of current proposals for reform.

Relief arrangements, we will argue, are ancillary to economic arrangements. Their chief function is to regulate labor, and they do that in two general ways. First, when mass unemployment leads to outbreaks of turmoil, relief programs are ordinarily initiated or expanded to absorb and control enough of the unemployed to restore order; then, as turbulence subsides, the relief system contracts, expelling those who are needed to populate the labor market. Relief also performs a labor-regulating function in this shrunken state, however. Some of the aged, the disabled and others who are of no use as workers are left on the relief rolls, and their treatment is so degrading and punitive as to instill in the laboring masses a fear of the fate that awaits them should they relax into beggary and pauperism. To demean and punish those who do not work is to exalt by contrast even the meanest labor at the meanest wages. These regulative functions of relief are made necessary by several strains toward instability inherent in capitalist economics.

"Regulating the Poor." From "The Relief of Welfare," *Trans-action, Vol. 8*, No. 7, May, 1971, pp. 31–39, 52–53 from Frances Fox Piven and Richard A. Cloward, *Regulating the Poor* (New York: Pantheon Books).

LABOR AND MARKET
INCENTIVES

All human societies compel most of their members to work, to produce the goods and services that sustain the community. All societies also define the work their members must do and the conditions under which they must do it. Sometimes the authority to compel and define is fixed in tradition, sometimes in the bureaucratic agencies of a central government. Capitalism, however, relies primarily upon the mechanisms of a market—the promise of financial rewards or penalties —to motivate men and women to work and to hold them to their occupational tasks.

But the development of capitalism has been marked by periods of cataclysmic change in the market, the main sources being depression and rapid modernization. Depressions mean that the regulatory structure of the market simply collapses; with no demand for labor, there are no monetary rewards to guide and enforce work. By contrast, during periods of rapid modernization—whether the replacement of handicraft by machines, the relocation of factories in relation to new sources of power or new outlets for distribution, or the demise of family subsistence farming as large-scale commercial agriculture spreads— portions of the laboring population may be rendered obsolete or at least temporarily maladjusted. Market incentives do not collapse; they are simply not sufficient to compel people to abandon one way of working and living in favor of another.

In principle, of course, people dislocated by modernization become part of a labor supply to be drawn upon by a changing and expanding labor market. As history shows, however, people do not adapt so readily to drastically altered methods of work and to the new and alien patterns of social life dictated by that work. They may resist leaving their traditional communities and the only life they know. Bred to labor under the discipline of sun and season, however severe that discipline may be, they may resist the discipline of factory and machine, which, though it may be no more severe, may seem so because it is alien. The process of human adjustment to such economic changes has ordinarily entailed generation of mass unemployment, distress and disorganization.

Now, if human beings were invariably given to enduring these travails with equanimity, there would be no governmental relief systems at all. But often they do not, and for reasons that are not difficult to see. The regulation of civil behavior in all societies is intimately dependent on stable occupational arrangements. So long as people are fixed in their work roles, their activities and outlooks are also fixed; they do what they must and think what they must. Each behavior and attitude is shaped by the reward of a good harvest or the penalty of a bad one, by the factory paycheck or the danger of losing it. But mass unemployment breaks that bond, loosening people from the main institution by which they are regulated and controlled.

Moreover, mass unemployment that persists for any length of time diminishes the capacity of other institutions to bind and constrain people. Occupational behaviors and outlooks underpin a way of life and determine familial, communal and cultural patterns. When large numbers of people are suddenly barred from their traditional occupations, the entire network of social control is weakened. There is no harvest or paycheck to enforce work and the sentiments that uphold work; without work, people cannot conform to familial and communal roles; and if the dislocation is widespread, the legitimacy of the social order itself may come to be questioned. The result is usually civil disorder—crime, mass protests, riots—a disorder that may even threaten to overturn existing social and economic arrangements. It is then that relief programs are initiated or expanded.

Western relief systems originated in the mass disturbances that erupted during the long transition from feudalism to capitalism beginning in the sixteenth century. As a result of the declining death rates in the previous century, the population of Europe grew rapidly; as the population grew, so did transiency and beggary. Moreover, distress resulting from population changes, agricultural and other natural disasters, which had characterized life throughout the Middle Ages, was now exacerbated by the vagaries of an evolving market economy, and outbreaks of turbulence among the poor were frequent. To deal with these threats to civil order, many localities legislated severe penalties against vagrancy. Even before the sixteenth century, the magistrates of Basel had defined twenty-five different categories of beggars, together with appropriate punishments for each. But penalties alone did not always deter begging, especially when economic distress was severe and the numbers affected were large. Consequently, some localities began to augment punishment with provisions for the relief of the vagrant poor.

CIVIL DISORDER AND RELIEF

A French town that initiated such an arrangement early in the sixteenth century was Lyons, which was troubled both by a rapidly growing population and by the economic instability associated with the transition to capitalism. By 1500 Lyons' population had already begun to increase. During the decades that followed, the town became a prosperous commercial and manufacturing center—the home of the European money market and of expanding new trades in textiles, printing and metalworking. As it thrived it attracted people, not only from the surrounding countryside, but even from Italy, Flanders and Germany. All told, the population of Lyons probably doubled between 1500 and 1540.

All this was very well as long as the newcomers could be absorbed by industry. But not all were, with the result that the town came to be plagued by beggars and vagrants. Moreover, prosperity was not continuous: some trades were seasonal and others were periodically troubled by foreign competition. With each economic downturn, large numbers of unemployed workers took to the streets to plead for charity, cluttering the very doorsteps of the better-off classes. Lyons was most vulnerable during periods of bad harvest, when famine not only drove up the cost of bread for urban artisans and journeymen but brought hordes of peasants into the city, where they sometimes paraded through the streets to exhibit their misfortune. In 1529 food riots erupted, with thousands of Lyonnais looting granaries and the homes of the wealthy; in 1530, artisans and journeymen armed themselves and marched through the streets; in 1531, mobs of starving peasants literally overran the town.

Such charity as had previously been given in Lyons was primarily the responsibility of the church or of those of the more prosperous who sought to purchase their salvation through almsgiving. But this method of caring for the needy obviously stimulated rather than discouraged begging and created a public nuisance to the better-off citizens (one account of the times describes famished peasants so gorging themselves as to die on the very doorsteps where they were fed). Moreover, to leave charity to church or citizen meant that few got aid, and those not necessarily according to their need. The result was that mass disorders periodically erupted.

The increase in disorder led the rulers of Lyons to conclude that the giving of charity should no longer be governed by private whim. In 1534, churchmen, notables and merchants joined together to establish a centralized administration for disbursing aid. All charitable donations were consolidated under a central body, the "Aumone-Generale," whose responsibility was to "nourish the poor forever." A list of the needy was established by a house-to-house survey, and tickets for bread and money were issued according to fixed standards. Indeed, most of the features of modern welfare—from criteria to discriminate the worthy poor from the unworthy, to strict procedures for surveillance of recipients as well as measures for their rehabilitation—were present in Lyons' new relief administration. By the 1550s, about 10 percent of the town's population was receiving relief.

Within two years of the establishment of relief in Lyons, King Francis I ordered each parish in France to register its poor and to provide for the "impotent" out of a fund of contributions. Elsewhere in Europe, other townships began to devise similar systems to deal with the vagrants and mobs cast up by famine, rapid population growth and the transition from feudalism to capitalism.

England also felt these disturbances, and just as it pioneered in developing an intensively capitalist economy, so it was at the forefront in developing nation-wide, public relief arrangements. During the closing years of the fifteenth century, the emergence of the wool industry in England began to transform agricultural life. As sheep raising became more profitable, much land was converted from tillage to pasturage, and large numbers of peasants were displaced by an emerging entrepreneurial gentry which either bought their land or cheated them out of it. The result was great tumult among the peasantry, as the Webbs were to note:

When the sense of oppression became overwhelming, the popular feeling manifested itself in widespread organised tumults, disturbances and insurrections, from Wat Tyler's rebellion of 1381, and Jack Cade's march on London of 1460, to the Pilgrimage of Grace in 1536, and Kett's Norfolk rising of 1549 —all of them successfully put down, but sometimes not without great struggle, by the forces which the government could command.

Early in the sixteenth century, the national government moved to try to forestall such disorders. In 1528 the Privy Council, anticipating a fall in foreign sales as a result of the war in Flanders, tried to induce the cloth manufacturers of Suffolk to retain their employees. In 1534, a law passed under Henry VIII attempted to limit the number of sheep in any one holding in order to inhibit the displacement of farmers and agricultural laborers and thus forestall potential disorders. Beginning in the 1550s the Privy Council attempted to regulate the price of grain in poor harvests. But the entrepreneurs of the new market economy were not so readily curbed, so that during this period another method of dealing with labor disorders was evolved.

Early in the sixteenth century, the national government moved to replace parish arrangements for charity with a nation-wide system of relief. In 1531, an act of Parliament decreed that local officials search out and register those of the destitute deemed to be impotent and give them a document authorizing begging. As for those who sought alms without authorization, the penalty was public whipping till the blood ran.

Thereafter, other arrangements for relief were rapidly instituted. An act passed in 1536, during the reign of Henry VIII, required local parishes to take care of their destitute and to establish a procedure for the collection and administration of donations for that purpose by local officials. (In the same year Henry VIII began to expropriate monasteries, helping to assure secular control of charity.) With these developments, the penalties for beggary were made more severe, including an elaborate schedule of branding, enslavement and execution for repeated offenders. Even so, by 1572 beggary was said to have reached alarming proportions, and in that year local responsibility for relief was more fully spelled out by the famous Elizabethan Poor Laws, which established a local tax, known as the poor rate, as the means for financing the care of paupers and required that justices of the peace serve as the overseers of the poor.

After each period of activity, the parish relief machinery tended to lapse into disuse, until bad harvests or depression in manufacturing led again to widespread unemployment and misery, to new outbreaks of disorder, and then to a resuscitation and expansion of relief arrangements. The most illuminating of these episodes, because it bears so much similarity to the present-day relief explosion in the United States, was the expansion of relief during the massive agricultural dislocations of the late eighteenth century.

Most of the English agricultural population had lost its landholdings long before the eighteenth century. In place of the subsistence farming found elsewhere in Europe, a three-tier system of landowners, tenant farmers and agricultural workers had evolved in England. The vast majority of the people were a landless proletariat, hiring out by the year to tenant farmers. The margin of their subsistence, however, was provided by common and waste lands, on which they gathered kindling, grazed animals and hunted game to supplement their meager wages. Moreover, the use of the commons was part of the English villager's birthright, his sense of place and pride. It was the disruption of these arrangements and the ensuing disorder that led to the new expansion of relief.

By the middle of the eighteenth century, an increasing population, advancing urbanization and the growth of manufacturing had greatly expanded markets for agricultural products, mainly for cereals to feed the urban population and for wool to supply the cloth manufacturers. These new markets, together with the introduction of new agricultural methods (such as cross-harrowing), led to large-scale changes in agriculture. To take advantage of rising prices and new techniques, big landowners moved to expand their holdings still further by buying up small farms and, armed with parliamentary Bills of Enclosure, by usurping the common and waste lands which had enabled many small cottagers to survive. Although this process began much earlier, it accelerated rapidly after 1750; by 1850, well over 6 million acres of common land —or about one-quarter of the total arable acreage—had been consolidated into private holdings and turned primarily to grain production.

For great numbers of agricultural workers, enclosure meant no land on which to grow subsistence crops to feed their families, no grazing land to produce wool for home spinning and weaving, no fuel to heat their cottages, and new restrictions against hunting. It meant, in short, the loss of a major source of subsistence for the poor.

New markets also stimulated a more businesslike approach to farming. Landowners demanded the maximum rent from tenant farmers, and tenant farmers in turn began to deal with their laborers in terms of cash calculations. Specifically, this meant a shift from a master-servant relationship to an employer-employee relationship, but on the harshest terms. Where laborers had previously worked by the year and frequently lived with the farmer, they were now hired for only as long as they were needed and were then left to fend for themselves. Pressures toward short-term hiring also resulted from the large-scale cultivation of grain crops for market, which called for a seasonal labor force, as opposed to mixed subsistence farming, which required year-round laborers. The use of cash rather than produce as the medium of payment for work, a rapidly spreading practice, encouraged partly by the long-term inflation of grain prices, added to the laborer's hardships. Finally the rapid increase in rural population at a time when the growth of woolen manufacturing continued to provide an incentive to convert land from tillage to pasturage produced a large labor surplus, leaving agricultural workers with no leverage in bargaining for wages with their tenant-farmer employers. The result was widespread unemployment and terrible hardship.

None of these changes took place without resistance from small farmers and laborers who, while they had known hardship before, were now being forced out of a way of life and even out of their villages. Some rioted when Bills of Enclosure were posted; some petitioned the Parliament for their repeal. And when hardship was made more acute by a succession of poor harvests in the 1790s, there were widespread food riots.

Indeed, throughout the late eighteenth and early nineteenth centuries, the English countryside was periodically beseiged by turbulent masses of the displaced rural poor and the towns were racked by Luddism, radicalism, trade-unionism and Chartism, even while the ruling classes worried about what the French Revolution might augur for England. A solution to disorder was needed, and that solution turned out to be relief. The poor relief system—first created in the sixteenth century to control the earlier disturbances caused by population growth and the commercialization of agriculture—now rapidly became a major institution of English life. Between 1760 and 1784, taxes for relief—the poor rate—rose by 60 percent; they doubled by 1801, and rose by 60 percent more in the next decade. By 1818, the poor rate was over six times as high as it had been in 1760. Hobsbaum estimates that up to the 1850s, upwards of 10 percent of the English population were paupers. The relief system, in short, was expanded in order to absorb and regulate the masses of discontented people uprooted from agriculture but not yet incorporated into industry.

Relief arrangements evolved more slowly in the United States, and the first major relief crisis did not occur until the Great Depression. The inauguration of massive relief-giving was not simply a response to widespread economic distress, for millions had remained unemployed for several years without obtaining aid. What finally led the national government to proffer aid was the great surge of political disorder that followed the economic catastrophe, a disorder which eventually led to the convulsive voting shifts of 1932. After the election, the federal government abandoned its posture of aloofness toward the unemployed. Within a matter of months, billions of dollars were flowing to localities, and the relief rolls skyrocketed. By 1935, upwards of 20 million people were on the dole.

The contemporary relief explosion, which began in the early 1960s, has its roots in agricultural modernization. No one would disagree that the rural economy of America, especially in the South, has undergone a profound transformation in recent decades. In 1945, there was one tractor per farm; in 1964 there were two. Mechanization and other technological developments, in turn, stimulated the enlargement of farm holdings. Between 1959 and 1961, one million farms disappeared; the 3 million remaining farms averaged 377 acres in size—30 percent larger than the average farm ten years earlier. The chief and most obvious effect of these changes was to lessen the need for agricultural labor. In the years between 1950 and 1965 alone, a Presidential Commission on Rural Poverty was to discover, "New machines and new methods increased farm output in the United States by 45 percent, and reduced farm employment by 45 percent." A mere 4 percent of the American labor force now works the land, signalling an extraordinary displacement of people, with accompanying upheaval and suffering. The best summary measure of this dislocation is probably the volume of migration to the cities; over 20 million people, more than 4 million of them black, left the land after 1940.

Nor were all these poor absorbed into the urban economic system. Blacks were especially vulnerable to unemployment. At the close of the Korean War, the national nonwhite unemployment rate leaped from 4.5 percent in 1953 to 9.9 percent in 1954. By 1958, it had reached 12.6 percent, and it fluctuated between 10 and 13 percent until the escalation of the war in Vietnam after 1964.

These figures pertain only to people unemployed and looking for work. They do not include the sporadically unemployed or those employed at extremely low wages. Combining such additional measures with the official unemployment measure produces a subemployment index. This index was first used in 1966—well after the economic downturns that characterized the years between the end of the Korean War and the escalation of the war in Vietnam. Were subemployment data available for the "Eisenhower recession" years, especially in the slum-ghettoes of the larger central cities, they would surely show much higher rates than prevailed in 1966. In any event, the figures for 1966 revealed a nonwhite subemployment rate of 21.6 percent compared with a white rate of 7.6 percent.

However, despite the spread of economic deprivation, whether on the land or in the cities, the relief system did not respond. In the entire decade between 1950 and 1960, the national AFDC caseload rose by only 17 percent. Many of the main urban targets of migration showed equally little change: the rolls in New York City moved up by 16 percent, and in Los Angeles by 14 percent. In the South, the rolls did not rise at all.

But in the 1960s, disorder among the black poor erupted on a wide scale, and the welfare rolls erupted as well. The welfare explosion occurred during several years of the greatest domestic disorder since the 1930s—perhaps the greatest in our history. It was concurrent with the turmoil produced by the civil-rights struggle, with widespread and destructive rioting in the cities, and with the formation of a militant grassroots movement of the poor dedicated to combating welfare restrictions. Not least, the welfare rise was also concurrent with the enactment of a series of ghetto-placating federal programs (such as the antipoverty program) which, among other things, hired thousands of poor people, social workers and lawyers who, it subsequently turned out, greatly stimulated people to apply for relief and helped them obtain it. And the welfare explosion, although an urban phenomenon generally, was greatest in just that handful of large metropolitan counties where the political turmoil of the mid- and late 1960s was the most acute.

The magnitude of the welfare rise is worth noting. The national AFDC caseload rose by more than 225 percent in the 1960s. In New York City, the rise was more than 300 percent; the same was so in Los Angeles. Even in the South, where there had been no rise at all in the 1950s, the rolls rose by more than 60 percent. And most significant of all, the bulk of the increase took place after 1965—that is, after disorder reached a crescendo. More than 80 percent of the national rise in the 1960s occurred in the last five years of the decade. In other words, the welfare rolls expanded, today as at earlier times, only in response to civil disorder.

While muting the more disruptive outbreaks of civil disorder (such as rioting), the mere giving of relief does nothing to reverse the disintegration of lower-class life produced by economic change, a disintegration which leads to rising disorder and rising relief rolls in the first place. Indeed, greatly liberalized relief-giving can further weaken work and family norms. To restore order in a more fundamental sense the society must create the means to reassert its authority. Because the market is unable to control men's behavior a surrogate system of social control must be evolved, at least for a time. Moreover, if the surrogate system is to be consistent with normally dominant patterns, it must restore people to work roles. Thus even though obsolete or unneeded workers are temporarily given direct relief, they are eventually succored only on condition that they work. As these adjustments are made, the functions of relief arrangements may be said to be shifting from regulating disorder to regulating labor.

RESTORING ORDER
BY RESTORING WORK

The arrangements, both historical and contemporary, through which relief recipients have been made to work vary, but broadly speaking, there are two main ways: work is provided under public auspices, whether in the recipient's home, in a labor yard, in a workhouse or on a public works project; or work is provided in the private market, whether by contracting or indenturing the poor to private employers, or through subsidies designed to induce employers to hire paupers. And although a relief system may at any time use both of these methods of enforcing work, one or the other usually becomes predominant, depending on the economic conditions that first gave rise to disorder.

Publicly subsidized work tends to be used during business depressions, when the demand for labor in the private market collapses. Conversely, arrangements to channel paupers into the labor market are more likely to be used when rapid changes in markets or technology render a segment of the labor supply temporarily maladapted. In the first case, the relief system augments a shrunken labor market; in the other, its policies and procedures are shaped to overcome the poor fit between labor demand and supply.

Public work is as old as public relief. The municipal relief systems initiated on the Continent in the first quarter of the sixteenth century often included some form of public works. In England, the same statute of 1572 that established taxation as the method for financing poor relief charged the overseers of the poor with putting vagrants to work. Shortly afterwards, in 1576, local officials were directed to acquire a supply of raw goods—wool, hemp, iron—which was to be delivered to the needy for processing in their homes, their dole to be fixed according to "the desert of the work."

The favored method of enforcing work throughout most of the history of relief was the workhouse. In 1723, an act of Parliament permitted the local parishes to establish workhouses and to refuse aid to those poor who would not enter; within ten years, there were said to be about fifty workhouses in the environs of London alone.

The destitute have also sometimes been paid to work in the general community or in their own homes. This method of enforcing work evolved in England during the bitter depression of 1840–1841. As unemployment mounted, the poor in some of the larger cities protested against having to leave their communities to enter workhouses in order to obtain relief, and in any case, in some places the workhouses were already full. As a result, various public spaces were designated as "labor yards" to which the unemployed could come by the day to pick oakum, cut wood, and break stone, for which they were paid in food and clothing. The method was used periodically throughout the second half of the nineteenth century; at times of severe distress, very large numbers of the able-bodied were supported in this way.

The first massive use of public work under relief auspices in the United States occurred during the 1930s when millions of the unemployed were subsidized through the Works Progress Administration. The initial response of the Roosevelt administration was to appropriate billions for direct relief payments. But no one liked direct relief—not the president who called for it, the Congress that legislated it, the administrators who operated it, the people who received it. Direct relief was viewed as a temporary expedient, a way of maintaining a person's body, but not his dignity; a way of keeping the populace from shattering in despair, discontent and disorder, at least for a while, but not of renewing their pride, of bringing back a way of life. For their way of life had been anchored in the discipline of work, and so that discipline had to be restored. The remedy was to abolish direct relief and put the unemployed to work on subsidized projects. These reforms were soon instituted—and with dramatic results. For a brief time, the federal government became the employer of millions of people (although millions of others remained unemployed).

Quite different methods of enforcing work are used when the demand for labor is steady but maladaptions in the labor supply, caused by changes in methods of production, result in unemployment. In such circumstances, relief agencies ordinarily channel paupers directly into the private market. For example, the rapid expansion of English manufacturing during the late eighteenth and early nineteenth centuries produced a commensurately expanded need for factory operatives. But it was no easy matter to get them. Men who had been agricultural laborers, independent craftsmen or workers in domestic industries (i.e., piecework manufacturing in the home) resisted the new discipline. Between 1778 and 1830, there were repeated revolts by laborers in which local tradesmen and farmers often participated. The revolts failed, of course; the new industry moved forward inexorably, taking the more dependent and tractable under its command, with the aid of the relief system.

The burgeoning English textile industry solved its labor problems during the latter part of the eighteenth century by using parish children, some only four or five years old, as factory operatives. Manufacturers negotiated regular bargains with the parish authorities, ordering lots of fifty or more children from the poorhouses. Parish children were an ideal labor source for new manufacturers. The young paupers could be shipped to remote factories, located to take advantage of the streams from which power could be drawn. (With the shift from water power to steam in the nineteenth century, factories began to locate in towns where they could employ local children; with that change, the system of child labor became a system of "free" child labor.) The children were also preferred for their docility and for their light touch at the looms. Moreover, pauper children could be had for a bit of food and a bed, and they provided a very stable labor supply, for they were held fast at their labors by indentures, usually until they were twenty-one.

Sometimes the relief system subsidizes the employment of paupers—especially when their market value is very low—as when the magistrates of Lyons provided subsidies to manufacturers who employed pauper children. In rural England during the late eighteenth century, as more and more of the population was being displaced by the commercialization of agriculture, this method was used on a very large scale. To be sure, a demand for labor was developing in the new manufacturing establishments that would in time absorb many of the uprooted rural poor. But this did not happen all at once: rural displacement and industrial expansion did not proceed at the same pace or in the same areas, and in any case the drastic shift from rural village to factory system took time. During the long interval before people forced off the land were absorbed into manufacturing, many remained in the countryside as virtual vagrants; others migrated to the towns, where they crowded into hovels and cellars, subject to the vicissitudes of rapidly rising and falling markets, their ranks continually enlarged by new rural refugees.

These conditions were not the result of a collapse in the market. Indeed, grain prices rose during the second half of the eighteenth century, and they rose spectacularly during the Revolutionary and Napoleonic wars. Rather, it was the expanding market for agricultural produce which, by stimulating enclosure and business-minded farming methods, led to unemployment and destitution. Meanwhile, population growth, which meant a surplus of laborers, left the workers little opportunity to resist the destruction of their traditional way of life— except by crime, riots and incendiarism. To cope with these disturbances, relief expanded, but in such a way as to absorb and discipline laborers by supporting the faltering labor market with subsidies.

The subsidy system is widely credited to the sheriff and magistrates of Berkshire, who, in a meeting at Speenhamland in 1795, decided on a scheme by which the Poor Law authorities would supplement the wages of underemployed and underpaid agricultural workers according to a published scale. It was a time when exceptional scarcity of food led to riots all over England, sometimes suppressed only by calling out the troops. With this "double panic of famine and revolution," the subsidy scheme spread, especially in counties where large amounts of acreage had been enclosed.

The local parishes implemented the work subsidy system in different ways. Under the "roundsman" arrangement, the parish overseers sent any man who applied for aid from house to house to get work. If he found work, the employer was obliged to feed him and pay a small sum (6 d) per day, with the parish adding another small sum (4 d). Elsewhere, the parish authorities contracted directly with farmers to have paupers work for a given price, with the parish paying the combined wage and relief subsidy directly to the pauper. In still other places, parish authorities parcelled out the unemployed to farmers, who were obliged to pay a set rate or make up the difference in higher taxes. Everywhere, however, the main principle was the same: an underemployed and turbulent populace was being pacified with public allowances, but these allowances were used to restore order by enforcing work, at very low wage levels. Relief, in short, served as a support for a disturbed labor market and as a discipline for a disturbed rural society. As the historians J. L. Hammond and Barbara Hammond were to say, "The meshes of the Poor Law were spread over the entire labour system."

The English Speenhamland plan, while it enjoys a certain notoriety, is by no means unique. The most recent example of a scheme for subsidizing paupers in private employ is the reorganization of American public welfare proposed in the summer of 1969 by President Richard Nixon; the general parallel with the events surrounding Speenhamland is striking. The United States relief rolls expanded in the 1960s to absorb a laboring population made superfluous by agricultural modernization in the South, a population that became turbulent in the wake of forced migration to the cities. As the relief rolls grew to deal with these disturbances, pressure for "reforms" also mounted.

Key features of the reform proposals included a national minimum allowance of $1,600 per year for a family of four, coupled with an elaborate system of penalties and incentives to force families to work. In effect, the proposal was intended to support and strengthen a disturbed low-wage labor market by providing what was called in nineteenth century England a "rate in aid of wages."

ENFORCING LOW WAGE
WORK DURING PERIODS
OF STABILITY

Even in the absence of cataclysmic change, market incentives may be insufficient to compel all people at all times to do the particular work required of them. Incentives may be too meager and erratic, or people may not be sufficiently socialized to respond to them properly. To be sure, the productivity of a fully developed capitalist economy would allow for wages and profits sufficient to entice most of the population to work; and in a fully developed capitalist society, most people would also be reared to want what the market holds out to them. They would expect, even sanctify, the rewards of the market place and acquiesce in its vagaries.

But no fully developed capitalist society exists. (Even today in the United States, the most advanced capitalist country, certain regions and population groups—such as southern tenant farmers—remain on the periphery of the wage market and are only partially socialized to the ethos of the market.) Capitalism evolved slowly and spread slowly. During most of this evolution, the market provided meager rewards for most workers, and none at all for some. There are still many for whom this is so. And during most of this evolution, large sectors of the laboring classes were not fully socialized to the market ethos. The relief system, we contend, has made an important contribution toward overcoming these persisting weaknesses in the capacity of the market to direct and control men.

Once an economic convulsion subsides and civil order is restored, relief systems are not ordinarily abandoned. The rolls are reduced, to be sure, but the shell of the system usually remains, ostensibly to provide aid to the aged, the disabled and such other unfortunates who are of no use as workers. However, the manner in which these "impotents" have always been treated, in the United States and elsewhere, suggests a purpose quite different from the remediation of their destitution. These residual persons have ordinarily been degraded for lacking economic value, relegated to the foul quarters of the workhouse, with its strict penal regimen and its starvation diet. Once stability was restored, such institutions were typically proclaimed the sole source of aid, and for a reason bearing directly on enforcing work.

Conditions in the workhouse were intended to ensure that no one with any conceivable alternatives would seek public aid. Nor can there by any doubt of that intent. Consider this statement by the Poor Law Commissioners in 1834, for example:

> In to such a house none will enter voluntarily; work, confinement, and discipline will deter the indolent and vicious: and nothing but extreme necessity will induce any to accept the comfort which must be obtained by the surrender of their free agency, and the sacrifice of their accustomed habits and gratifications. *Thus the parish officer, being furnished an unerring test of the necessity of applicants, is relieved from his painful and difficult responsibility: while all have the gratification of knowing that while the necessitous are abundantly relieved, the funds of charity are not wasted by idleness and fraud.*

The method worked. Periods of relief expansion were generally followed by "reform" campaigns to abolish all "outdoor" aid and restrict relief to those who entered the workhouse—as in England in 1722, 1834 and 1871 and in the United States in the 1880s and 1890s—and these campaigns usually resulted in a sharp reduction in the number of applicants seeking aid.

The harsh treatment of those who had no alternative except to fall back upon the parish and accept "the offer of the House" terrorized the impoverished masses in another way as well. It made pariahs of those who could not support themselves; they served as an object lesson, a means of celebrating the virtues of work by the terrible example of their agony. That, too, was a matter of deliberate intent. The workhouse was designed to spur men to contrive ways of supporting themselves by their own industry, to offer themselves to any employer on any terms, rather than suffer the degraded status of pauper.

All of this was evident in the contraction of relief which occurred in the United States at the close of the Great Depression. As political stability returned, emergency relief and work relief programs were reduced and eventually abolished, with many of those cut off being forced into a labor market still glutted with the unemployed. Meanwhile, the Social Security Act had been passed. Widely hailed as a major reform, this measure created our present-day welfare system, with its categorical provisions for the aged, the blind and families with dependent children (as well as, in 1950, the disabled).

The enactment of this "reform" signalled a turn toward the work-enforcing function of relief arrangements. This became especially evident after World War II during the period of greatly accelerated agricultural modernization. Millions were unemployed in agriculture;

millions of others migrated to the cities where unemployment in the late 1950s reached extremely high levels. But few families were given assistance. By 1960, only 745,000 families had been admitted to the AFDC rolls. That was to change in the 1960s, as we have already noted, but only in response to the most unprecedented disorder in our history.

That families without jobs or income failed to secure relief during the late 1940s and the 1950s was in part a consequence of restrictive statutes and policies—the exclusion of able-bodied males and, in many places, of so-called employable mothers, together with residence laws, relative responsibility provisions and the like. But it was also—perhaps mainly—a consequence of the persistence of age-old rituals of degradation. AFDC mothers were forced to answer questions about their sexual behavior ("When did you last menstruate?"), open their closets to inspection ("Whose pants are those?"), and permit their children to be interrogated ("Do any men visit your mother?"). Unannounced raids, usually after midnight and without benefit of warrant, in which a recipient's home is searched for signs of "immoral" activities, have also been part of life on AFDC. In Oakland, California, a public welfare caseworker, Bennie Parish, refused to take part in a raid in January 1962 and was dismissed for insubordination. When he sued for reinstatement, the state argued successfully in the lower courts that people taking public assistance waive certain constitutional rights, among them the right to privacy. (The court's position had at least the weight of long tradition, for the withdrawal of civil rights is an old feature of public relief. In England, for example, relief recipients were denied the franchise until 1918, and as late as 1934 the constitutions of fourteen American states deprived recipients of the right to vote or hold office.)

The main target of these rituals is not the recipient who ordinarily is not of much use as a worker, but the able-bodied poor who remain in the labor market. It is for these people that the spectacle of the degraded pauper is intended. For example, scandals exposing welfare "fraud" have diffuse effects, for they reach a wide public—including the people who might otherwise apply for aid but who are deterred because of the invidious connotations of being on welfare. Such a scandal occurred in the District of Columbia in 1961, with the result that half of all AFDC mothers were declared to be ineligible for relief, most of them for allegedly "consorting with men." In the several years immediately before the attack, about 6,500 District of Columbia families had applied for aid annually; during the attack, the figure dropped to 4,400 and it did not rise for more than five years—long after that particular scandal itself had subsided.

In sum, market values and market incentives are weakest at the bottom of the social order. To buttress weak market controls and ensure the availability of marginal labor, an outcast class—the dependent poor—is created by the relief system. This class, whose members are of no productive use, is not treated with indifference, but with contempt. Its degradation at the hands of relief officials serves to celebrate the virtue of all work and deters actual or potential workers from seeking aid.

THE CURRENT CALL
FOR REFORM

From our perspective, a relief explosion is a reform just because a large number of unemployed or underemployed people obtain aid. But from the perspective of most people, a relief explosion is viewed as a "crisis." The contemporary relief explosion in the United States, following a period of unparalleled turbulence in the cities, has thus resulted in a clamor for reform. Similar episodes in the past suggest that pressure for reform signals a shift in emphasis between the major functions of relief arrangements—a shift from regulating disorder to regulating labor.

Pressure for reform stems in part from the fiscal burden imposed on localities when the relief rolls expand. An obvious remedy is for the federal government to simply assume a greater share of the costs, if not the entire cost (at this writing, Congress appears likely to enact such fiscal reform).

However, the much more fundamental problem with which relief reform seeks to cope is the erosion of the work role and the deterioration of the male-headed family. In principle, these problems could be dealt with by economic policies leading to full employment at decent wages, but there is little political support for that approach. Instead, the historic approach to relief explosions is being invoked, which is to restore work through the relief system. Various proposals have been advanced: some would force recipients to report regularly to employment offices; others would provide a system of wage subsidies conditional on the recipient's taking on a job at any wage (including those below the federal minimum wage); still others would inaugurate a straight-forward program of public works projects.

We are opposed to any type of reform intended to promote work through the relief system rather than through the reform of economic policies. When similar relief reforms were introduced in the past, they presaged the eventual expulsion of large numbers of people from the rolls, leaving them to fend for themselves in a labor market where there was too little work and thus subjecting them once again to severe economic exploitation. The reason that this happens is more than a little ironic.

The irony is this: when relief is used to enforce work, it tends to stabilize lower-class occupational, familial and communal life (unlike direct relief, which merely mutes the worst outbreaks of discontent). By doing so, it diminishes the proclivities toward disruptive behavior which give rise to the expansion of relief in the first place. Once order is restored in this far more profound sense, relief-giving can be virtually abolished as it has been so often in the past. And there is always pressure to abolish large-scale work relief, for it strains against the market ethos and interferes with the untrammeled operation of the market place. The point is not just that when a relief concession is offered up, peace and order reign; it is, rather, that when peace and order reign, the relief concession is withdrawn.

The restoration of work through the relief system, in other words, makes possible the eventual return to the most restrictive phase in the cycle of relief-giving. What begins as a great expansion of direct relief, and then turns into some form of work relief, ends finally with a sharp contraction of the rolls. Advocates of relief reform may argue that their reforms will be long-lasting, that the restrictive phase in the cycle will not be reached, but past experience suggests otherwise.

Therefore, in the absence of economic reforms leading to full employment at decent wages, we take the position that the explosion of the rolls is the true relief reform, that it should be defended, and that it should be expanded. Even now, hundreds of thousands of impoverished families remain who are eligible for assistance but who receive no aid at all.

c h a p t e r 2

The foundations:
charity begins at home

DAVID HOROWITZ WITH DAVID KOLODNEY

At the turn of the century, when John D. Rockefeller Sr. com-
manded his "Standard Oil gang" from the elegant boardroom at 26
Broadway, the name "Rockefeller" conjured something far different
from the present visions of vaguely liberal Republicanism, high-minded
philanthropy and subsidized ballet. As one biographer recalls, "For 40
years—from 1872 to 1914—the name of John D. Rockefeller was the
most execrated name in American life. It was associated with greed,
rapacity, cruelty, hypocrisy and corruption. . . . The attorney generals of half a dozen states clamored for his imprisonment. La Follette
called him the greatest criminal of the age. . . ."

When it is considered that a Rockefeller in the White House has
become a possibility—for many, even a desire—it is possible to appreciate the massive beautification program, the political face lifting, that
has taken place over the last 50 years. The public image of robber
barons like the Rockefellers and of American capitalism itself—has
been cleaned up beyond recognition. It has taken a great effort and
the subsidized bad memory of history; but the greatest credit is due to
the royal families themselves, the Rockefellers and the Fords, who by
dint of circumstance and through the devices of their lawyers have
turned a new institutional face upon the world, at once benign and
inscrutable: the nonprofit, charitable foundation.

As might be expected, however, more is to be found in these foundations than the mere stuff on which images are built.

The income of the 596 largest tax-exempt foundations is more than
twice the net earnings of the nation's 50 largest commercial banks. The
annual income of the Ford Foundation alone exceeds that of the
world's biggest bank and has totaled almost two billion dollars over
the last 30 years. The Rockefeller Foundation, starting life with $34.4

"The Foundations: Charity Begins at Home" from David Horowitz with David
Kolodney, "The Foundations: Charity Begins at Home," from *Ramparts* 7, no. 11
(April, 1969): 39–48. Reprinted by permission of Noah's Ark, Inc.

million in 1913, accumulated over the next half century another $876.2 million—three-fourths of it from stock income and capital gains.

But even more important, the foundations sustain the complex nerve centers and guidance mechanisms for a whole system of institutional power. To a remarkable and not accidental degree, this power has both characterized and defined American society and its relations with the rest of the world in the 20th century.

HOW THE GREAT PHILANTHROPIC FOUNDATIONS WERE BORN

As the century turned and the Gilded Age tarnished into the Age of Frenzied Finance, it was evident that the wanton, headlong joy-ride of economic grab and ruin that had produced a Rockefeller was producing a popular reaction of serious import. "We have been cursed with the reign of gold long enough," Eugene Debs told wildly cheering crowds. "We are on the eve of a universal change." Populism had already put 15 men into Congress and was making a serious bid for power as a third party. Its enemy, said agrarian rebel Tom Watson, was "monopoly—monopoly of power, of place, of privilege, of wealth, of progress."

As the mood of the country became increasingly rebellious, it became clear that some sacrifice would have to be made if the edifice of corporate power and privilege was to be maintained. John D. Rockefeller, whose Standard Oil Trust was the first, biggest and most notorious of the giant trusts—the living symbol of monopoly itself—was keenly aware that no one could make a more delicious and satisfying sacrificial offering than himself, not only because he exemplified all the system's excesses, but also because his interventions in politics, both as bankroller and prompter, had made important enemies, most notably Teddy Roosevelt.

By 1909 there seemed no way, even for Rockefeller, to stem the tide of antitrust actions and lawsuits which reached their culmination that year in a court order to dissolve the Standard Trust itself. It was primarily in response to all this that Rockefeller's defensive campaign of strategic philanthropy was launched. He had begun seriously laying its groundwork as early as 1903, when he announced the formation of his first big philanthropy, the General Education Board, following Teddy Roosevelt's ascension to the Presidency. On March 2, 1910, Rockefeller finally asked the United States Congress to grant a special charter for a great new "Benevolent Trust." This was the auspicious start of the Rockefeller Foundation. Time was clearly of the essence: less than a year earlier, Congress had submitted to the states the 16th Amendment, authorizing an income tax; just five days before applying for the charter, Rockefeller attorneys had filed their last, futile appeal with the Supreme Court to block the dissolution of the Standard Oil Trust.

The hatred attached to Rockefeller's name and the fear which his power inspired were so widespread at this time that Congress rejected the proposal for the Foundation charter. It was dubbed "the kiss of Judas Iscariot" by the press, "a Trojan horse." In the end, Rockefeller was forced to relinquish his request and content himself with a charter issued by the State of New York in May 1913. With the issuance of this charter, he surrendered a small portion of his wealth, not to the plebian control of the state, but to a select group of Foundation trustees whose discretion he could count on: John D. Rockefeller Jr.; his son-in-law, Harold McCormick of the International Harvester McCormicks: and, lest nepotism be charged, his servant, Rev. Frederick T. Gates, as "business and benevolent advisor."

The breakup of the Standard Oil Trust, the outstanding triumph of the trust-busting Progressive Era, was seen as a serious limitation of Rockefeller's monopolistic economic preeminence. However, knowledgeable men in the world of high finance weren't placing any bets against him. The day after the dissolution of Standard Oil, activity on the Big Board added a prodigious $200 million to the company's market value, including $56 million to Rockefeller's own holdings (substantially more than his initial $34 million "gift" to the new Foundation). And those who had thought that Rockefeller's power over the fragments of the old trust was really gone were surprised when a corporate battle royal a few years later demonstrated that reports of its death had been greatly exaggerated.

On May 28, 1929, in the wake of the Teapot Dome scandal, a bitter corporate battle erupted over control of the erstwhile trust subsidiary, Standard Oil Company of Indiana. Indiana's President Robert W. Stewart had been linked in shady business deals with Harry Sinclair of Sinclair Oil (whose bribe to the secretary of the Interior was at the center of the Teapot Dome affair). When the new scandal broke, the president of the Rockefeller Foundation, John D. Rockefeller Jr., publicly demanded Stewart's resignation—a presumptuous, even insolent demand for a stockholder with only 4.5 percent of Indiana Standard's common shares.

Stewart stood his ground against the upstart philanthropist, making full use of his managerial position to rebuff the attack. On Stewart's recommendation, the board of directors voted a dividend of $116,-000,000, payable to the holders of Indiana Standard's 14 million outstanding shares, proving to the stockholders the desirability of the current management. But Rockefeller Jr. had a few aces up his sleeve.

When the crunch came, he voted against Stewart—not only his own shares but also those of the Rockefeller Foundation, the General Education Board, other Rockefeller endowments and his sister's trust fund, as well as the stock held by the Harkness, Pratt and Whitney families, all Rockefeller partners in the original Standard Trust and still family and corporate allies.

Leading the Rockefeller forces in the proxy fight was Charles Evans Hughes, former secretary of State—dubbed by his critics, "secretary for Oil"—and a distinguished trustee of the Rockefeller Foundation. When the dust settled, Rockefeller had won 60 percent of the votes and the ousted Stewart had to content himself with a $50,000-a-year pension which the directors awarded him for past services.

This kind of amiable camaraderie has continued to exist between the Rockefeller Foundation and the companies of the old Standard Oil Trust, according to Congressman Wright Patman's report on tax-exempt foundations. In 1962, when Standard Oil of New Jersey needed an extra million of its own shares to purchase the Olin Gas and Oil Company but was reluctant to make a new stock issue, it had only to ask the Rockefeller Foundation, which sold it the necessary shares.

Of course the covert reintegration of Rockefeller's formally shattered empire is not often laid open to view as it was in this corporate gathering of the tribe. And the uses to which this potential for central control are put are not well understood, not only because of the secrecy with which corporate and financial leaders shroud their decisions and modes of operation, but more importantly because the academic professions—heavily subsidized by the Rockefellers and Fords—have shown a singular lack of interest in its alliances, power configurations and interests.

Despite this failure, the scope and strength of the financial network that binds together a continuing Rockefeller imperium can be indicated by the known holdings just of the charitable Rockefeller trusts (not to speak of family trusts, personal and other direct holdings). Of course the main wealth of the Rockefeller Foundation itself flows from the fortune's primal source, the Standard Oil Company of New Jersey. The Foundation is today probably Jersey Standard's largest stockholder, with 4.3 million shares worth several hundred million dollars. In addition the Foundation owns two million shares of Standard Oil of Indiana, 230,000 of Standard Oil of California, 300,000 of Socony Mobil (Standard of New York), 300,000 of Continental Oil, and 100,000 of the Union Tank Car Company (often referred to as John D. Rockefeller's "secret weapon" in the oil monopolization business). And there's more, for the superstructure of the Rockefeller empire extends through another dozen foundations, and for these too the taproot is sunk deep in Rockefeller oil. According to the 1962 Patman Report, six other noncommercial Rockefeller foundations own another 3.5 million shares of Jersey Standard, 300,000 of Socony Mobil, 450,000 of Ohio Oil—and so it goes.

These foundation holdings, combined with personal holdings and a matrix of over 75 family trusts, afford the Rockefellers control of an inconceivably vast economic empire. In 1967, the assets of Standard Oil of New Jersey alone were valued at $15 billion. The combined assets of Socony Mobil, Jersey Standard, Indiana Standard and California Standard, in all of which the Rockefellers were major stockholders, amounted to $30.5 billion. Other Rockefeller-dominated interests include the world's second largest commercial bank, the Chase Manhattan ($17.7 billion); the second and third largest insurance companies, Metropolitan and Equitable ($24.6 and $13 billion); Eastern Airlines ($829 million); Consolidated Natural Gas ($1 billion); Union Tank Car ($367.8 million); Itek ($63 million); and Rockefeller Center ($300 million). This must be considered only a partial listing, but its grand total—$88 billion—is revealing nonetheless.

As the Patman Committee Report indicates, the Rockefeller Foundation was built in part as a secure repository designed to insulate a great fortune from the legal and political assaults that plague overtly commercial institutions. It was a disguised tax-free holding company. But it was not *only* that or it would be neither disguised nor untaxed nor as potent and portentous an instrument as it has become. A philanthropic cover must have some substantial reality to it if it is effectively to protect the underlying corporate structure. This duality of commercial interest and charitable form was the genius in the Foundation's architecture. Forced to dispense huge resources to keep its status, it salvaged something from the situation by understanding that it had a unique opportunity for private interest to operate on the cultural, political and social life of the society. Suspicion and resistance are forestalled by the assumption that what is nonprofit is disinterested and what is charitable is beneficial. The Rockefeller Foundation is only one of a phalanx of similar and related institutions. Indeed, it has even been to some extent upstaged by a later entrant on the scene.

The Ford Foundation is the Everest of the cultural-social trust field. Its assets exceed $3 *billion,* which is more than the gross national product of Cuba, and four times those of the second-place Rockefeller Foundation. Its annual income from securities is $150 million. In the period of a year and a half beginning in 1956, it "gave away" $500,-000,000, which is like giving away Time, Inc., Magnavox, General Mills, Pepsi-Cola, or even American Motors. The Ford Foundation represents the largest charitable dispenser in history; it is also without doubt the one whose genesis was most firmly rooted in greed.

Henry Ford was anything but a charitable man in his lifetime, and the greatest of all the philanthropic foundations was in fact not the outgrowth of generosity at all, but of Ford's own overweening perversity. In 1935, Ford, along with his son Edsel, owned 97 percent of the third largest industrial corporation in the world. He considered this his crowning achievement, and he could not comprehend that in the world of modern business, it was a disaster. All the time that his compeers, the Rockefellers, Mellons and others, were occupied with diluting their "ownership" in vast industrial empires (at the same time securing the reins of tax-protected control through foundations, trusts and various other holding devices), Ford was busily buying out his partners in simpleminded pursuit of exclusive, total, personal possession of his very own motor company.

But just as the "sage of Dearborn" was reaching the frenzied peak of the megalomania that dominated his later years, the national climate was becoming increasingly dangerous for such nakedly exposed riches. The speculative boom of the '20s had collapsed into the chasm of the Great Depression; the thievery of the "economic royalists" was being denounced in public hearings, while unarmed hunger marchers were being shot down at the Ford plant in Dearborn, Michigan. Out of the South, neo-Populist Huey Long was marshaling national support behind his share-the-wealth campaign, and in 1935 FDR recommended that federal taxes be used as a weapon against "unjust concentration of wealth and power." The Wealth Tax of that same year fixed high income, gift and estate taxes (70 percent for sums in excess of $50 million). Finally it all sank in. Within months, the papers establishing a Ford Foundation were completed.

If Henry and Edsel Ford had left their Ford stock to the Ford children, the heirs would have had to sell *most* of the shares they received just to pay the inheritance taxes. So Ford's lawyers arranged for him to will only 10 percent of the stock to the Ford children and 90 percent to the Ford Foundation. The Foundation stock, however, was designated "non-voting," a thoughtful gesture which kept control of the company firmly in the hands of the family. The Ford lawyers also provided that the inheritance taxes on the shares passed on to the Ford family would be paid out of the Foundation's shares as its first philanthropy.

Like the Rockefellers', the Fords' foundation program has always emphasized self-help, and they have always helped themselves. In 1961, the Fords needed a million Ford shares to acquire and absorb Philco Corporation. The Foundation—whose charter stipulates that it is "for charitable purposes, and nothing else"—was charitable to a fault; it even settled for four dollars per share less than the market value of the stock, amounting to a four million dollar discount. But then the market value was itself twice the value which the modest Ford Foundation carried on its books, so that the Foundation was doubling its money on the deal (tax-free, naturally).

Though the Ford Foundation is not quite so charitable to other companies, it has never been one to let a nonprofit status stand in the way of a little business. During the period 1950–1962, for example, the Ford Foundation made loans of at least $300 million to commercial organizations.

In the first 15 years of its existence, while Henry Ford was still alive, the Ford Foundation prudently avoided throwing money around in the loose showy manner of some charities. Its frugal philanthropy of those years added up to about $20 million, mostly trickling to "local" projects like the Detroit symphony and the Ford museum and hospital. Then, in the next 16 years, from 1951 to 1967, the Foundation poured out $2.6 billion, or a thousand times the previous rate. The story behind this sudden largesse underlines the unique character of this type of institution. It is an anomalous creature of unique circumstances; not really a charity, its prodigious levels of spending are imposed by external conditions and the only really pertinent question becomes who presides over its expenditures and for what ends.

The mere transfer of Ford stocks to the Ford Foundation in 1937 had not fully solved the Ford family crisis over control of their motor company. For while Congress has in its time turned a blind eye toward many tax-exempt "charitable" holding companies for commercial enterprises, the mammoth Ford enterprise was too big and blatant to be ignored indefinitely. Moreover, certain very powerful constituents began to get restless. These were not constituents of the letter writing class, but included Chrysler and General Motors. What they found particularly annoying was the dividend policy that Ford's peculiar stockholding arrangement permitted.

The family, whose 10 percent of the stock held all the votes, was not particularly concerned with high dividends, since 90 percent of the stock on which they would be paid was locked away in the Foundation. And since that 90 percent was in no position to complain, Ford Motor Company was able to put only half as much of its profits into dividends as Chrysler was, leaving the rest for a reinvestment and expansion program which powered Ford's forward surge in the auto market. By April 1954, the very important constituents were visibly losing their patience: "If General Motors or Chrysler earned no money and paid no dividends this year," complained the Corporate Director, a business monthly, "management heads would roll and equity credit would be seriously impaired. . . . It is our belief that in this case and in many others, federal legislation is needed that will prohibit any charitable foundation . . . from owning more than ten percent of any business enterprise."

The Ford Foundation, not wanting to force anyone to such drastic measures, immediately took steps to sell 15 percent of its Ford Motor stock to the public (a figure that was later upped to 22 percent) and even to spend its income, amounting to $100 million and more annually. After two decades, forced by the sheer weight of its own resources, the Foundation finally got down to philanthropic business.

Obviously, nominally philanthropic institutions like Rockefeller and Ford fail to coincide with the popular conception of a charitable institution or an altruistic mission to uplift the poor. They were after all designed first for the purpose of preserving wealth, not undermining it. This is why the largest area of foundation support has been research and higher education: the development of techniques and the training of the social elite.

"The problem of our age," Andrew Carnegie said in *The Gospel of Wealth,* is not the redistribution but "the proper *administration* of wealth, that the ties of brotherhood may still bind together the rich and poor in harmonious relationship." For the foundations, this effort takes many forms, from charting national policies designed to make the world safe for Standard Oil to engineering a proper course of moderation for America's black minority.

HOW CHARITY CAN BE ARTFULLY DISPENSED AND NOT ONLY BENEFIT THE RECEIVER BUT MAKE HIM A RESPONSIBLE CITIZEN AS WELL

At the outset of the '60s, the NAACP and the Urban League were on the right wing of the civil rights movement. Financed by white wealth, they preached an accommodationist line and upheld the business values of the system. As Booker T. Washington had, they denounced the militants and radicals. "Where the builders differ from the burners," remarked Whitney Young, director of the Rockefeller-financed Urban League, "is that we want to win victories within the framework of the system."

Young's remark was cited in a special Time essay on "Black Power and Black Pride" which appeared in December 1967. This was the third year of black uprisings in the United States and the second of the slogan "Black Power," which symbolized the new independence of the black movement from white influence—and restraint—and the program of self-reliance for black people. Four months later, Martin Luther King was assassinated, an event which put the quietus to non-violent agitation and confrontation. The dynamic of organized political action passed to the militants who had coined the term "Black Power" and whose guiding figure was not the preacher Martin Luther King but the assassinated prophet Malcolm X.

What Malcolm recognized in 1964—that the black man had a stake in national liberation struggles against the white imperialist powers all over the world—became clear to others after the U.S.'s massive escalation of its intervention in Viet-Nam in 1965. One year to the day before his assassination, King had mounted the pulpit in New York's Riverside Church to denounce the American government as "the greatest purveyor of violence in the world today," and to declare the black man's stake in opposing the war in Viet-Nam, in which "we are on the side of the wealthy and the secure while we create a hell for the poor." As King pointed out, Washington was ready to squander billions to preserve the status quo in Asia, but offered no more than pennies to modify and alleviate the suffering which their system caused at home; willing to spend $350,000 to kill a single yellow peasant in Asia, but only $54 to train a black laborer in the United States.

While King was gravitating towards a position of more serious confrontation with the system, Malcolm's disciples were explicitly identifying themselves with the revolutionary liberation movements of the Third World. In the summer of 1967, Stokely Carmichael appeared as the honored guest of the Tri-Continental Conference of revolutionary movements in Havana. The rhetoric was becoming anti-imperialist and anti-capitalist. ("Our enemy," Carmichael told the delegates, "is white Western imperialist society.") And meanwhile the cities were burning.

The first-line response to the militant black uprisings and organizations was of course the big stick of Law and Order, as the repression of SNCC and the Black Panther Party showed. But along with the frame-ups and police terror, a highly sophisticated program was being launched by forces of the status quo in the glass-enclosed New York headquarters of the $3 billion Ford Foundation.

In 1966, McGeorge Bundy left his White House position as Special Assistant for National Security ("I have learned," he once told an interviewer, "that the United States is the engine and mankind is the train") to become president of the Ford Foundation. Bundy was an exponent of the sophisticated approach to the preservation of the international status quo. Rejecting what he called "either/or" politics, he advocated "counterinsurgency and the Peace Corps . . . an Alliance for Progress and unremitting opposition to Castro; in sum, the olive branch and the arrows." The arrows of course would be taken care of by the authorities, from the CIA and the American military to Mayor Daley, while the foundations were free to pursue the olive branch side. Since they were "private" and non-governmental, they could leave the task of repression to their friends in other agencies while they pursued a benevolent, enlightened course without apparent hypocrisy.

In the spring of the following year, the Foundation announced a half-million dollar grant to Kenneth Clark's newly organized and militant-sounding Metropolitan Applied Research Center (MARC), created "to pioneer in research and action in behalf of the powerless urban poor in Northern Metropolitan areas." MARC promptly named Roy Innis, chairman of the militant Harlem chapter of the Congress on Racial Equality (CORE), as its first civil rights "fellow-in-residence." Then on May 27, it sponsored a secret meeting of civil rights leaders (nine major groups were represented) which announced a joint effort to calm racial tension in the city of Cleveland.

Cleveland, coincidentally, had been since 1961 the scene of a major attempt on the part of the Ford Foundation and major economic interests in the area to cool racial tensions. These attempts had ended in failure, and Cleveland had erupted during the previous summer. The enlightened economic powers of the city were now backing a black man for mayor, as a climax to their tepid campaign for an end to conflict. Now all eyes were on the November elections, and the candidacy of Carl Stokes, a Negro with what *Time* characterized as "moderate, constructive" programs and business backing. Cyrus Eaton, liberal lord of the greatest industrial fortune of the area, was backing Stokes, as were the electric power companies, who had an added incentive in that the candidate had promised to divest the city of its income-producing transit and electric systems and turn them over to private companies.

Into this situation trod the Ford Foundation, announcing on July 14 that it was giving $175,000 to CORE for work in the Cleveland area, which included voter registration. CORE accepted the grant, and helped Stokes, a Democrat and supporter of the Viet-Nam war, win the election. This was quite a position for militants who at one time had talked of forming a third party and whose opposition to the war in Viet-Nam had predated that of Martin Luther King Jr. Robert Allen, a black activist, explains CORE's turnabout in this way: "In the first place, they needed money. Floyd McKissick in 1966 had become national director of an organization which was several hundred thousand dollars in debt, and his espousal of black power scared away potential financial supporters. Secondly, CORE's militant rhetoric but reformist definition of black power as simply black control of black communities appealed to Foundation officials who were seeking just those qualities in a black organization which hopefully could tame the ghettos. From the Foundation's point of view, old-style moderate leaders no longer exercised any real control, while genuine black radicals were too dangerous. CORE fit the bill because its talk about black revolution was believed to appeal to discontented blacks, while its program of achieving black power through massive injections of [white] governmental business and Foundation aid seemingly opened the way for continued corporate domination of black communities by means of a new black elite."

In July 1967, a black power conference was held in Newark, financed by 50 white corporations. Then at the end of the month, the most massive rebellion to date took place in the Motor City of Detroit, leaving 45 blacks dead and millions of dollars worth of property damage in its wake. On August 1, the day after troops left the city, 22 American leaders called on the nation to revise its priorities and bring more resources to bear on domestic problems, and announced the formation of an Urban Coalition to do just that. The Urban Coalition, headed by John Gardner, former secretary of Health, Education and Welfare and former president of the Carnegie Foundation, included moderate Negro leaders Roy Wilkins of the NAACP and Whitney Young of the National Urban League, as well as labor leaders, big city mayors and businessmen like David Rockefeller and Gerald Phillippe, chairman of the board of General Electric and trustee of the National Industrial Conference Board, a foundation-financed policy organization. The funds for the Urban Coalition were to be provided by the Rockefeller Brothers Fund Inc., the Carnegie Foundation and the Ford Foundation. Regional coalitions between labor, Negroes, businessmen and politicians were to be formed (the New York coalition was headed by Christian Herter Jr., vice president of Standard Oil of New York) and they were to work in close cooperation with the National Alliance of Businessmen headed by Henry Ford II. Not surprisingly, the coalition placed primary emphasis not on massive income redistribution and federal reconstruction and rebuilding programs, but on the vigorous involvement of the private sector in the crises in the cities by commitment of investment, job training, hiring and "all other things that are necessary to the full employment of the free enterprise system, and also to its survival."

This basic strategy of salvation was echoed in the Report of the Special Advisory Commission on Civil Disorders (the Kerner Commission) which had been empowered by the President at the same time (July 27, 1967, in the wake of the Detroit insurrection) to look into the causes of riots and prescribe remedial action. "We conclude," declared the Commission report, "that maximum utilization of the tremendous capability of the American free enterprise system is a crucial element in any program for improving conditions, in both our urban centers and our rural poverty areas, which have brought us to the present crisis." The Commission also noted that more than 85 percent of the current annual gross national product is attributable to the private business sector, but it failed to draw the obvious conclusion that if free enterprise has been "the mainspring of the national economy," it has also been the mainspring of an economy that has produced the poverty and blight which are at the source of the present crisis.

That the Kerner Commission should agree so heartily with the Urban Coalition is not surprising. The head of the Commission's Advisory Panel on Private Enterprise, which drew these conclusions, was Tex Thornton, chairman of the board of Litton Industries [See David Horowitz, "Proving Poverty Pays: Big Brother as a Holding Company, in this volume, pp. 141–156.] Thornton's right-hand man, Roy Ash, had represented Litton on the Urban Coalition. Similarly, Vice Chairman John Lindsay, Roy Wilkins and I. W. Abel of the Commission all doubled as members of the privately sponsored group.

While vigorously repressing—i.e., killing, jailing, framing, ostracizing—Black Power advocates for whom Black Power meant confrontation with the system and agitation for revolutionary change, the rich white establishment and its press began to promote recognition of the reasonable connotations which the term "Black Power" had in the mouths of "responsible militants." As the Wall Street Journal reported in July 1968, "Black Power" is being "newly defined in a way that may not be quite so frightening to the white man"—and particularly to Wall Street Journal readers. "What now seems to be happening in the tortuous history of race relations in America," commented the Journal, "is that the black man is coming of age." While maintaining that "extremist blacks, and their radical ideas must be purged," the Journal noted that "White America is the majority, and the new black leadership, while adopting more of a 'do-it-ourselves' stance, still does not want a complete break with the rest of America."

Black Power as self-help within the system, then, was the Journal's preferred interpretation, and it was pleased to find that the black organizations, which are heavily subsidized by Journal readers on the one hand and savagely repressed by the forces of law and order on the other, are coming around to this point of view: "What is really being said now, in different ways by different leaders, is that the black man is beginning to feel strong enough to rely more on himself and less on the white man. This new emphasis on self-help is, in a sense, a return to the turn-of-the-century philosophy of Booker T. Washington. . . ."

NONPROFIT INSTITUTIONS
AND PROFITABLE EMPIRES

In 1911, the American Tobacco Trust, which had done for tobacco what Rockefeller did for oil, was "dissolved" by Supreme Court order. The founder of the trust, James Buchanan Duke, had been an admirer of Rockefeller, and two of the six men who controlled it were Rockefeller partners in Standard Oil. When Duke died in 1925, he left his fortune tied up in the Duke Endowment, a philanthropic foundation which is today worth more than $600 million, the largest such institution after the big three of Ford, Rockefeller and Carnegie, and itself a microcosmic model of what such foundations are all about.

Duke's lawyers had spent ten years perfecting the indenture of his Endowment, which made Trinity College, in Durham, North Carolina, the principal beneficiary of the fund, on the condition that it change its name to Duke University, which it promptly did. The indenture also "recommended" that securities of the Duke Power Company be "the prime investment" of the Endowment (which today holds 68 percent of the stock of Duke Power) and also stipulated that the trustees manage the Duke Power Company and the Doris Duke Trust (set up for the Duke heirs). To make the system airtight and perpetual, the indenture also provided that none of the holdings of the Endowment in Duke Power could be sold without the unanimous consent of the trustees—who were all affiliated with the company and associated tobacco, banking and legal interests, and among whom Doris Duke was to be a prominent member. Furthermore, it was stipulated that the income of the Endowment had to be distributed, after Duke University received its share, in designated percentages to hospitals, colleges, "superannuated preachers, their widows or orphans," and rural Methodist churches and seminaries. All these recipients, according to the terms of the indenture, must be situated in areas of North and South Carolina served by Duke Power. "Thus," as Dwight MacDonald aptly observed, "the interests of Duke's heirs, his power company, his customers, his foundation and God are all cunningly knotted together." Or, as Duke himself is reported to have said just before he died: "What I mean is, I've got 'em fixed so they won't bother it after I'm gone."

What Duke had sewed up, of course, was more than mere *income*—a secondary consideration at those stratospheric levels (*"What,"* Governor Rockefeller is reputed to have once asked an aide, "is 'take-home' pay?"). He had set his seal to a system of *power*, based on concentrated wealth. To this day, the Duke system is not only interlocked with former companies of the dissolved trust (for example, R. J. Reynolds, the number-one tobacco producer) and with non-Duke major economic

interests in the area, but with the New York financial matrix as well.
Thus the chairman of the Duke Endowment is also on the executive
committee of the board of directors of Morgan Guaranty and is a director of General Motors and the Penn-Central Railroad. Political
power in North Carolina, according to Professor V. O. Key, the leading
authority on the subject, is in the hands of a tight economic oligarchy,
which naturally includes the institutional trust system that "Buck"
Duke left behind.

Not everyone would agree. Dwight MacDonald, for example, con-
trasts the "narrow" conception of the Duke Endowment with that of
the Rockefeller, Ford and Carnegie Foundations. To be sure, the operations of the Rockefeller Foundation, for example, stretch far beyond the environs of New York, New Jersey, or even the 50 states.
But then oil has more widely dispersed sources of profit and supply
than tobacco: two-thirds of Jersey Standard's net income is derived
from operations in 52 countries overseas. Moreover, as the energy
source of modern industry, oil has a vastly more significant role to play
in contemporary society and international politics.

One can readily appreciate why the Rockefeller Foundation, with
more than half of its income flowing from the Standard Oil companies, should spend fully 75 percent of its revenue on the creation of
elites, modernization of infrastructures and purchases of goodwill overseas. In 1966, for example, the Foundation spent a million dollars on
higher education and elite training in Nigeria, or about *ten times* the
amount of its grants in Arkansas, Mississippi, Missouri, Virginia, West
Virginia and South Carolina combined. A cynic might observe that the
difference between the local and overseas underdeveloped regions is
that Nigeria is scheduled to become the biggest oil producing region
after the Middle East, and the danger of a nationalist-oriented elite
emerging to threaten the oil privileges of various corporations, including the Standard Oil Companies of New York and California, is very
real.

In any case, the concerned interest of the Big Three Foundations
is in the international "responsibilities" of American power. This is
evident in the prominence on their boards of financiers and indus-
trialists reflecting those businesses with by far the largest stake in the
overseas economic frontier. The most important international bank,
the Rockefellers' Chase Manhattan, has been prominently represented
on both the Ford and Rockefeller Foundation boards. The ubiquitous
John J. McCloy, once chairman of the board of Chase and the second
president of the so-called World Bank, one of the key institutions in
managing the expansion of U.S. private enterprise in the underdeveloped world, was one of the key figures in setting up the Ford Foundation after the transfer of Ford Motor stock, and he became chairman

of the board of the Foundation. Another dual trustee is Eugene Black, also a former president of the World Bank and also a director of Chase and trustee of the Ford Foundation.

Equally well represented with Chase is the Standard Oil Company itself (whose directors, naturally, also have regular seats on Chase). John Foster Dulles, long-time attorney for Standard Oil, was chairman of the board of the Rockefeller Foundation, while Arthur H. Dean, Dulles' law partner, has been a prominent Carnegie trustee, as Grayson Kirk has been of Standard Oil of New York (Socony Mobil). There are of course two Fords on the Ford Foundation, and naturally John D. Rockefeller III occupies a central position in the Rockefeller philanthropy. The circle becomes complete, as one might expect, when David Rockefeller, president of the Chase Manhattan Bank, sits on the board of the Carnegie Endowment for International Peace, while Morris Hadley, McCloy's law partner, is in the Carnegie Corporation.

There is a point to the intermarriages. These are no longer family trusts, but class institutions; they are conscious not merely of parochial economic interest but of the necessity of preserving a total social system, international in scope, on which their wealth, power, prestige—in a word, their whole way of life—depends.

Of course the chief guardian of the international economic frontier (and the rights of Chase Manhattan and Standard Oil abroad) is the U.S. government in Washington. Naturally the sights of the stewards of wealth are pointed in that direction, with the idea of shaping the ends and instruments of foreign policy. We live, however, in a pluralist democracy composed of an infinite number of competing interest groups, in which no collective or class dominates and where the self-interest of each is transformed via the matrix of competition into the interest of all—or so our leading social scientists, liberally financed by the Rockefeller, Ford and Carnegie Foundations, tell us. The unsophisticated and unbenefacted layman may retain the suspicion that a select few of these interest groups are more equal than others.

Take the AFL-CIO and the Rockefeller Foundation, two prominent organizations on the American scene. The AFL-CIO has 16 million members who make up the bulk of the most politically conscious working people in the country, from steelworkers to social workers, from printers to teachers. Its members pay the bulk of the individual income taxes that go to support the various activities of the federal government; while many millionaires pay no taxes at all, 61 percent of all individual federal income tax is paid by people with annual incomes of less than $15,000. These people also provide the bulk of the young sons who go off to fight on the overseas frontier. Yet in the history of pluralist America since the New Deal, only one union official has been graced with the privilege—and influence—of a post in the U.S. Cabinet.

The Rockefeller Foundation is a somewhat more exclusive club than the AFL-CIO, with a staff of less than 250 persons, the most important of whom generally belong to the upper echelons of the American social structure and hence pay considerably less taxes, lay down far fewer lives and are related to an infinitely smaller cross-section of the American people than are the members of the AFL-CIO. Yet the Rockefeller Foundation, in the open competition of pluralist interest groups, has found fortune standing consistently in its corner.

Trustees of the Rockefeller Foundation have been appointed to major cabinet posts in every administration since Truman (in addition to several important undersecretaryships), including secretary of Defense, secretary of the Treasury, and two secretaries of State. (They have done less well with Nixon, garnering only secretary of Agriculture.) Once having gotten to Washington, moreover, they have tended to stay. John Foster Dulles, the Foundation's chairman from 1950 to 1952, completed seven years of an eight-year term as secretary of State, being removed only by death, while his protégé, Dean Rusk, president of the Foundation from 1952 to 1961, filled out a full eight years in office. With opportunities for power like that, it is no wonder that the Rockefeller Foundation is organized more as an institution for mobilizing, training and offering a base to elites, than as a charitable institution, and that it spent half as much on administrative expenses in its plush New York office alone as it gave out in grants in the entire United States in the year 1966.

The foundations, however, are only the beginning, the base of the network of organizations through which the nerve centers of wealth impress their will on Washington. This network, the ganglia of foundation intelligence, is composed of a panoply of "independent" research and policy organizations, jointly financed and staffed by the foundations and the corporate community, which as a group set the terms and define the horizon of choice for the long-range policies of the U.S. government.

In addition to the Council on Foreign Relations, the foundation corporation complex has set up and directs the Brookings Institution, the National Bureau of Economic Research, the National Planning Association, the Foreign Policy Association, the Twentieth Century Fund, the National Industrial Conference Board and the Committee for Economic Development, as well as a whole bevy of institutions inside the universities.

As Philip Mosely, director of studies of the CFR, observed in a recent article, the foundations have been primarily responsible for the availability of academic research and scholarship to government (and of course for choosing which representatives of the academy shall gain this access). Does the government need policy studies? The Council on Foreign Relations, the Brookings Institution and the Committee on Economic Development would be happy to provide them. Strategic studies? There's always the RAND Corporation (which got its start as an independent research corporation through the Ford Foundation) and its progeny, the Stanford Research Institute, the Institute for Defense Analysis and others—all presided over, shaped and generally originated by the corporate elite which circulates from industry to philanthropy to government with infinite elegance and ease.

II

Welfare for the rich

Those who take the meat from the table
Teach contentment.
Those for whom the taxes are destined
Demand sacrifice.
Those who eat their fill speak to the hungry
Of wonderful times to come.
Those who lead the country into the abyss
Call ruling too difficult
For ordinary folk.

—BERTOLT BRECHT

. . . let it be remembered that we can never presume to aim at the extinction of poverty. . . . For, from the order of providence, which has designed that society should consist of various ranks, mutually dependent on each other, from the constitution of man, from the corruption of our nature, from the vicissitudes of life, from the different subordinations of society, as well as from the declaration of the scriptures, we are assured that "the poor shall never cease out of the land" (Deut. xv. 11) and "the poor we shall have with us always" (Mark xiv, 7). Moreover, such a constitution of society, under the government of infinite wisdom, conduces materially to the extent and variety of our obligations, and the increase of our comforts. The vast amount of real poverty, and the fear of its relentless oppression, are powerful stimulants to forecast and industry.[1]

In this section, Howard Wachtel and Larry Sawers of the faculty of the Department of Economics and Political Economy, American University, and Howard Sherman, assistant professor of economics at the University of California at Riverside, scrutinize the distributive impact of government policies on poor, average-income, and well-to-do groups in America. Wachtel and Sawers' findings suggest that government spending programs may substantially benefit higher-income groups.

[1] Charles Burroughs, Rector of St. John's Church, "A Discourse Delivered in the Chapel of the New Alms-House, in Portsmouth, New Hampshire, December 15, 1834, on the Occasion of its Being First Opened for Religious Services" (Portsmouth, N.H.: J. W. Foster, 1835), pp. 8–9.

Sherman criticizes the Nixon administration's premise that "all Americans will benefit from more profits" by arguing that increased monopoly profits tend to lower wages and to create more inflation and unemployment rather than the reverse. Sherman's conclusions, written early in 1972, appear even truer now than when they were written. During the intervening year and a half, profits have continued to climb, inflation has risen to the highest point since 1947, the real incomes of many groups of wage earners as well as social security and welfare recipients have declined, and beef dinners and home ownership have become out of reach for many middle- as well as low-income groups.[2]

[2] Readers interested in reading more concerning the relationship between capitalism and inflation are referred to Jacob Morris, "The Crisis of Inflation," *Monthly Review* 25, no. 4 (September, 1973): 1–22; and *The Review of Radical Political Economics,* "Special Issue on The New Economic Policy," 4, no. 4 (August 1972).

chapter three

Government spending
and the distribution of income

HOWARD M. WACHTEL AND LARRY SAWERS

> *To clamor for* equal or even equitable distribution *on the basis of the wages system is the same as to clamor for* freedom *on the basis of the slavery system. What you think just or equitable is out of the question. The question is: What is necessary and unavoidable with a given system of production.*[1]

In this paper, we present a conceptual framework that enables us to understand the economic activities of the government and the impact of this activity on the distribution of income. We do not attempt to produce a comprehensive *measurement* of the impact of total government expenditures, but we do survey a wide variety of Federal government programs and assess their distribution impact.[2]

An expanded version of this paper was presented at the 13th General Conference of the International Association for Research in Income and Wealth (Balatenfured, Hungary, September 1973). Copyright © by Howard M. Wachtel and Larry Sawers 1973.

The research for this paper was facilitated by a Faculty Summer Research Grant from The American University.

1 K. Marx, "Wages, Price and Profit," in Karl Marx and Frederick Engels, *Selected Works* (Moscow: Foreign Languages Publishing House, 1962), 1: 426 (emphasis in original).

2 Gillespie, the Tax Foundation, and Herriot and Miller have attempted precise quantitative estimates of the aggregate redistributive impact of tax and expenditure policy of the government. The results one obtains from this process derive more from the distributive assumption than from any hard facts. For example, depending on whether we assume that the benefits of so-called public goods (like military expenditures) are distributed according to wealth, income, or on a *per capita* basis, one finds redistribution towards higher- or lower-income groups. This does not seem to be an adequate scientific method. Wherever possible, we will present quantitative estimates of the specific government activities we are analyzing, but frequently we are unable to do so. Indeed, it may be conceptually meaningless to attempt a comprehensive measurement since more than one person or group can benefit from the same expenditure. At any rate, existing data and our energies to analyze them are limited.

We have been somewhat selective in our choice of government activities for the present analysis. Social welfare activities are given prominent attention since this is the area of government activity that purports to be the most redistributive toward lower-income groups. By challenging previous analyses, we hope to show that social welfare expenditures are far less redistributive toward lower-income groups than commonly believed, and, in some important instances, they are redistributive toward the higher income groups.

The major areas of federal government expenditure that we ignore are spending on transportation and spending on military and ancillary activities (space, international affairs and finance, CIA, interest on the national debt, and atomic energy development). Military and ancillary expenditures can be easily subsumed within the framework of this paper. There exists a voluminous literature which describes how these activities benefit the dominant classes and we shall not attempt to summarize the argument here. (See, for example, Magdoff for a simple statement of the argument.) Space and time limitations have prevented us from analyzing government transportation policy in this paper. In addition to its outlays on goods and services analyzed in this paper, the government undertakes a considerable variety of administrative and regulatory activities whose benefits far exceed actual outlays. We believe that, for example, the activities of the FDA, the Federal Reserve System, or the judiciary can be readily understood within the framework of this paper, but a careful treatment of this subject is beyond the scope of the present analysis.

I. THEORY OF THE STATE AND SOCIAL WELFARE EXPENDITURES

The question of how the effects of federal social welfare expenditures on interpersonal income distribution are analyzed lies at the heart of the differing liberal and radical theories of the state. The dominant liberal pluralist model views the society as divided along "interest group" lines with each interest group protecting and attempting to further its objectives. The role of the state in this view is a neutral *arbiter*, mediated through the electoral process, receiving "informational inputs," weighing the political pressures it is under, assessing the voting strength of the various interest groups seeking its favor, and so forth. What results in the mixture of governmental actions is largely a function of the number of votes each interest group can muster and the shrewdness with which it can organize its forces. Standing somewhere in between are the mediating representatives of the state in the form of political parties. Though these mediating political parties may have ideological biases that color their predilections, for the most part these parties are sufficiently malleable to bend with political pressures. And over time, as ideological concerns give way to pragmatic political ones, the parties become more and more alike in their goals of interest-group aggregation and mediation. The key elements of this view of the state are mediation, increasing neutrality of ideological preconception, and growth of the number of interest groups represented through the political process.

In contrast, the radical perspective views the state as part and parcel of the capitalist economic and social system. And that system has certain institutions that are essential to its survival, certain norms that must be protected, certain ideological underpinnings that cannot be undermined, and certain functions that it must perform smoothly. With the transformation of capitalism into monopoly capitalism, the role of the state has taken on many more complex forms than it had under competitive capitalism. It was relatively easy for Lenin to identify the dominant state role as one of preserving and stabilizing the property relations of a capitalist economy, i.e., the state as the "dictatorship of the bourgeoisie." Moreover, the class dominance of that earlier system was also more easily identifiable and less subject to serious debate. Today, however, many of these same attributes of the state are hidden behind more complex state institutions, with an obfuscating ideology, supported by important mediating institutions that prevent people from identifying the objective functions of the state in monopoly capitalist society. In what follows, we will consider several radical hypotheses about state action in the social welfare field.

First, it is important to recognize that the state influences the process by which people obtain income, and thereby structures the *pretax, preexpenditures income distribution*. Michelson (p. 78) offers an example of this: if the government only has purchasing contracts with white construction companies that employ only white, then blacks will end up with lower incomes. Enter the government's tax and transfer programs and it appears that the state redistributes income from whites to blacks. But the need for such a redistributive policy originated with the government's own action. The government creates a redistributive function for itself by establishing the initial conditions that require a redistributive policy. Michelson concludes (p. 78) with reference to government redistributive policy towards blacks:

The consequence of government action . . . is to reduce their before tax income, then pay some of that loss back, and then claim a net redistribution in their favor!

Michelson (p. 77) succinctly captures the fundamental point of a radical analysis of state redistributive policy when he argues that "The

entire impact of the government cannot be measured by only calcu-
lating redistribution from property after income has initially been
biased toward property." Gordon (1972, p. 321) has provided a useful
summary of this important proposition:

In modern industrial societies, the state has sweeping distributive impact on
the lives of its citizens. Only a few of those distributive effects result from
tax-and-transfer adjustments of the market distribution of income. The government not only pays wages and profits to individual "owners" of labor and
capital, but it also confers rights to engage in economic activities differentially
among individuals.

The government, therefore, benefits certain groups in society by purchasing goods and services from them rather than from other groups.
An even more important distributive activity of the government is in
defining and maintaining the institutional structure in which (as in
the above example) one group can benefit by owning enterprises that
sell to the government and another group is forced to sell its labor
to the first group to avoid destitution. By defining and enforcing property relations and markets in labor and capital, the state ensures the
domination of those who own productive property. Furthermore, the
government supports a wide array of socializing institutions (schools,
the nuclear family) that support those property relations.[3]

The state's long-run objectives become coincident with the long-run
objectives of the dominant classes in society—namely, *system-maintenance*.[4] At all costs, the fundamental economic and social system must

[3] We shall not attempt here to outline a general theory of state action in capitalist
society since our concern here is with only a part of government activity, that which
is thought of as social welfare expenditures. For a general discussion of the state, see
Miliband, Moore, and O'Connor.

[4] The implicit assumption is that maintaining the system is *not* in the best interests of the nondominant classes (or at least not in the interests of the majority
of the population). The argument is not couched solely in terms of income, that
the dominant classes receive more than their fair share. The dominant classes do
receive enormous sums for the mere ownership of property, an "activity" that is not
productive and thus should not be remunerated. (Property may in some sense be
productive—though orthodox Marxists would dissent—but the act of *owning*
property is not productive in any sense). Political economists argue that aside from
its maldistribution of income, the capitalist system is essentially dehumanizing and
alienating. Those outside the dominant classes are essentially unable to control their
lives. They are controlled by owners of property through ostensibly neutral markets
and through the state over which they have little influence. Life in capitalist society
is reduced to little more than the consumption of commodities, a process that can
never yield satisfaction (satiation) since there are always others who consume more
commodities and thus one can never have "enough." In noncapitalist societies,

be maintained, including property relations, market relations, social relations of production, markets in capital, labor, and land, and so on. However, within this long-run objective there is room for a variety of short-run activities that are either offensive, in the sense that they propel the interest of the dominant class forward, or defensive in the sense that they are concessions made to groups potentially threatening to the long-run objectives of system maintenance. Other things equal, the state would undertake redistributive policies that benefit the dominant class. But other things are not equal and this is the dialectic that produces short-run social welfare programs that benefit somewhat the subordinate classes.

Such activities have become more prevalent in recent years in the United States due to the growing economic surplus in monopoly capitalism and the intensification of the dynamics of inequality inherent in the system's normal operation. One of the uses of this surplus, along with such things as military expenditures, is increased social welfare expenditures to "buy off" the intense discontent fostered by the very system of monopoly capitalism that provides the growing surplus.

In the absence of any offsetting tendencies, inequality becomes more severe over time in monopoly capitalism. This occurs for two reasons. First, the economic system is dynamically disequalizing, what Marxists refer to as the "Law of Uneven Development." (See Bluestone, 1972[a] and Wachtel, 1973[b].) In the acquisition of human capital, individuals starting in a family with more economic wealth and more human capital will tend to acquire relatively more human capital. Moreover, the complementarity of the early socialization process and one's network of acquaintances acquired during elite schooling reinforces any unevenness in the acquisition of human capital itself. The same is true with physical capital: firms that start out with more physical capital and a larger share of the market have important economic

---

work is an expression of ones humanity; in capitalist societies it becomes its negation. One can hardly improve upon Marx's formulation of a century ago:

. . . all means for the development of production transform themselves into means of domination over, and exploitation of, the producers; they mutilate the labourer into a fragment of a man, degrade him to the level of an appendage of a machine, destroy every remnant of charm in his work and turn it into hated toil; they estrange from him the intellectual potentialities of the labor-process in the same proportions as science is incorporated in it as an independent power; they distort the conditions under which he works, subject him during the labor-process to a despotism the more hateful for its meanness . . . Accumulation of wealth at one pole is, therefore, at the same time accumulation of misery, agony, of toil, slavery, ignorance, brutality, mental degradation. (*Capital*, 1:645)

Stabilizing or maintaining the system is thus in the short- and long-term interests of the dominant classes. It *may* be in the short-term interests of others, but is never in their long-term interests.

advantages in information, market control, research and development, and investment funds to exacerbate the inequality over time. Diminishing returns to investment are easily offset by control of the market and control over information. This accounts for the increasing concentration and centralization in monopoly capitalist product markets, reaching its present heights in the form of conglomerates and multinational corporations. Finally, the state reinforces these tendencies, especially in its purchasing policies, primarily in the area of defense purchases. Here is where the militarism of monopoly capitalism's need to provide stable and hospitable national states in other countries intersects with the dynamics of uneven development at home. The defense establishment provides both: places to invest in other countries to export the growing domestic surplus and financially attractive contracts and investment subsidies at home to the powerful defense corporations.

To the extent that uneven development is cumulative—that is, it becomes more and more severe in each time period—then the state must penetrate into society more and more to offset the socially destructive aspects of uneven development. The extent to which the state will mitigate the growing tendencies towards inequality is conditioned by the need to prevent total societal breakdown, or put differently, to perform its system maintenance function. The extent to which the state will be forced to offset the dynamics of uneven development will depend on the political strength of the forces adversely affected by the dynamics of inequality. The extent to which this occurs depends on the unity of classes thrown in motion against the dominant class. Hence, the state will have to move faster and faster just to keep up. This explains the sharp increase in social welfare activities of the state since the Second World War, along with a stable income distribution. The state has entered the market to offset the negative aspects of the disequalizing tendencies just enough to forestall large-scale social unrest, which in this instance has meant the preservation of the existing distribution of income. In times of crisis, when solutions are sought, the political economist predicts that solutions to any problem will favor the interests of the dominant class and the long-run stability of the system. In the 1930s, rural poverty was a problem. Cash transfers to persons living in rural areas could have solved the problem, but breaking the work-income nexus for anyone but the abjectly poor would have serious destabilizing consequences. Instead, commodity price supports were instituted, and these subsidies to farmers have mostly benefited the wealthy farmers and agri-business. Farm laborers and migrant workers have, of course, been left out in the cold. If by mistake in a moment of duress, the government is forced because of political expediency into pursuing a program that is dissonant with the interests of the wealthy, these programs are quietly phased out as soon as the moment of crisis has passed. The Farm Security Administration (FSA), created in 1937, helped tenant farmers buy their farms, established cooperatives, and made loans and grants for rehabilitation purposes. One prominent program even benefited migrant workers. But (Aaron [b] pp. 147–48):

> Widespread political opposition, to FSA's allegedly "socialistic" and "impractical" farming projects, its promotion of "pressure groups," its attempts to "regiment" clients and "destroy their individualism, initiative and self-respect" led to its replacement.

In 1946, the Farmers Home Administration (FmHA) supplanted the FSA. The activities of the FmHA differ from its precursor, not because "the nature of the farm problem and the national perception of that problem have changed," as Aaron (b, p. 148) attempts to argue, but because the FSA was challenging the *status quo*. The FmHA now has a $5 billion program of financing homes in rural, small town, and suburban areas; only seven percent of the loans of the agency, whose predecessor was established to deal with rural poverty, go to farmers (Aaron b, p. 146). The destabilizing programs of the old FSA have been excised, and the new sanitized version receives generous treatment in the Congress.

Although this dimension to social welfare expenditures is the most general observation one can make, there are important exceptions that should not be overlooked. As the material forces of the economy advance, more and more segments of the labor force become redundant. Being no longer necessary for productive purposes due to increases in productivity, these segments of the labor force can be permanently removed, in some cases with the provision of a transfer payment. For example, the social security system created in the 1930s had the effect of cutting the size of the labor force substantially, thereby reducing the measured rate of unemployment "overnight" by substantial amounts. This segment was granted a transfer payment; however, other segments of the population have been eliminated from the labor force without the grant of a transfer. For example, child and women labor laws accomplished this result in the earlier part of this century. It is quite possible that today we face a more generalized problem of this type where a substantial segment of the labor force is economically redundant in the sense that they do not have the skills required to function with our existing level of technology in an economy organized along monopoly-capital lines.[5] For these people, some form of perma-

---

[5] This need not be the case in a rationally planned socialist economy, but this question lies outside the concerns of the present paper.

nent income-maintenance program may be the state's solution (Gordon, 1972, p. 323).

Within this conceptual framework, we can now investigate the distributional impact of government social welfare expenditures, starting with the broad category of transfer payments.

II. TRANSFER PAYMENTS

Transfer payments are a general category of income received by individuals that is neither in exchange for a labor service nor accrues as a result of ownership of capital. They are *categorical* in the sense that rights to the receipt of a transfer are based on qualifications under some category by virtue of age, physical incapacity, veteran's status, and the like. Transfer payments are wide-ranging in their scope, embracing social security, railroad retirement, government pensions, veteran's disability pensions and veteran's compensation, unemployment insurance, workmen's compensation, and public assistance.

In the discussion that follows, we will focus on the distributional effects of several of the larger forms of transfer payments. We will not be able to present any precise quantitative estimate of the distributional impact of transfers, but will suggest the direction and mode of analysis appropriate to the initial steps that must be taken if such estimates are to be made in the future.

First, it is worth noting the pervasiveness of transfer payments in the American economy. As table 1 shows, every segment of the income distribution received transfer payments of some kind in 1966. Moreover, the size of the transfer payment is essentially invariant with respect to pretransfer income above the poverty cutoff of $4,000. The heavy concentration of individuals in the lower-income brackets in this table is a result of the large weight that social security payments have in the total, thus rendering the concentration of transfer recipients biased toward lower-income categories that have virtually no income. Overall, forty-one percent of all households received some form of transfer payment in 1966, with slightly higher proportions receiving transfer payments among the poverty population below $4,000.

Decomposing aggregate transfer payments into their constituent parts reveals some interesting patterns.

1. SOCIAL SECURITY

Let us first consider social security (Old Age and Survivors Disability Insurance—OASDI) since this category of transfer is reputed to be one of the more redistributive of all social welfare programs. Moreover, its large size in the aggregate warrants a careful analysis.

Table 2 shows the distribution of OASDI payments among income

TABLE 1: DISTRIBUTION OF HOUSEHOLDS RECEIVING TRANSFER PAYMENTS BY INCOME OTHER THAN TRANSFER PAYMENTS, 1966

Nontransfer Income	Percent Distribution of Households Receiving Transfer Payments	Average Transfer Payment	Proportion Receiving Payments
$ 0– 499	30.1%	$1,885	.89
500– 999	6.9	1,893	.74
1,000– 1,499	5.7	1,830	.68
1,500– 1,999	4.2	1,638	.62
2,000– 2,499	3.3	1,486	.51
2,500– 2,999	2.9	1,692	.49
3,000– 3,499	3.1	1,572	.42
3,500– 3,999	2.4	1,751	.39
4,000– 4,499	2.7	1,166	.32
4,500– 4,999	2.6	1,198	.36
5,000– 5,999	5.4	1,307	.29
6,000– 6,999	5.9	1,207	.31
7,000– 7,999	5.1	1,134	.27
8,000– 8,999	3.6	1,030	.22
9,000– 9,999	3.2	1,061	.23
10,000–11,999	5.3	1,735	.23
12,000 and over	7.4	1.176	.21
Total	100.0	$1,575	.41

Source: Irene Lurie, "The Distribution of Transfer Payments Among Households," in The President's Commission on Income Maintenance Studies, *Technical Studies* (Washington: Government Printing Office, 1970), pp. 146 and 151.

groups and the average size of the benefit in 1966. The average payments are essentially invariant with respect to income for incomes over the poverty level of $4,000. Monthly benefits were higher in 1971 for higher paid workers, but the ratio of benefits of previous earnings declines as earnings rise (table 3). An individual in 1971 with average monthly earnings of $750 (during his/her working life) would be receiving $296 per month or thirty-nine percent of earnings, while a lower paid worker earning $250 per month would receive only $145.60 or fifty-eight percent of previous earnings. But inevaluating the redistributive aspects of a social welfare program it is not sufficient to simply describe the small amount of redistribution in favor of those with lower incomes that derives from the payment structure. The tax that supports the program must be analyzed simultaneously as well as associated deductions from the benefit structure for income received from various sources. These issues are discussed below.

Some have argued that the social security tax and transfer program is essentially an intergenerational transfer. This argument has two interpretations: First, the tax and transfer program is a transfer from

TABLE 2: DISTRIBUTION OF HOUSEHOLDS RECEIVING OASDI BY INCOME OTHER THAN OASDI, PUBLIC ASSISTANCE, AND VETERANS PENSIONS, 1966

Income Other Than OASDI, Public Assistance and Veterans Pensions	Percent Distribution of Households Receiving OASDI	Average OASDI Benefit
$ 0– 499	27.5%	$1,144
500– 999	11.1	1,275
1,000– 1,499	9.3	1,332
1,500– 1,999	7.0	1,314
2,000– 2,499	4.9	1,419
2,500– 2,999	3.9	1,410
3,000– 3,499	3.6	1,358
3,500– 3,999	2.5	1,423
4,000– 4,499	2.6	1,019
4,500– 4,999	2.5	1,246
5,000– 5,999	4.5	1,201
6,000– 6,999	4.1	1,207
7,000– 7,999	3.3	1,232
8,000– 8,999	2.7	1,183
9,000– 9,999	1.8	1,264
10,000–11,999	3.6	1,121
12,000 and over	5.2	1,138
Total	100	$1,235

Source: Irene Lurie, "The Distribution of Transfer Payments Among Households," in The President's Commission on Income Maintenance Studies, *Technical Studies* (Washington: Government Printing Office, 1970), p. 146.

those presently working to those who have retired from the labor force as a result of the statutory retirement provisions. Second, the social security program represents a transfer of income for the same individual between the period she or he works and the period of retirement. Whichever of these interpretations is valid and both seem to be highly

TABLE 3: RATIOS OF OLD AGE AND SURVIVORS INSURANCE BENEFITS TO SELECTED AVERAGE MONTHLY EARNINGS, 1971 BENEFITS SCHEDULES

Average Monthly Earnings of Insured Worker During Working Years	Monthly Benefit, Single Retired Workers	Ratio of Benefit to Prior Earnings
($)	($)	
250	145.60	0.58
417	198.80	0.48
583	251.80	0.43
750	296.00	0.39

Source: Charles L. Schultze, et al., *Setting National Priorities: The 1973 Budget* (Washington: The Brookings Institution, 1972), p. 181.

speculative and unsupported by any careful empirical work), they both tend to ignore the very regressive structure of taxes that supports the social security program.

The tax that supports the social security program is in equal part a payroll tax paid by employers and a tax on wages and salaries paid by the employee. However, there is a ceiling placed on those wage and salary earnings subject to the tax (on both the employer and employee side). For example, the maximum taxable earnings were set at $7800 (ignoring the most recent amendments) for the 1968–1987 period! However, at the same time the total tax (both employer and employee share) was to rise from 8.8 percent to 11.8 percent. The effect of increasing the tax while holding the ceiling on taxable wages and salaries fixed is to increase sharply the regressivity of the tax.

As a consequence of the sharp ceiling on taxable wages and salaries, the tax rates are highly regressive, as table 4 shows. The effective tax

TABLE 4: EFFECTIVE TAX RATES ON INCOME OF A FIVE PERCENT PAYROLL TAX ON EMPLOYERS AND EMPLOYEES, BY INCOME CLASSES, 1964

Income Class ($)	Effective Rate of Payroll Tax (%)[a]
1,000– 2,000	8.1
2,000– 3,000	8.4
3,000– 4,000	8.9
4,000– 5,000	9.3
5,000– 6,000	9.4
6,000– 7,000	9.5
7,000– 8,000	9.4
8,000–10,000	8.4
10,000–15,000	6.3
15,000–25,000	3.9
25,000 or more	1.5

Source: Joseph A. Pechman, Henry J. Aaron, and Michael R. Taussig, *Social Security— Perspectives for Reform* (Washington: The Brookings Institution, 1968), p. 307.

[a] Based on assumption that employer share of tax is borne by employee in the form of lower wages.

rate rises somewhat up to $8,000 and then falls sharply thereafter, leaving a low-wage worker paying about nine percent of wages and salary earnings while a high salaried professional earning over $15,000, paying four percent or less.

The regressivity of the social security tax is only the tip of the iceberg. Brittain has shown that the *employer's* share of the social security tax is shifted *backward* to the employee, resulting in lower wages than would have been paid in the absence of the social security tax (Brittain 1971, p. 111):

The long-run result appears to be that employers in the aggregate avoid the burden of their contribution via a trade-off between the tax and the real wages and salaries.

As a consequence, previous estimates on the redistributive impact of the social security tax have been overstated (Brittain 1971, p. 122):

The conclusion that labor bears the tax makes clear its burden on low income groups is greater than generally realized. It also implies that its impact on income distribution is typically regressive.

But the story does not end here. The tax-transfer and penalty system is severely class-biased in that, first, only *labor income* is taxed leaving the principal source of income for the upper portions of the income distribution (*capital income*) untaxed.

Second, retired people (up to age seventy-two are limited to the amount of wage and salary earnings they can acquire before they start to lose their social security benefits. In 1972, an individual was able to earn only $1,680 before she or he began to forfeit social security benefits. However, this restriction applies only to income from wages and salaries but not to income from capital. An individual can receive unlimited amounts of rent, interest, dividends, private pensions, income from trusts, capital gains, and other forms of capital income without forfeiting a penny in social security.

Third, since poor people (especially blacks) die at an earlier age because of the inaccessability of private markets for health care, poorer life-long nutrition, and dangerous work conditions the system is further biased against lower paid workers and blacks who are unable to live to benefit from the payment system to the same extent as higher-income white people. Equity would suggest that taxes be differentiated by income class and by race in order to compensate for the earlier age of death of poorer people and of blacks.

2. VETERAN'S PROGRAMS

Table 5 presents data for three veteran's programs in 1966: Veteran's Disability Benefits, Veteran's Compensation, and Veteran's Pensions. Departing from the pattern in social security, the recipients of Veteran's Compensation are more heavily concentrated in the higher-income brackets, but this pattern is not replicated in the other two veteran's programs. There are several interesting points worth noting about these data: first, with the exception of Veteran's Pensions, the distribution of benefits over income groups is fairly constant. Second, the average benefit levels exhibit no clear patterns; in some instances

TABLE 5: DISTRIBUTION OF HOUSEHOLDS RECEIVING VETERANS DISABILITY BENEFITS BY INCOME OTHER THAN VETERANS DISABILITY BENEFITS AND PUBLIC ASSISTANCE, 1966

Income Other Than Veterans Disability Benefits and Public Assistance	Percent Distribution of Households Receiving Veterans Disability Benefits	Average Veterans Disability Benefit	Percent Distribution of Households Receiving Veterans Compensation	Average Veterans Compensation Benefit	Percent Distribution of Households Receiving Veterans Pensions	Average Veterans Pensions
$ 0- 499....	7.7%	$1,068	2.1%	$1,157	14.0%	$1,053
500- 999....	5.8	1,066	1.7	1,235	10.4	1,035
1,000- 1,499....	6.5	957	2.7	1,321	10.7	853
1,500- 1,999....	5.3	856	1.5	1,030	9.5	825
2,000- 2,499....	5.7	977	2.0	968	10.0	979
2,500- 2,999....	5.9	1,180	2.4	1,188	10.0	1,140
3,000- 3,499....	3.8	1,227	2.0	1,273	5.8	1,210
3,500- 3,999....	3.6	1,324	1.2	2,320	6.4	1,108
4,000- 4,499....	3.5	707	2.5	796	4.7	654
4,500- 4,999....	3.7	898	2.9	1,245	4.5	644
5,000- 5,999....	6.5	854	3.1	1,349	10.4	686
6,000- 6,999....	6.4	1,078	8.8	1,349	3.6	327
7,000- 7,999....	6.1	828	11.5	828	0	0
8,000- 8,999....	5.5	715	10.3	715	0	0
9,000- 9,999....	3.8	973	7.2	973	0	0
10,000-11,999....	7.5	674	14.2	674	0	0
12,000 and over...	12.7	691	23.9	691	0	0
Total...........	100.0%	$ 917	100.0%	$ 914	100.0%	$ 920

Source: Irene Lurie, "The Distribution of Transfer Payments Among Households," in The President's Commission on Income Maintenance Studies, *Technical Studies* (Washington: Government Printing Office, 1970), p. 147.

higher-income groups receive higher average benefits while in other instances lower-income groups receive higher benefits.

3. PUBLIC ASSISTANCE

For many the phrase "social welfare spending" connotes public assistance, a category that embraces several programs: old age assistance, aid to the blind and permanently disabled, and aid to families with dependent children (AFDC). As with veteran's programs, there is no specific tax levied to collect funds for these programs. Consequently, the regressivity or progressivity of the tax side of these programs must be analyzed within the context of the tax system as a whole.

Table 6 presents the data on public assistance as a group. The heavy concentration of public assistance in the very lowest income groups

TABLE 6:   DISTRIBUTION OF HOUSEHOLDS RECEIVING PUBLIC ASSISTANCE
BY INCOME OTHER THAN PUBLIC ASSISTANCE, 1966

Income Other Than Public Assistance	Percent Distribution of Households Receiving Public Assistance	Average Public Assistance Payment
$ 0– 499......................	39.2%	$1,423
500– 999......................	16.6	930
1,000– 1,499......................	9.5	989
1,500– 1,999......................	5.3	1,032
2,000– 2,499......................	4.1	768
2,500– 2,999......................	3.9	970
3,000– 3,499......................	2.2	918
3,500– 3,999......................	2.2	568
4,000– 4,499......................	1.4	667
4,500– 4,999......................	1.7	702
5,000– 5,999......................	3.4	975
6,000– 6,999......................	2.5	708
7,000– 7,999......................	2.3	765
8,000– 8,999......................	1.8	740
9,000– 9,999......................	.9	623
10,000–11,999......................	1.6	921
12,000 and over....................	1.2	837
Total...........................	100.0	1,098

Source: Irene Lurie, "The Distribution of Transfer Payments Among Households," in The
President's Commission on Income Maintenance Studies, *Technical Studies* (Washington:
Government Printing Office, 1970), p. 148.

results from the fact that many of the public assistance programs provide transfers for people who are not capable of working at all. No
doubt this program is redistributive to lower-income groups in the conventional sense without taking account of the system maintenance
function (discussed above) that many of these programs, especially
AFDC, provides. With the exception of households with virtually no
other source of income, the average public assistance payment is
roughly constant across all income groups.

4. UNEMPLOYMENT INSURANCE AND
WORKMEN'S COMPENSATION

The final two transfer payments that will be discussed here are
lumped together, Unemployment Insurance and Workmen's Compensation, since both are programs provided to workers who are either disabled physically or economically (unemployed) by the vicissitudes of
the economic system. Both are supported in part by payroll taxes
levied on employers but probably shifted backward onto the employees
wage, in the same manner in which the employer's share of the social

security tax is shifted backward. Both vary according to state law (more in benefits than in taxes).

Unemployment Insurance is spread fairly evenly over the income distribution in terms of households receiving some benefits (table 7).

TABLE 7: DISTRIBUTION OF HOUSEHOLDS RECEIVING UNEMPLOYMENT INSURANCE BY INCOME OTHER THAN UNEMPLOYMENT INSURANCE, PUBLIC ASSISTANCE, AND VETERANS PENSIONS, 1966

Income Other Than Unemployment Insurance, Public Assistance, and Veterans Pensions	Percent Distribution of Households Receiving Unemployment Insurance	Average Unemployment Insurance Benefit
$ 0– 499	1.4%	$793
500– 999	.9	505
1,000– 1,499	1.6	521
1,500– 1,999	3.1	385
2,000– 2,499	4.7	535
2,500– 2,999	4.4	477
3,000– 3,499	4.1	383
3,500– 3,999	3.7	383
4,000– 4,499	3.9	419
4,500– 4,999	6.2	393
5,000– 5,999	8.7	439
6,000– 6,999	11.4	389
7,000– 7,999	10.5	369
8,000– 8,999	8.8	295
9,000– 9,999	6.7	348
10,000–11,999	9.8	378
12,000 and over	9.9	384
Total	100.0	$399

Source: Irene Lurie, "The Distribution of Transfer Payments Among Households," in The President's Commission on Income Maintenance Studies, *Technical Studies* (Washington: Government Printing Office, 1970), p. 149.

And like most of the other programs we have encountered, the average benefit level is roughly constant over all income groups above the $4,000 poverty level. The pattern is slightly different for Workmen's Compensation; the concentration of households participating is more skewed toward the higher-income groups, while the average benefit level is slightly progressive (table 8).

Not all the recipients of public assistance are completely outside the labor force. Many are sporadically employed in the secondary sector of the economy. They move between government social welfare programs and jobs—the one being a substitute for the other (see Harrison). For these individuals, public assistance takes on more of the appearance of a *wage supplementation program*, providing these

TABLE 8: DISTRIBUTION OF HOUSEHOLDS RECEIVING WORKMEN'S COMPENSATION BY INCOME OTHER THAN WORKMEN'S COMPENSATION, PUBLIC ASSISTANCE, AND VETERANS PENSIONS, 1966

Income Other Than Workmen's Compensation, Public Assistance, and Veterans Pensions	Percent Distribution of Households Receiving Workmen's Compensation	Average Workmen's Compensation Benefit
$ 0– 499	1.6%	$1,193
500– 999	1.2	1,834
1,000– 1,499	1.9	765
1,500– 1,999	2.4	655
2,000– 2,499	2.4	731
2,500– 2,999	3.6	818
3,000– 3,499	2.7	881
3,500– 3,999	4.7	442
4,000– 4,499	4.0	702
4,500– 4,999	4.2	648
5,000– 5,999	9.0	428
6,000– 6,999	11.4	442
7,000– 7,999	10.0	443
8,000– 8,999	5.3	425
9,000– 9,999	9.0	470
10,000–11,999	11.2	342
12,000 and over	15.4	471
Total	100.0	513

Source: Irene Lurie, "The Distribution of Transfer Payments Among Households," in The President's Commission on Income Maintenance Studies, *Technical Studies* (Washington: Government Printing Office, 1970), p. 149.

members of the secondary labor force with a bare minimum income between their low-paying jobs. In these circumstances, public assistance benefits the *employer* in low-wage industries as well as the direct recipient of public assistance, a common feature of most poor laws dating back to the Elizabethan period. This point has been conceded in an official government document, the 1968 *Manpower Report of the President* (p. 98):

Public assistance often served as a form of wage supplementation for the low-paid, partially employed worker. Welfare status did not necessarily represent a sharp break with the labor force, as the theory of assistance would imply.

The argument advanced here is not that these transfer programs are redistributive toward higher-income groups, although in the case of a major program, social security, it probably is when account is taken of the tax structure and class bias of the program. However, one point is clear: these transfer programs, which are the cornerstone of the redistribution policies of the state, are far *less* redistributive toward the poor than either the government or economists propose. When coupled with a much reduced level of redistribution in transfer programs, the overall redistributive results of state policy are much more open to serious question.

We turn next to the overall issue of federal government *subsidies,* a classification scheme introduced by the Joint Economic Committee of the U.S. Congress.

III. FEDERAL SUBSIDIES

Another aggregative approach to the problem of analyzing the distributional impact of federal government expenditures has recently been advanced by the Joint Economic Committee (JEC) of the U.S. Congress in their work on *subsidies.* They define a subsidy as:

the provision of Federal economic assistance, at the expense of others in the economy, to the private sector producers or consumers of a particular good, service or factor of production. The Government receives no equivalent compensation in return, but conditions the assistance on a particular performance by the recipient—a quid pro quo—that has the effect of altering the price or costs of the particular good, service, or factor to the subsidy recipient, so as to encourage or discourage the output, supply, or use of these items and the related economic behavior. (JEC, 1972, p. 18)

Included in their definition of subsidies are: explicit cash payments, implicit payments through a reduction of a specific tax liability, implicit payments by means of loans at interest rates below the government borrowing rate or from loan guarantees, implicit payments through provisions of goods and services at prices or fees below market value, implicit payments through Government purchases of goods and services above market price, and implicit payments through government regulatory agencies that alter particular market prices (JEC, 1972, p. 18). Their empirical work excludes some of the larger elements of subsidies in the economy—subsidies implicit in international tariffs and quotas and subsidies provided in connection with defense purchases above market prices (including subsidies in the form of progress payment and subsidies attained via government regulatory activities) [JEC, 1972, p. 19]. In addition, subsidies from state and local governments are also excluded.

Even with these important exclusions from the calculation of subsidies, the JEC estimated the amount of federal subsidies to be over $63 billion in 1970, with the vast majority of the subsidies provided

TABLE 9: SUBSIDIES BY FINANCIAL FORM, 1970

Form of Subsidy	1970 (millions of $)
Cash payment subsidy	11,801
Federal tax subsidy	38,480
Federal credit subsidy	4,183
Benefit-in-kind subsidy	9,245
	63,709

Source: Joint Economic Committee, *The Economics of Federal Subsidy Programs* (Washington: Government Printing Office, 1972), pp. 26, 31, 34, 38, 39, and 40.

to *producers* rather than consumers (JEC, 1972, pp. 4 and 5). A breakdown of those subsidies by financial form is provided in table 9, and a breakdown of subsidies by program is provided in table 10.

TABLE 10: SUBSIDIES BY PROGRAM, 1970

Program	1970 (millions of $)
Agricultural subsidies	5,202
Food subsidies	1,593
Medical care subsidies	8,740
Manpower training subsidies	2,541
Education subsidies	3,604
International trade subsidies	1,183
Housing subsidies	8,425
Natural resource subsidies	3,034
Transportation subsidies	672
Commerce and economic development subsidies	19,623
Subsidies not elsewhere classified	9,092
	63,709

Source: Joint Economic Committee, *The Economics of Federal Subsidy Programs* (Washington: Government Printing Office, 1972), pp. 87, 99, 105, 114, 125, 140, 152, 167, 181, 187.

In the discussion that follows, we will examine the interpersonal distributional effect of some of these financial forms of subsidies and subsidy programs in more detail, starting with the largest financial form of subsidy payment, *federal tax subsidies.*

1. FEDERAL TAX SUBSIDIES

There is little or no conceptual difference between an outright subsidy to an organization or group of people and a tax loophole that benefits that same organization or group. The only difference between receiving a check for a certain sum and paying less taxes of that same amount is that in the former case the subsidy is more visible and public. For this very reason economists have traditionally argued against implicit subsidies since they tend to obfuscate the true nature of transfers. These implicit subsidies that derive from erosion of the tax base are truly enormous. A recent study has shown that for the federal personal income tax alone, an additional $77 billion in revenue would be collected if loopholes could be plugged (Pechman and Okner, p. 23).

It is difficult to give a precise definition of a tax subsidy. Some argue it is merely a lower tax than some ideal, and thus is inherently value-ladden and ambiguous. Some honest and intelligent persons believe for reasons other than pecuniary self interest that capital gains should be taxed at a lower rate than other kinds of income. For them, favorable treatment of capital gains is not a loophole, but a just and rational means of achieving allocative efficiency. The following discussion of the major tax subsidies in the federal tax structure follows the lead of most orthodox public finance theorists who view tax subsidies as deviations from horizontal equity. A useful operational definition of a tax subsidy (or loophole) posits the existence of a tax subsidy wherever income is taxed differentially solely dependent upon the *source* of the income. That is, not all dollars of income are taxed at the same rate as a function of the income source, so a dollar of capital gains income is taxed at a lower rate than a dollar of wage and salary income.[6]

Accordingly, personal income is defined as the sum of consumption, net of the change in the value of assets, and net of direct taxes. Corporate income is defined as receipts minus costs (including depreciation of assets). The exemption of income from taxation takes place in a number of ways, but the quantitatively most important loopholes in the federal personal income tax are as follows.

Capital gains. Only one-half of net realized long-term gains are taxed, with a maximum tax rate of twenty-five percent to thirty-five percent. Furthermore, capital gains completely escape taxation if passed from generation to generation by bequest, and are taxable if transferred by gift only if the assets are later sold. If the favorable treatment of capital gains were ended, yearly federal personal income tax revenues would rise by an estimated $9.3 billion. If capital gains realized on gifts and bequests were taxed, revenues would rise by an additional $4.4 billion (Pechman and Okner, p. 23).

6 A comprehensive definition of personal income is discussed in Boris Bittker, et al. See also Goode and Pechman, pp. 67–104. For a discussion of the corporate income tax base, see Pechman, pp. 107–9 and Musgrave, pp. 164–71.

State and local bond interest. Interest on bonds issued by state and local governments is exempted from taxation. This leads to a revenue loss of $1.2 billion (Pechman and Okner, p. 23).

Interest on life insurance savings. Interest on savings accumulated on straight life insurance policies, unlike other interest, is not taxable. This leads to a revenue loss of $2.7 billion (Pechman and Okner, p. 23).

Home owners' preferences. Home owners do not pay tax on the imputed rent from the ownership of their homes. Furthermore, mortgage interest and property taxes may be deducted from taxable income. These ommissions lead to a revenue loss of $9.6 billion (Pechman and Okner, p. 23).

Transfer payments. The failure to treat transfer payments as taxable income leads to a revenue loss of $13.1 billion.

Divident exclusion. Up to $100 of dividend income is excluded from taxable income leading to a revenue loss of $0.7 billion.

Income splitting. Husbands and wives may treat income as if it were divided equally between them. This leads to large tax savings for middle and upper income families and discriminates against the unmarried. Revenue loss from this loophole is $21.5 billion (Pechman and Okner, p. 23).

The following tax subsidies derive from both the personal and corporate income taxes, but the revenue loss to the Treasury is much greater for the corporate tax.

Depreciation allowances. Before 1954, assets could be depreciated according to the "straight line" method, i.e., by a constant percentage each year. Since 1954, various methods of accelerated depreciation have been allowed. "The more rapid recovery of capital, made possible by accelerated depreciation, offers an interest (time-discount) gain to investors and permits growing firms to finance more of their capital requirements from retained earnings. Moreover, it reduces risk and uncertainty" (Herber, p. 246). A precise, quantitative estimate of this tax subsidy is unavailable.

Depletion allowance. Taxpayers may deduct twenty-two percent of receipts from the sale of gas and oil (other minerals at lower rates) from their taxable income to allow for depletion of mineral deposits. In addition all costs of exploration and development of oil and gas wells are treated as expenses rather than as depreciable invest-

ment. The revenue loss from favorable treatment of depletion is about
$1.2 billion (Pechman, p. 130).

The following loopholes are associated only with the corporate income tax.

Investment credit. Beginning in 1962, business firms have
been permitted to deduct as a credit against their tax liability a percentage of the value of their new investment. This percentage varies
with the expected service life of the asset. In 1969, this cost the Federal
Treasury about $2.5 billion (Pechman, p. 127).

Financial institutions. Banks have been allowed to maintain
a reserve for bad debts that greatly exceeded actual loss experience,
thereby lowering tax liabilities by significant amounts. This loophole
has cost the Treasury billions but is gradually being plugged up.

The most striking aspect of this list of tax subsidies is that all but
two of them—the exclusion of transfer income and income splitting—
are associated with the ownership of property. With respect to the personal income tax, all of these provisions, except the exclusion of transfer income, benefit high-income taxpayers more than low-income taxpayers. But this is not very remarkable; it only means that the tax
structure is less progressive than the nominal rates would lead one to
believe. What is salient about the erosion of the personal income tax
base is that almost all of the large loopholes favor unearned (property)
income over earned income.

Likewise with the corporate income tax. It is not surprising that the
provisions mentioned above lower the average tax rate. But it is interesting to note that all of the above provisions favor firms that are
capital intensive more than those that are labor intensive.

The tax breaks given home owners under the personal income tax
offer substantial savings to middle-income households, i.e., the benefits
are not reserved for the rich. However, this is consistent with the national policy to favor home ownership over rentals in order to give
even the middle-income strata a feeling that they have a stake in
society. (See discussion of housing subsidies below.) The income splitting provision can be easily understood as part of a general policy to
favor the nuclear family over other modes of family organization.

We have discussed above the major sources of tax-base erosion in the
federal tax structure. In addition, there are hundreds of other possible
deductions and exemptions, none of which are individually as important as the ones described above, but together they represent an enormous drain on the Treasury. The value of these deductions and exemptions is equal to the deduction or exemption times the marginal
tax rate. Since high-income taxpayers have higher marginal tax rates,

these deductions and exemptions are worth proportionately more to them. Thus, the benefits flow disproportionately to the affluent.

The larger tax subsidies are unequally distributed among income groups, with higher-income groups receiving disproportionately higher tax subsidies. In table 11, we present data for the overall distribution

TABLE 11: TAX SUBSIDIES BY INCOME GROUP, 1972

Income Group (thousands of $)	Average Annual Tax Subsidy ($)		
	Total	Capital Gains	Tax-Exempt Interest on Bonds
3	16	—	—
3–5	148	1	—
5–10	340	9	—
10–15	651	24	1
15–20	1,181	55	1
20–25	1,931	120	4
25–50	3,897	534	24
50–100	11,911	3,795	205
100–500	41,480	22,630	3,630
500–1,000	202,752	165,000	19,167
over 1,000	720,448	640,667	36,333

Source: Philip M. Stern, "Statement Before Joint Economic Committee," in Joint Economic Committee, *Hearings Before the Subcommittee on Priorities and Economy in Government* (Washington: Government Printing Office, 1972), pp. 80–81.

of tax subsidies, along with data for tax subsidies for tax-exempt interest on bonds and for capital gains, by income group. At the upper reaches of the income distribution (individuals earning $1 million or more), the average tax subsidy amounted to over $720,000 in 1972.

The unequal distributional impact of personal income tax exemptions is repeated in the corporate income tax through a variety of subsidies (usually called "tax incentives") that benefit the larger corporations disproportionately. In 1971, for example, eleven of the top forty-five corporations in the Fortune 500 list paid corporate income taxes of ten percent or less, on a "taxable income" of nearly two- and three-quarter billions of dollars (JEC, 1973, p. 8). The acceleration of this trend toward unequal tax subsidies among corporations has exacerbated the trend toward concentration in American industry.

Next we will discuss the distributional impact of some of the larger program subsidies—agricultural subsidies, manpower training subsidies, and housing subsidies.

2. FEDERAL AGRICULTURAL SUBSIDIES

Born in the midst of desperate rural poverty during the Great Depression, agricultural programs have come to epitomize the unequal distribution of federal government expenditures. Beyond the static distributional impact that federal agricultural programs have had, there are also some important *qualitative* and *dynamic* dimensions of agricultural programs. The original rhetoric of our agricultural programs was highly egalitarian: to relieve the exteme conditions of poverty in rural areas and to mitigate the seasonal and cyclical fluctuations in farm income. However, the farm programs have drastically altered the structure of farming in the United States. First, the program fostered the *corporatization* of farming through its technical assistance offered through the Agricultural Extension Program. Second, it fostered the *concentration* of farm ownership through its subsidy programs and its technical assistance programs. Third, to accomplish this, millions of previously independent farmers were forced to leave their independent, self-reliant existence and enter the labor market as wage laborers. (See Wachtel, 1971, p. 12.) Thus, the classic pattern of capitalist development was telescoped in agriculture in the past forty years: millions of small-scale owners became *decapitalized,* forming the pool of wage laborers for the large-scale, concentrated, corporate farming structure that dominates the landscape today.

The result of this policy is the highly unequal distribution of farm benefits revealed in table 12. With Gini Coefficients ranging from .40 to .80 for program benefits, the farm program typifies the unequal distribution of federal government expenditures. But these data do not even tell the whole story. Farm programs are severely class-biased in that owners of farms are paid not to produce, but the workers displaced by this curtailment of production are *not* paid not to work!

3. FEDERAL MANPOWER TRAINING SUBSIDIES

Manpower training appears to be the most permanent, if not the only survivor, of the social welfare "experimentation" of the 1960s. From its modest beginnings in 1964, when $142 million was spent on manpower training, the program has grown to close to 1.5 billion dollars in 1971, with 1.5 million enrollees. The conventional argument views these training programs as solely redistributive in that it enhances economic opportunity for individuals by augmenting their human capital.

However, this does not represent a complete analysis of the distributive impact of this program. Over the years, manpower training programs have increasingly taken on the character of training subsidies for the largest of our corporations (see Wachtel, 1971, pp. 12–16). One indicator of this is the trend away from generalized institutional training, which maximizes benefits, to the individual worker to job-specific or on-the-job training, (OJT) which maximizes benefits to the employer. On-the-job training as a percent of MDTA programs increased

TABLE 12: DISTRIBUTION OF FARM INCOME AND COMMODITY PROGRAM BENEFITS BY FARM SIZE, MID-1960s
Percent of total income or benefits

Source and Year	Lower 20 Percent	Lower 40 Percent	Lower 60 Percent	Top 40 Percent	Top 20 Percent	Top 5 Percent	Gini Concentration Ratio[a]
Farmer and farm manager total money income, 1963	3.2	11.7	26.4	73.6	50.5	20.8	0.468
Program benefits							
Sugar cane, 1965	1.0	2.9	6.3	93.7	83.1	63.2	0.799
Cotton, 1964	1.8	6.6	15.1	84.9	69.2	41.2	0.653
Rice, 1963	1.0	5.5	15.1	84.9	65.3	34.6	0.632
Wheat, 1964							
Price supports	3.4	8.3	20.7	79.3	62.3	30.5	0.566
Direct payments	6.9	14.2	26.4	73.6	57.3	27.9	0.480
Total	3.3	8.1	20.4	79.6	62.4	30.5	0.569
Feed grains, 1964							
Price supports	0.5	3.2	15.3	84.7	57.3	24.4	0.588
Direct payments	4.4	16.1	31.8	68.2	46.8	20.7	0.405
Total	1.0	4.9	17.3	82.7	56.1	23.9	0.565
Peanuts, 1964	3.8	10.9	23.7	76.3	57.2	28.5	0.522
Tobacco, 1965	3.9	13.2	26.5	73.5	52.8	24.9	0.476
Sugar beets, 1965	5.0	14.3	27.0	73.0	50.5	24.4	0.456
Agricultural conservation program, 1964							
All eligibles	7.9	15.8	34.7	65.3	39.2	n.a.	0.343
Recipients	10.5	22.8	40.3	59.7	36.6	13.8	0.271

Source: Charles L. Schultze, *The Distribution of Farm Subsidies; Who Gets the Benefits?* (Washington: The Brookings Institution, 1971), p. 16.

n.a.: not available.

[a] The higher the Gini coefficient, the more unequal is the distribution.

from five percent in 1964 to twenty percent in 1966, to forty-one percent in 1968. The General Accounting Office (p. i), a conservative auditor of federal programs, has reached the same conclusion:

OJT contracts had served primarily to reimburse employers for OJT which they would have conducted even without the Government's financial assistance. These contracts were awarded even though the intent of the program was to induce *new or additional training efforts* beyond those usually carried out (emphasis in original).

In addition, to these more "indirect" means of corporate subsidy, other programs were introduced that did not mask their direct-subsidy character. In particular, the JOBS program provided training subsidies to members of the National Alliance of Businessmen, an elite group of large corporations drawn primarily from among the more liberal members of the Fortune 500. In 1971, $169 million was allotted to this program.

In sum, the benefits of training, though normally examined by means of looking at rates of return to the individuals trained (which generally are low or close to zero), should properly be examined in their total context by assigning benefits to the corporate recipient of the subsidy as well. If this were done, any supposed redistribution toward low-income groups would be mitigated if not completely eliminated.

4. FEDERAL HOUSING SUBSIDIES

The federal government has a wide variety of programs that directly affect the housing market. After surveying these programs, one perceives a consistent and coherent housing policy. By examining what the federal government does with respect to housing—not what it says —one can isolate three major themes:

1. most government subsidies of housing are directed toward encouraging home ownership;
2. most of what the government has done in the housing field has been to subsidize or aid in other ways mortgage lenders, the construction industry, or land speculators;
3. a small amount of housing subsidies have gone to groups in the population that were temporarily insurrectionary—urban, low-income populations in the late 1960s—in order to quell their dissent.

This list is not exhaustive, but it accounts for most of the government's activity with regard to housing.

a. Tax subsidy of housing. A major thrust of housing policy in the United States has been to encourage home ownership for middle-income families. The most important programs that encourage home ownership are tax subsidies for home ownership, insurance of mortgage credit through the Federal Housing Administration, the Veterans Housing Administration, and the Farmers Home Administration, and various federal credit institutions such as the Federal National Mortgage Administration, the Government National Mortgage Administration, the Federal Home Loan Bank Board, and the Federal Savings and Loan Insurance Corporation. Liberals, operating under a paradigm that views the government as a mediating agency, are baffled when they see most of the benefits of government housing programs going to middle-

and upper-income families. Referring to the largest single housing-subsidy program (tax subsidies) one observer writes: "With respect to any conceivable policy objective, the pattern of tax benefits seems to be capricious and without rationale" (Aaron [b], p. 20). The rationale for encouraging home ownership is obvious and it is precisely the "alleged, but unsubstantiated, benefits accruing to the community when households come to own their own homes. . . ." (Aaron b, p. 70). A government commission has made explicit these benefits to the community."

Home ownership encourages social stability and financial responsibility. It gives the homeowner a financial stake in society with a built-in inflation hedge. . . . It helps eliminate the "alienated tenant" psychology (Douglas Commission, p. 401).

By making the homeowner into a minicapitalist and property owner, the government housing policy fosters a petty bourgeois mentality in the middle-income stratum. The major programs that encourage home ownership are as follows:

The federal income tax gives preferential treatment to homeowners by allowing them to deduct from taxable income all interest on their mortgage and their property taxes. Furthermore, the imputed rental income is untaxed, and capital gains on owner-occupied housing is not normally taxable.[7] This tax subsidy amounts to nearly ten billion dollars each year—more than ten times as much as the next largest housing subsidy (Pechman and Okner, p. 23). Not surprisingly, these benefits, whose level depends upon one's marginal tax rate (i.e., one's "tax bracket"), flow disproportionately to upper income families. Over one-third of the $10 billion goes to families with incomes of $15,000 or more per year (Aaron [a], p. 571). The homeowners preferences are worth on the average only 66 cents per year to the lowest income group but over $6,000 to the highest income group (Stern [b], p. 60). These provisions benefit the "average" taxpayer by offsetting about fifteen percent of his or her annual housing cost and about one-third of the housing cost for those at the $50,000 income level (Douglas Commission, p. 400).

b. Mortgage credit. The federal government, since the early 1930s, has created a number of institutions that have dramatically increased the availability of mortgage credit. These programs have both encouraged homeownership by middle-income persons and at the same

---

[7] If, within a year after selling the principal residence, the owner buys another house costing at least as much, the capital gains are tax-free. Otherwise, capital gains are taxed at one-half the normal rate with a maximum of twenty-five percent.

time have been an enormous boon to the mortgage banking industry. Home mortgages in 1966 amounted to $225 billion with $555 million in new mortgages being written every year (Stone, p. 27). Mortgage lending is a giant industry and has gained enormously from a government policy that results in millions of families demanding mortgages.

In the depression of the 1930s, the mortgage market collapsed and the government intervened in order to give a boost to the construction industry as well as bail out the homeowner (Aaron [b] p. 77). Housing starts fell by ninety percent from 1929 to 1934, and the industry was in a crisis (Douglas Commission, p. 94). Before federal mortgage insurance, mortgage interest rates were relatively high, repayment periods short (seven to ten years) and down payments were high (thirty-five percent or more). Periodic payments were for interest only, with the principal due at the expiration of the mortgage. The Federal Housing Administration (FHA), created in 1935, was willing to insure mortgages with much longer repayment periods (up to twenty-five years by 1938), low down payments (as little as ten percent by 1938, no down payment on inexpensive houses by 1965), with the principal amortized over the period of the loan (Douglas Commission, p. 96). The home buyer paid an insurance premium of one-half percent of the principal per year. Note that contrary to any other kind of insurance, the one insured against risk (the lender) does not pay the premium. The buyer who is not insured against any loss pays the premium. In 1944, the Veterans Housing Administration (VHA) was created to insure mortgages for veterans and servicemen. The program is similar to the FHA except that the buyer pays no premium. In 1946, the Farmers Home Administration (FmHA) was created to insure mortgages and other credit in rural and small towns (including suburbs) where credit is traditionally difficult to obtain. (Despite its name, most of the credit that FmHA insures is not extended to farmers).

The benefits of federal mortgage insurance extend beyond those actually covered by the insurance. Noninsured lenders have been able to see that long repayment periods and low down payments are not necessarily a bad risk. Furthermore, the competitive pressures from federally insured mortgages have put pressure on noninsured lenders to liberalize their terms. Since 1965, only about fifteen percent of all mortgages have been insured by FHA, but the impact of the federal mortgage guarantee since 1935 has been to revolutionize the mortgage market (Aaron b, p. 27). FHA is not a true subsidy. The agency normally turns a small profit, although this would probably vanish in the event of a major depression—but the federal guarantees have created major institutional change.[8]

8 "VHA generated measurable subsidies of about $141 million in 1966" (Aaron [a] p. 572).

Another group of federally sponsored institutions aids the home-owner. In 1938, the Federal National Mortgage Association (FNMA) was legislated to create a secondary mortgage market. The Congressional mandate has varied over the years, but the thrust of FNMA has been to encourage investors to enter the mortgage market. FNMA increased the liquidity of lenders by allowing them to sell off mortgages. Secondly, FNMA encouraged new money to enter the mortgage market by offering its shares on the short term securities market. Both of these features make mortgages attractive to those who do not want their money tied up for long periods. Furthermore, FNMA can partially isolate the mortgage market from cyclical variations in other securities markets. FNMA was so successful that pressures were generated to turn it over to private investors. This process was completed by 1968. The Government National Mortgage Association (GNMA) was then created to take over the unprofitable activities of the FNMA, which is now entirely private. In recent years, FNMA has acquired up to forty-four percent of all mortgages (fourth quarter, 1969) (Aaron [b], p. 96).

The Federal Home Loan Bank Board was created in 1932 to regulate mortgage bankers in the same fashion as the Federal Reserve System has regulated commercial banks. In addition, the Federal Savings and Loan Insurance Corporation insures depositors in Savings and Loan Associations in much the same way as the Federal Deposit Insurance Corporation insures depositors in commercial banks. By rationalizing and stabilizing the mortgage industry, these two institutions favored the growth of the mortgage market.

c. Housing the poor. The thrust of federal housing policy has been to subsidize home ownership among middle-income groups and to structure the mortgage industry to encourage home ownership and enhance the profitability of mortgage lending, construction, and real estate development. Neither of these policies directly aid the lower-income strata since a house is far too expensive for most low-income families to purchase. The poor in this country are largely housed in the discarded dwellings of the more affluent. When housing becomes obsolete, expensive to maintain, or the character of the neighborhood shifts "adversely," the affluent leave, turning their houses over to those whose income is a notch lower. Thus, housing "filters down" to the poor.

Decent low-cost housing is rarely built in the United States. Liberals and conservatives typically blame this on the rapidly rising wages of construction workers, but this assertion is contradicted by the fact that, because of rising labor productivity in construction, the labor share of housing costs actually fell between 1950 and 1966 (Stone, p. 29). (The annual incomes of construction workers have not kept up with those in manufacturing.) The true reason for the high and rising cost of housing is the money going to the land speculator and creditor. According to Stone (p. 29), "During the last few decades land has been the fastest rising major element in the cost of new housing." The interest cost of the builders' working capital accounts for about ten percent of the price of a new house (Stone, p. 28). After the house is bought, interest is the single largest component of housing expense. On a thirty-year, seven-percent mortgage, interest payments will exceed the principal by forty percent. Thus, one of the most important reasons why housing is expensive is that in this economy, with a chronic tendency towards inflation, the government has seen fit to maintain interest rates at high levels. For higher-income families, the government subsidizes a portion of these enormous interest costs via the federal income tax, but lower-income families receive no such subsidy (except for several small programs, the more important of which were begun only in 1968). Most low-income families receive housing through the filtering process that is in part maintained by state action. Beyond its effect on the filtering process, the government has other housing programs that directly affect the poor: public housing, urban renewal, and other housing subsidies of the poor.

d. Public housing. Two and one-half million people live in federally subsidized public housing, and over three-quarters of the households living in public housing have incomes of less than $4,000 per year (Aaron [b], pp. 108, 115). In 1966, tenants of public housing received a subsidy of over one-half a billion dollars as measured by the difference between rents charged public housing tenants and equivalent private housing (Aaron [b], p. 123). Benefits have risen substantially since 1966 as the number of units of public housing has increased (Aaron [a], p. 571). Federal outlays on public housing are currently just over one billion dollars per year (Aaron [b], p. 113). Thus, public housing represents the largest single housing subsidy directed at the poor.

Originally, however, public housing was not conceived as a program to aid the lowest strata of society. Federal subsidy of public housing was initiated during the 1930s "to provide for the temporarily indigent middle class" (Gordon [b], p. 361). A second major reason for public housing was to rescue the construction industry, which was suffering from severe depression. When World War II ended the economic collapse of the 1930s, public housing came to be seen as a part of the mobilization effort and was used to build housing, much of it temporary in nature, for defense workers (Gordon [b], p. 109). After successfully serving its original purposes, federal subsidy of public housing was very nearly ended in 1949. The Korean War gave the program new life by exacerbating housing shortages; public housing reached a peak in 1951 that it would not match again until the late 1960s. The Eisenhower administration was decidedly hostile to public housing, and he program fared only slightly better in the Kennedy-Johnson era. It was not until the urban racial insurrections of the mid-1960s forced the government to act that public housing again found favor in Washington as a part of the "war on poverty." In sum, federal aid to public housing was not originally a program to aid the poor, but was designed to meet other needs. As these needs vanished, the program continued, grudgingly giving a few crumbs to the poor. Most recently, the crumbs have been larger in response to dissidence among the disadvantaged.

Public housing is a grudging gift to the poor for another reason. Housing projects "almost inevitably consist of tall, standardized, prison-like structures completely isolated from other communities and other facilities" (Gordon [b], p. 362). Operating subsidies are so stingy that a public housing project rapidly becomes a slum due to the lack of maintenance and repair. Public housing, then, is an alienating, inhuman monstrosity, but it is at the same time better housing than what one can buy on the private market at a similar cost. Furthermore, "most projects have extremely low vacancy rates and long waiting lists for admission" (Aaron [b], p. 108). Public housing, despite its many drawbacks, meets a crying need of the poor for better and more housing.

In the public mind's eye, public housing is seen as a major attempt to relieve the housing problems of the poor—a perception that stands in sharp contrast to the facts. Instead, we see that:

[c]ongress has never appropriated enough money to make public housing work, local public housing authorities have not even spent what little money the federal government has authorized, and those to whom our institutions have given control over public housing have no intention of redirecting the program in order to improve dramatically its contribution to the low-income housing stock in urban areas" (Gordon [b], p. 361).

e. Urban renewal. Urban renewal is normally thought of as a program that is essentially housing-oriented, and additionally, a program designed to increase the supply of housing for low-income households. In actual fact, neither of these popular conceptions is true.

Urban renewal, begun in 1949, is a program that buys up urban land, clears the property, builds needed infrastructure, and then sells the land to private developers. The subsidy, which goes to the developer and the new user of the land, comes from several sources. First, plans for urban renewal are normally announced considerably ahead of time, often years before the acquisition of the land takes pace. As soon as an area is designated for renewal, property owners understandably reduce their maintenance and repair outlays and the neighborhood begins to deteriorate physically. As residents move out, it becomes increasingly difficult to find new tenants. Rising vacancy rates lead to vandalism and accelerated deterioration. Businesses begin to close their doors. In short, the community that has existed in the urban renewal area disintegrates and property values fall. When the urban renewal authority takes possession of property, it pays the current market value, not the value of the property at the time that the area was designated for urban renewal. Property owners often bear a considerable loss, which becomes in effect a subsidy to the new users of the land.

A second source of subsidy arises from the fact that the property owners are forced to sell their land whether or not they wish to. For the first time in the history of this country, the government's right of eminent domain has been used to acquire land from one set of private owners in order to give the land to another set of private citizens. Property owners are remunerated at the "fair market value," as determined ultimately by the courts, but it is clear that many property owners would not choose to sell if they had the choice. Another way of saying the same thing is that the price they would voluntarily accept for their property is higher than the amount they are forced to accept, and this difference, therefore, is a subsidy to the new users of the land.

A third source of subsidy arises from the fact that businesses are reimbursed for only the physical assets that they lose. A small shop may have spent a generation building a clientele within a community, and its "goodwill" is by far its most important asset. If it leases a store front and holds its inventory on credit, the shop may have only a few hundred dollars in tangible assets. Yet it would be obviously impossible to start up a new business elsewhere with only that much cash. Thus, the shopkeeper is wiped out. One study has shown that over three-fifths of the 750 small businesses displaced by one urban renewal project never reopened (cited in Ives, p. 75). The size of the subsidy to the new owners is the difference between what the shopkeepers would voluntarily accept as payment to move and the far smaller sum that they actually do receive.

The fourth source of subsidy is the actual "write-down," which is the difference between the urban renewal authority's outlay for acquisition, clearance, and site improvement of the land and the smaller sum that the private developers pay. The federal government pays two-thirds to three-quarters of the write-down, depending on the size of the sponsoring jurisdiction. By 1967, the federal government had spent over six billion dollars on the program. But most of the subsidy of the new property owners was paid by the former property owners, not the government.

The new uses of urban renewal land are typically upper-middle-income or upper-income housing or cultural and commercial facilities that service these income groups. Some low- and moderate-income housing has been built on urban renewal land as well as some public housing, but this has not been the thrust of the program. In the postwar period, the well-to-do have found the suburban frontier steadily receding. Instead of merely grumbling about the increased time and distance of commuting, they have made attempts to reconvert downtown areas to their own ends. (See Edel.) It was difficult to do this through the private market. First, it would be far too expensive merely to buy up the land; an enormous subsidy was required—most of which came from the slum dweller—and, thus, government subsidy and condemnation powers were necessary. Second, even if subsidized, enormous amounts of money were required. Redevelopment had to be done by the square mile, not by the acre, in order to insulate the new arrivals from their impecunious neighbors. Governmental assistance was required because it was difficult to assemble the requisite amount of private capital. And third, land assemblage in such large tracts in urban areas is very difficult because of unclear titles, persons refusing to sell altogether, or a few holdouts who demand astronomical sums. Thus, condemnation powers were necessary. The urban renewal program of the Housing Act of 1949 suited the needs of the affluent admirably. Urban renewal, then, is best seen as a land grab by the affluent, who simply decided what part of the city they wanted and then dispossessed the largely poor and black populations with little regard for their welfare.

Urban renewal, to emphasize again, has not been a program to subsidize housing for the poor. In fact, it has done quite the opposite by reducing the supply of low cost housing and thereby driving up the price of that which remains. Not only did the total stock of low-cost housing decrease, but urban renewal did not even remove the worst dwelling units from the housing stock. From the early fifties, urban renewal concentrated on the "gray" areas rather than on the slums *per se* (Douglas Commission, p. 156).

Urban renewal has benefited the dominant class in another way. The program has generated significant amounts of political conflict, often along racial lines. In some cities, it came to be called "Negro removal." The middle-class lashed back at nonwhites who, displaced by renewal, were moving into their neighborhoods. Thus urban renewal has exacerbated racial divisions outside the dominant class, thereby strengthening its power.

By the late 1960s, in response to popular uprisings by urban poor, the urban renewal program became increasingly deflected from its original goals. Control over urban renewal programs increasingly shifted to community-based groups who were interested in improving housing for the poor rather than displacing them.

f. Other housing subsidies of the poor. The federal government has a number of other housing programs that generate a subsidy for the poor. The most important ones are homeownership and rental assistance, below-market interest-rate loans on multifamily housing, and rent supplements.[9] The federal government, since the 1930s, has sponsored numerous housing programs (in addition to public housing) that have benefited low-income groups in some way, but it was not until the late 1960s that, in response to urban racial insurrection, it made more than token subsidies of low-income housing. These subsidies, taken together, are currently about half the size of federal outlays on public housing and are far less than housing subsidies of those with higher incomes.

Howeownership and rental assistance began in 1968 with the passage of the National Housing Act. Participants pay a certain percentage of their income for mortgage amortization or rent, and the federal government pays the difference. The maximum subsidy for homeownership assistance (SECTION 235) was the difference between amortization (for thirty years) at market interest rates and amortization at one percent, or about sixty percent in 1970 (Aaron [a], p. 578). The maximum rental assistance (SECTION 236) was about forty-four percent of market rents in 1970 (Aaron [a], p. 578). Most beneficiaries of the programs have incomes of between $3,000 and $7,000. The subsidy to low-income families is expected to be $450 million in 1972 (Aaron [a], p. 579).

Low-income groups probably do not receive the major share of the subsidy from this program. In purchasing a house under SEC. 235, the family pays a fixed amount no matter how much the house costs and the federal government pays the rest. This has allowed real estate speculators to buy up nearly worthless property and sell it to unsophisticated purchasers—often with hard-sell tactics at exorbitant markups. The new owners often do not have the resources to pay the enormous repair and maintenance expenditures on a dwelling that is unfit for habitation. The new owners default, giving themselves a bad credit rating. FHA picks up the tab. It is possible for FHA to auction

---

[9] For a complete list of housing-subsidy programs, see Aaron [b], Appendix A.

off the same house to the same speculator so that the process may repeat itself.

A recent government study concluded that "speculator profits of sixty to seventy percent on houses held for less than eight weeks are not uncommon" (Committee on Government Operations, p. 4). In Detroit, FHA is expected to acquire 18,000 to 20,000 houses (up from 1150 in 1968) in the near future, and might lose as much as $200 million in Detroit alone (Committee on Government Operations, p. 4). Losses in other cities are sizable. Thus, the subsidy of real estate speculators through FHA insurance probably exceeds the subsidy to homeowners. The report also showed that FHA collaborated with the mortgage industry in this raid on the Treasury (Committee on Government Operations, pp. 4–6).

A precursor to the SEC. 236 program was the below-market interest-rate loans on multifamily housing. The program was begun in 1961, but did not get off the ground until the late 1960s when it became a part of the larger federal housing effort being used to quell urban discontent. This program allowed builders to pay in effect only three percent interest on mortgage debt. With market rates of nine percent, a rent reduction of thirty-seven percent was possible (Aaron [a], p. 581). In 1970, the subsidy amounted to $28 million, most of which went to households with income between $3000 and $8000 (Aaron [a], p. 578). The program was plagued from the beginning by congressional antipathy and administrative delays and has now been abandoned in favor of rental assistance under Title 236. Aaron comments:

One important reason for the program's demise was its limited appeal to profit-oriented developers or investors. Nonprofit and cooperative developments were sponsored by various civic, religious, charitable, or public service organizations, whose motives for building housing were varied but not confined to thirst for profit. Limited dividend corporations, restricted to a 6 percent annual yield on equity investment before taxes, must reduce rents if their profits go higher. Why would profit-oriented builders, developers, or investors be willing to participate in a program with such stringent limitations? (Aaron [a], p. 132)

They did not, of course, and they pressured the Congress to subsidize housing for the poor in a manner that was profitable for owners of large amounts of wealth.

Another program to subsidize housing for low-income groups is the rent-supplement program. A limited dividend corporation or cooperative constructs an apartment building and the federal government contracts to supplement that part of rent payments that exceeds twenty-five percent of the family's income. The contract expires after forty years, and tenants are required to pay at least thirty percent of the fair market rent. Beneficiaries are poor; eligible families have incomes below public-housing limits. When originally proposed in 1965, the program was to have 500,000 units constructed in the first four years. But by 1972, fewer than 46,000 units have been started and the subsidy in 1972 was only $91 million.

The major federal programs that subsidize housing for low-income groups are public housing and several sections of the Housing Act of 1968. As was pointed out earlier, public housing was not originally designed for the poor; significant amounts of public housing designed for the poor only began in the 1960s. In addition, during the last five years, urban renewal has increasingly become a program to aid rather than hurt the poor. It becomes clear that these programs are in response to the growing militancy of the civil rights movement and the urban racial unrest of the mid-1960s. The last major rebellions occurred in 1968. At present there is no longer any need to "buy off the poor with crumbs," and therefore the Nixon Administration's proposed budget for 1973 allocates *no* new funding for any of these programs.[10] (It is not yet clear how Congress will react or if their reaction makes any difference.) These programs have served their purpose and are now no longer needed. Most of the federal subsidies of housing, however, have never gone to the poor but instead to middle- and upper-income groups, land owners, and financiers. The recent "economy" moves, of course, do not touch these far larger subsidizes to the privileged.

IV. CONCLUDING REMARKS

As we indicated at the outset, no attempt has been made to produce a summary, quantitative measure of the distributional impact of government expenditures. Rather, we have tried to introduce an alternative theoretical perspective that pertains to this question, and have presented a mode of analysis appropriate to that perspective by examining selected government programs. The conclusions we draw, therefore, are tentative but suggestive. Earlier studies of net fiscal incidence (i.e., benefits of government expenditures plus transfers minus taxes) have shown that the overall incidence of the government is highly redistributive toward the poor. The latest of these studies has shown that those with incomes under $2000 annually receive substantial net benefits, while those with incomes above $10,000 receive less in

---

[10] It is not clear at this writing (March 1973) how many of these programs will receive continued support via revenue sharing.

benefits than they pay in taxes (Herriot and Miller, p. 19). The present paper, applying a different theoretical perspective, finds, on the other hand, that the government programs studied yield substantial benefits to the higher-income classes (though low-income groups may also benefit from these programs). By ignoring the effect of the government on pretax, pretransfer income, and by ignoring the system-maintenance functions of many government programs (even those that are ostensibly directed toward helping the poor), the orthodox analysts have committed a fatal methodological error. Their finding of redistribution away from the rich and to the poor is, we conclude, consequently erroneous.

The analysis of this paper is largely qualitative, rather than quantitative. In part this is required by the paucity of data that can be brought to bear on these issues. The U.S. government, which generates most of the data that American Social Scientists use, has not devoted a great deal of energy in gathering statistics that could be used to measure the distributive effects of its programs. Additional data requirements for more refined analyses should be self-evident.

But there is a second reason why much of this paper is only qualitative in its analysis. There are many benefits that the government provides about which it makes no sense to attempt measuring with any precision. We have argued that the government, through a number of mechanisms, has created and maintains class divisions in society. It is meaningless to attempt to measure the benefits to classes at the top of the class hierarchy (or the costs to those at the bottom) of the government action that put them there. For example, one cannot measure in dollars the financial benefits to the dominant classes of the government's definition and enforcement of property relations. This function is system-defining, i.e., is crucial for the functioning of the capitalist system as such. Or again, according to the perspective of this paper, one function of the government is to buy off dissent and unrest through various ameliorative programs (welfare, manpower training, housing subsidies, and so forth). It makes no sense to measure the benefits of these programs to the dominant classes since, from the political economic perspective, without these programs the dominant classes would cease to be dominant. These programs have qualitative benefits, and thus our analysis of them has been largely qualitative. One of the conclusions of this paper is that more and better data cannot be a substitute for careful analysis within a proper theoretical perspective.

In addition to more data, we also need deeper theoretical explorations into the role of the state in the history of capitalism and in our contemporary phase of monopoly capitalism. Historical study of the role of the state can make a valuable contribution to the analysis of the qualitative as well as the quantitative impact of the government, which is normally treated in a more static sense. All of these observations point to a massive need to know more about the role of the state in distributional matters.

References

AARON, HENRY J. [a] "Federal Housing Subsidies." In U.S., Congress, Joint Economic Committee. *The Economics of Federal Subsidy Programs, Part 5 —Housing Subsidies,* pp. 571–98. 92nd Cong., 2nd Sess., Washington: Government Printing Office, 1972.

————. [b] *Shelter and Subsidies.* Washington: The Brookings Institution, 1972.

BERNSTEIN, HARRY. "U.S. Work Ethic: A Cherished Virtue or a Theoretical Dream." *Washington Post,* January 1, 1973, p. A3.

BITTKER, BORIS; GALVIN, CHARLES; MUSGRAVE, R. A.; and PECHMAN, JOSEPH A. *A Comprehensive Income Tax Base? A Debate.* New York: Federal Tax Press, 1968.

BLUESTONE, BARRY. [a] "Capitalism and Poverty in America: A Discussion." *Monthly Review* 24, no. 2 (June, 1972): 65–71.

————. [b] "Statement Prepared for the Joint Economic Committee: February 29, 1972." Mimeographed. Boston: Department of Economics, Boston College, 1972.

————; STEVENSON, MARY H.; BETWEY, CHARLES; and BACHMAN, WILLIAM. *Code Book for 1967 Merged Survey of Economic Opportunity—Industry— Occupation File.* Ann Arbor: Institute of Labor and Industrial Relations, n.d.

BOWLES, SAMUEL. "Education and the Reproduction of the Social Division of Labor." *Review of Radical Political Economics* 3, no. 4 (Fall–Winter, 1971): 1–30.

————. "Schooling and Inequality from Generation to Generation." *Journal of Political Economy* 8, no. 3, part 2 (May/ June, 1972): S219–S251.

BRITTAIN, JOHN A. "The Incidence of Social Security Payroll Taxes." *American Economic Review* 51, no. 1 (March, 1971): 110–25.

————. *The Payroll Tax for Social Security.* Washington: The Brookings Institution, 1972.

BROWN, RICHARD MAXWELL. "Historical Patterns of Violence in America." In GRAHAM, H. D.; and GURR, T. R. *Violence in America: Historical and Comparative Perspectives,* pp. 45–84. A report submitted to the National Commission on the Causes and Prevention of Violence. New York: Bantam, 1969.

The Douglas Commission (The National Commission on Urban Problems). *Building the American City,* U.S., Congress, House, 91st Cong., 1st Sess.

(House Document no. 91-34). Washington: Government Printing Office, 1968.

EDEL, MATTHEW. "Urban Renewal and Land Use Conflicts." *Review of Radical Political Economics* 3, no. 3 (Summer, 1971): 76–89.

GILLESPIE, W. IRWIN. "Effect of Public Expenditures on the Distribution of Income." In Richard A. Musgrave, ed. *Essays in Fiscal Federalism,* pp. 122–86. Washington: The Brookings Institution, 1965.

GINTIS, HERBERT. "Education, Technology, and the Characteristics of Worker Productivity." *American Economic Review* 61, no. 2 (May, 1971): 266–79.

GOODE, RICHARD A. *The Individual Income Tax.* Washington: The Brookings Institution, 1964.

GORDON, DAVID M. [a] "Class and the Economics of Crime," *Review of Radical Political Economics* 3, 3 (Summer, 1971), pp. 51–75.

GORDON, DAVID M. ed. [b] *Problems in Political Economy: An Urban Perspective.* Lexington, Mass.: D. C. Heath and Co., 1971.

———. "Taxation of the Poor and the Normative Theory of Tax Incidence." *American Economic Review* 57, no. 2 (May, 1972): 319–28.

HANSEN, W. LEE; and WEISBROD, BURTON A. *Benefits, Costs, and Finance of Public Higher Education.* Chicago: Markham Publishing Company, 1969.

HARRISON, BENNETT. "Public Employment and the Theory of the Dual Economy." In SHEPPARD, HAROLD L., et al., eds. *The Political Economy of Public Service Employment,* pp. 41–76. Lexington: D. C. Heath, 1972.

HARTMAN, ROBERT W. "Equity Implications of State Tuition Policy and Student Loans." *Journal of Political Economy* 80, no. 3, part 2 (May/June, 1972): S142–S171.

HERBER, BERNARD. *Modern Public Finance.* Homewood, Ill. Irwin Publishers, 1967.

HERRICT, ROGER A.; and MILLER, HERMAN P. "Changes in the Distribution of Taxes Among Income Groups: 1962 to 1968." Presented at the American Statistical Association, Fort Collins, Colorado, August, 1971.

HOBSON, JULIUS W. *The Damned Children.* Washington: Washington Institute for Quality Education, 1970.

IVES, RALPH; LLOYD, GARY W.; and SAWERS, LARRY. "Mass Transit and the Power Elite." *Review of Radical Political Economics* 4, no. 2 (Summer, 1972): 68–77.

KAUFMAN, RICHARD F. "MIRVing the Boondoggle: Contracts, Subsidy, and Welfare in the Aerospace Industry." *American Economic Review* 57, no. 2 (May, 1972): 288–95.

The Kerner Commission. *Report of the National Advisory Commission on Civil Disorders.* New York: Dutton, 1968.

LAMPMAN, ROBERT J. "Transfer Approaches to Distribution Policy." *American Economic Review, Papers and Proceedings* 60, no. 2 (May, 1970): 270–79.

LURIE, IRENE. "The Distribution of Transfer Payments Among Households." In the President's Commission on Income Maintenance Studies. *Technical Studies,* pp. 143–58. Washington: Government Printing Office, 1970.

MAGDOFF, HARRY. *The Age of Imperialism: The Economics of U.S. Foreign Policy.* New York: Monthly Review Press, 1969.

MARX, KARL. *Capital,* vol. 1. New York: International Publishers, 1967.

McLURE, CHARLES E., JR. "The Income Tax Treatment of Interest Earned on Savings in Life Insurance." In U.S., Congress, Joint Economic Committee. *The Economics of Federal Subsidy Programs: A Compendium of Paper. Part 3—Tax Subsidies,* pp. 370–405. 92nd Cong., 2nd Sess. Washington: Government Printing Office, 1972.

MICHELSON, STEPHAN. "The Economics of Real Income Distribution." *Review of Radical Political Economics* 2, no. 1 (Spring, 1970): 75–86.

MILLIBAND, RALPH. *The State in Capitalist Society.* New York: Basic Books, 1969.

MOORE, STANLEY. *The Critique of Capitalist Democracy: An Introduction to the Theory of the State in Marx, Engels, and Lenin.* New York: Paine-Whitman Publishers, 1957. Reprinted by Augustus Kelly Reprints, Englewood, N.J.

MUSGRAVE, PEGGY B. "Tax Preferences to Foreign Investment." In U.S. Congress, Joint Economic Committee. *The Economics of Federal Subsidy Programs: A Compendium of Papers. Part 2—International Subsidies,* pp. 176–219. 92nd Cong., 2nd Sess. Washington: Government Printing Office, 1972.

MUSGRAVE, RICHARD A. *The Theory of Public Finance.* New York: McGraw-Hill, 1959.

O'CONNOR, JAMES. *The Fiscal Crisis of the State* (forthcoming).

OTT, DAVID J.; and OTT, ATTIAT F. "The Tax Subsidy Through Exemption of State and Local Bond Interest." U.S., Congress, Joint Economic Committee. *The Economics of Federal Subsidy Programs: A Compendium of Papers. Part 3—Tax Subsidies,* pp. 305–16. 92nd Cong., 2nd Sess. Washington: Government Printing Office, 1972.

PECHMAN, JOSEPH A. *Federal Tax Policy.* Washington: The Brookings Institution, 1971.

————; AARON, HENRY J.; and TAUSSIG, MICHAEL K. *Social Security. Perspectives for Reform.* Washington: The Brookings Institution, 1968.

————; and OKNER, BENJAMIN A. "Individual Income Tax Erosion by Income Classes." In U.S., Congress, Joint Economic Committee, *The Economics of Federal Subsidy Programs, Part I—General Study Papers,* pp. 13–40. 92nd Cong., 2nd Sess. Washington: Government Printing Office, 1972.

PIVEN, FRANCES FOX; and CLOWARD, RICHARD A. *Regulating the Poor: The Functions of Public Welfare.* New York: Pantheon Books, 1971.

PRIEST, ALAN R. "The Budget and Interpersonal Distribution." *Public Finance* 23, nos. 1–2 (1968): 80–98.

SCHNITTKER, JOHN A. "The Distribution of Benefits from Existing and Prospective Farm Programs." Presented at the Symposium on Public Problems and Policies, Iowa State University for Agricultural and Economic Development, May 27, 1969.

SCHULTZE, CHARLES L. *The Distribution of Farm Subsidies. Who Gets the Benefits?* Washington: The Brookings Institution, 1971.

———; FRIED, EDWARD R.; RIVLIN, ALICE M.; and TEETERS, NANCY H. *Setting National Priorities: The 1973 Budget.* Washington: The Brookings Institution, 1972.

STERN, PHILIP M. [a] "Statement Before Joint Economic Committee." In U.S., Congress, Joint Economic Committee, *Hearings Before the Subcommittee on Priorities and Economy in Government,* pp. 77–89. 92nd Cong., 2nd Sess. Washington: Government Printing Office, 1972.

———. [b] "Uncle Sam's Welfare Program—For the Rich." *New York Times Magazine,* April 16, 1972, pp. 28–71.

STONE, MICHAEL. "Housing, Mortgages, and the State." *Upstart* 3 (December, 1971): 25–36.

SWEEZY, PAUL M. *The Theory of Capitalist Development.* New York: Modern Reader, 1968.

Tax Foundation, Inc. *Tax Burden and Benefits by Income Class, 1961 and 1965.* New York: Tax Foundation, Inc., 1967.

THUROW, LESTER C.; and LUCAS, ROBERT E. B. *The American Distribution of Income: A Structural Problem.* Washington: Government Printing Office, 1972.

The Union for Radical Political Economics. "Capitalism, Inequality, and Poverty." *Review of Radical Political Economics* 3, no. 3 (Summer, 1971).

U.S., Congress, House, Committee on Government Operations. "Defaults on FHA-Insured Home Mortgages—Detroit, Michigan." 92nd Cong., 2nd Sess. Washington: Government Printing Office, 1972.

U.S., Congress, Joint Economic Committee. *The Economics of Federal Subsidy Programs, Part I—General Study Papers.* 92nd Cong., 2nd Sess. Washington: Government Printing Office, 1972.

U.S., Congress, Joint Economic Committee. *Tax Subsidies and Tax Reform* Washington: Government Printing Office, 1973.

U.S., Department of Commerce, Office of Business Economics. *The National Income and Product Accounts of the United States, 1929–1965: Statistical Tables.* Washington: Government Printing Office, 1966.

U.S., Department of Labor, *Manpower Report of the President.* Washington: Government Printing Office, 1968.

U.S., General Accounting Office. *Improvements Needed in Contracting for On-the-Job Training Under the Manpower Development and Training Act of 1962.* Washington: General Accounting Office, 1970.

Urban America, Inc., and the Urban Coalition. *One Year Later: An Assessment of the Nation's Response to the Crisis Described by the National Advisory Commission on Civil Disorders.* Washington: The Urban Coalition, 1969.

WACHTEL, HOWARD M. "Capitalism and Poverty in America: Paradox or Contradiction?" *American Economic Review* 62, no. 2 (May, 1972): 187–94.

————. [a] "Class, Class Consciousness and Labor Market Stratification: A Marxian Analysis." Mimeographed. Washington: Department of Economics, American University, 1973.

————. "Looking at Poverty from a Radical Perspective," *Review of Radical Political Economics* 3, no. 3 (Summer, 1971), pp. 1–19.

————. [b] "Theses on Poverty and Inequality," *The American Economist* (forthcoming, 1973).

————; and BETSEY, CHARLES C. "Employment at Low Wages." *Review of Economics and Statistics* 54, no. 2 (May, 1972): 121–29.

chapter 4

Profits up; wages down

HOWARD SHERMAN

President Nixon's New Economic Policy (NEP) is based on his philosophy that "all Americans will benefit from more profits." [1] It reminds one of Charlie Wilson's philosophy that "what's good for General Motors is good for the country." It is the view of this paper, on the contrary, that more corporate profits to the monopolies tend to create *more* unemployment, inflation, and low wages. Therefore, while Nixon may succeed in raising monopoly profits, this tends to make most Americans worse off, not better off.

1. PROFITS AND PRICES

Most inflations in American history have been during wars. Prices rose rapidly and profit rates were very high during the Revolutionary War, the Civil War, and World Wars I and II. These inflations were of the classic *demand-pull* type. In each case, the government demand for military goods was almost unlimited. With a restricted amount of goods available and an upsurge in demand, prices rose rapidly. In the textbook language of Keynesian theory, inflation is caused by excess demand when the supply is already as high as full employment will permit.

The war-induced inflation of the 1965–1968 period at the height of the Vietnam War followed that pattern as military spending pushed up prices. Since 1968, however, Nixon has been forced to reduce the scale of military intervention in Vietnam. As a result the U.S. economy entered a recession in the period 1969–1972. Therefore, the inflation of recent years is a very different inflation than the usual condition of excess aggregate demand. The recession shows a deficiency of aggre-

"Profits Up; Wages Down" (editors title). From Howard Sherman, "Inflation, Profits and the New Economic Policy," *Review of Radical Political Economics* 4, no. 4 (August 1972). Reprinted by permission of *Review of Radical Political Economics*.

[1] Television speech, October 7, 1971.

gate demand, and thus we are faced with the situation—unique in American history—of inflation in the midst of recession in production and employment.

Although the American economy has been far from full employment, it has still had inflation. Between 1970 and 1971, the consumer price index rose 4.3% while the industrial production index declined very slightly and unemployment rose from 4.9% to 5.9%. Corporate profits, meanwhile, were growing from $75 billion to $85 billion.[2]

If inflation is not demand-pull—since we are far below full employment—then what is it? Most economists would agree that it is a *cost-push* inflation. There is bitter disagreement, though, on the meaning of that term. Conservatives believe the main rising cost is wages, and talk about wage-push inflation. Radicals believe the main rising "cost" is profits and talk about *profit-push* inflation.

Many conservatives allege that labor shortages and strong unions push up wages, forcing entrepreneurs to raise prices, and thus beginning a cost-push inflationary spiral. It is true that back in the 19th century in the early stages of U.S. industrial development, there may have been some shortages of workers during the railway booms. These shortages temporarily caused wage increases and made immigration necessary to get more cheap labor. Since that time, however, the peacetime U.S. economy has been characterized by labor surplus and unemployment (mainly among unskilled workers, but recently even including aerospace engineers). Moreover, unions have always been better at defending wages from cuts than in getting higher wages to keep up with price rises.

As a result, in almost all U.S. expansion periods, prices and profits have risen much faster than wages.[3] From 1960 to 1971, for example, incomes from unincorporated businesses, corporate profits, rents and interest rose by 88% while wages and salaries rose by only 59%. Moreover, while income from ownership (profits, rents and interest) remained at record highs throughout the period from 1965 to 1971, the average real income, or spending power, of a worker with three dependents failed to increase at all during those years of rapid inflation.[4] The conservative theory is therefore only hogwash, useful to bolster the arguments of big business. Wage increases have only been a *pretext* for previously decided price increases; the cost-push theory of inflation

---

[2] *Economic Report of the President for 1972* (Washington, D.C.: U.S. Government Printing Office, January, 1972), pp. 209, 223, 235, and 247.

[3] Plentiful data and further discussion of this point are presented in Howard Sherman, *Radical Political Economy* (New York: Basic Books, 1972), pp. 86–7.

[4] These data are from the *Economic Report of the President for 1972, op. cit.,* pp. 209 and 233.

has been used as a weapon against labor to hold down real wages and increase profits. Nixon follows this grand tradition.

Radicals tend to view the causes of inflation quite differently. *It is monopoly power that is held responsible for rising prices in the face of unemployment.* To make the point, some background facts of economic life are important.

The U.S. economy still has millions of very small enterprises but a few hundred corporate giants hold most of the wealth and do most of the production.[5] Profits are even more concentrated than assets. Over the long run (1931 to 1961, excluding the war years 1940 to 1947) the smallest class of corporations with under $50,000 in assets, made a negative rate of profit on investment—7.1%. Each larger asset class made a higher rate of profit. Those corporations over $50 million made a long-run profit rate of 10.4%.[6] The same is true when we classify industries according to the degree of economic concentration. The highly concentrated industries, such as automobiles or tobacco, have enormously high profit rates; while the more competitive areas, such as textiles or apparel, have very low profit rates. Finally, we find that the small corporations in the competitive industries have very unstable profit rates, going negative in mild recession; whereas the monopolies maintain their rate of profit come hell or high water.

How does this happen? Part of the answer is that in a recession, the small firms are forced to operate below the minimum technologically necessary scale of production, so they have higher costs per unit. This is true "cost-push," but operates only for the small firms, who have no power to raise prices, and therefore must suffer lower prices. If Nixon had talked only about small business profits being too low, he might have had a point.

The second reason for the higher profits and greater stability of the monopoly corporations, however, is their price-fixing power. Not only do they charge consumers high prices, but their power as buyer also allows them to pay low prices to small businesses and small farmers, and to pay low wages. It is important to note, however, that monopolies *do not always* push their prices as high as possible or keep their wages as low as possible. They have vast reserves and can afford (as small business cannot) to take a long view of profit maximization. The wise corporate manager keeps prices below the maximum possible

5 See Sherman, *Radical Political Economy, op. cit.*, pp. 99–101. Editorial note: The data which the author originally presented here have been omitted because of the extensive data and discussion of concentration in Michael Best's contribution to this issue.

6 *Ibid.*, pp. 106–9. Also see Howard Sherman, *Profits in the United States* (Ithaca, New York: Cornell University Press, 1968), p. 41 ff.

during the expansion upswing, increasing the company's slice of the market, both through "reasonable" pricing and massive advertising.

When the crunch comes—at the peak of the cycle as a crisis is approaching—with costs rising and consumer demand limited (by limited wages), the small firm can only watch its profit margin decline, since its prices are set by the competitive market. Not so the large oligopoly or monopoly firm. Since it had intentionally set its price a little below what the market would take, it may now use up part of the slack to raise its prices. Of course, wage increases are given as the excuse, even though they are merely a belated response to earlier price and profit rises. Higher wage costs would have no direct effect on prices if it were not that the oligopolistic structure of industry allows the giant firms freedom of price fixing within wide limits.

This is not an imaginary phenomenon. It is the record of all past cycle peaks. What is new is that monopoly prices no longer fall in a recession (presumably due in part to the secular increase in economic concentration). The shape of coming events was shown by Robert Lanzillotti in hearings before the Joint Economic Committee of Congress.[7] He showed that in the 1948 recession, prices in the more competitive industries fell by 8%, but they fell by only 2% in the more concentrated industries. In the recessions of 1953 and 1957, there was something new: even the more competitive prices fell only slightly, while *monopoly prices continued to rise*. This is the phenomenon that we find causing such havoc in the 1968 to 1971 period. Prices of the monopoly corporations continue to rise rapidly even in the face of unemployment.

It might also be mentioned that, in the good old days, small business usually gained back some of its relative position during prosperities. That is no longer the case. As early as the expansion from 1948 to 1953, Lanzillotti's pioneering report showed competitive prices rose by only 12% while monopoly prices rose by 23%. Similarly, in the expansion from 1954 to 1957, monopoly prices rose by 16%, while competitive prices rose by only 4.5%. The same thing occurred in all the prosperity periods of the 1960's. In the whole period to the present, monopoly prices rose most rapidly, while small business prices rose less (and wages lagged far behind). The cause of these phenomena is a long-run increase in economic concentration and monopoly power.

---

[7] Robert K. Lanzillotti in hearings before the Joint Economic Committee of Congress, *Employment, Growth, and Price Levels* (Washington, D.C.: U.S. Government Printing Office, 1959), p. 2238. Discussed fully in Sherman, *Radical Political Economy*, *op. cit.*, pp. 114–16.

2. THE NEP "SOLUTION"

As always, the right-wing economists, such as Milton Friedman, stick to the line that government need only stop interfering with business and everything will be fine. In this era of problems such as profit-push inflation and chronic unemployment, almost nobody accepts that solution. The most modern instruments acceptable to right-wing economists are the mild monetary measures, but these measures are continually shown to be inadequate.

The usual liberal Keynesian solution for unemployment was to increase aggregate demand (by more government spending or lower taxes); while their solution for inflation was to reduce aggregate demand (by less spending or more taxes). Under the present conditions of insufficient aggregate demand and unemployment, combined with profit-push inflation, these solutions are also inadequate. A small increase in demand, usually by military production or by cutting corporate taxes, does not necessarily stimulate output and employment; but is used by the dominant large corporations as a means of further raising prices for higher profits. A small decrease in demand, usually by cutting welfare spending or raising taxes, does not necessarily reduce most prices, but only leads to more unemployment.

The most daring liberal economists, such as John Kenneth Galbraith and Paul Samuelson, have recognized this new situation for some time. Since aggregate measures will no longer work, they advocate some form of direct control over individual prices and wages. Their dream seems to be that full employment can be reached by more government welfare spending, while direct controls hold down inflation. They have neglected several things, particularly the political reality (namely, that the capitalist state is naturally oriented toward capitalist interests). Yet the liberal arguments did convince the Democratic Congress; of course, the legislation was not passed because of rational arguments, but because of the political muscle of labor and a sector of business that favored it. At any rate, among Democrats the feeling was created that stand-by wage-price control would be an excellent political ploy. The Democrats could claim that they had passed legislation for a daring solution, but that the President was too conservative and unwilling to use it.

We all know that the President did decide to use this weapon given him by the liberals in Congress. He has not used the controls in the way that the liberals dreamed, but in a way that was quite predictable (given his capitalist orientation). Nixon and his administration seem to be representing only the few big businessmen rather than the millions and millions of working people. Can it be that they don't care about poverty, low wages, or unemployment? Nixon's New Economic Policy gives tax credits to big business, freezes welfare spending, carefully restricts most wages, but lets most prices increase, and has "voluntary" controls on profits. The dream has become a nightmare. The system of controls would seem to combine all the worst features of capitalism and centralized socialism. It is a directed economy in the interests of the large corporations.

It will be argued here that the following features will result from the Nixon Program: (1) As Friedman argues, controls will prevent efficient operation of the market, will lead to a vast bureaucracy, and will encourage corruption and repression; (2) As radicals point out, the program is accompanied by a large increase in America's already vast military spending; (3) As Samuelson argues, the program is pro-business and will shift the distribution of income from wages toward profits; and (4) As many liberals argue, the program does damn little for the unemployed. Radicals thus agree with *both* the conservative and liberal criticisms of the program. The program of regulated capitalism adds up to the worst of all possible worlds, and this dilemma will exist so long as the capitalist system continues. It is predictable that the controls would always be fixed in this way by a big business dominated administration (a liberal Democratic President might change their shape a little, but not much).

MORE PROFITS AND INEFFICIENCY

Conservatives such as Milton Friedman[8] are horrified at the violation of the First Commandment of *laissez-faire* economics: thou shalt not interfere with the market process of setting wages and prices. They have always argued that if prices are not set by competition in the market, then resources including capital and labor cannot be efficiently allocated.

If the government arbitrarily sets wages and holds prices to certain politically given levels, then how can a capitalist calculate (for profit maximization) what to produce or what technology to use? More precisely, a capitalist who follows the arbitrary prices set or allowed by government will not produce what consumers desire (even according to the preferences created by advertising), nor produce it in the cheapest possible way. Indeed, the monopolies would probably put less money and effort into production improvement (since prices are fixed), and more into corrupting administrators to raise prices (as they presently do in military procurement). Perhaps "corruption" is the wrong

8 Milton Friedman, *Newsweek* (August 30, 1971).

word; those who administrate the price controls mostly favor business interests because they are mostly pro-business by training and background—just as the present regulatory agencies always are. Thus government controls on wages and prices doom a capitalist economy to inefficiency—and, if continued, will create an enormous, inefficient, and possibly repressive bureaucracy.

MORE PROFITS AND MILITARY SPENDING

As expected the new Nixon budget proposes a $6.3 billion increase in military spending.[9] Remember the Nixon philosophy that "all Americans will benefit from more profits." From this point of view, military production must be the greatest benefit to all Americans —not only does military production have a guaranteed market, but the rate of profit is at least twice as high as for civilian industry (a point carefully documented by Senator Proxmire's investigations).[10] Of course, these profits are not distributed to all Americans, nor even to all businesses. According to the Department of Defense, between 1950 and 1967 the one hundred largest contractors received two-thirds of all military contracts; and just ten giant firms received almost one-third.[11]

MORE PROFITS AND INCOME DISTRIBUTION

Nixon's profit-oriented approach must seem strange when it is demonstrated that the inflation it was designed to control was mainly based on profit-push. The Administration appears to be relying on a variant of the trickle-down theory-high income for those at the top will result in a greater demand for the services of those at the bottom. (This comparative statics argument is quite different from the argument—to be examined in the next section—that in the expansion

[9] Executive Office of the President, *The Budget in Brief for 1973* (Washington, D.C.: U.S. Government Printing Office, 1972), p. 45.

[10] See discussion and data in Sherman, *Radical Political Economy, op. cit.,* pp. 141–5.

[11] For more extensive analysis of the role of military spending in the American economy, see two earlier issues of this *Review*: Michael Reich and David Finkelhor, "Capitalism and the 'Military-Industrial Complex': The Obstacles to Conversion," in Vol. 2, No. 4, Fall 1970. This article has been reprinted in T. Christoffel, D. Finkelhor and D. Gilbarg (eds.), *Up Against the American Myth* (New York: Holt, Rinehart, and Winston, 1970) and in R. Edwards, M. Reich and T. Weisskopf (eds.), *The Capitalist System* (Englewood Cliffs: Prentice-Hall, 1972); and the Special Issue on *The War and Its Impact on the Economy*, particularly the article on "Political Power and Military Spending," Vol. 2, No. 3, August, 1970.

phase of the cycle more corporate profits lead to more investment, which lead to more employment.) At the National Governors' conference in 1971, Spiro Agnew must have been thinking of the trickle-down theory when he said: "Rising corporate profits are good for the average man [sic] and are needed more than ever by the poor."

A look at recent data shows that the trickle-down theory leaves more than a little to be desired. Corporate profits were very high in the mid-1960's, yet very little seems to have trickled down to workers. According to official, understated, figures for 1966, at least 14% or 25,000,000 Americans were living in poverty (and there has been little change up through 1971).[12] This poverty line is based on an "economy diet," infrequent purchases of clothing, and minimal housing of the slum variety. Moreover, about 60% of Americans fall below what the Bureau of Labor Statistics calls a "moderate but adequate city worker's family budget." Of the bottom 60% of income receivers, whose budget was less than "adequate" by BLS standards, almost all were workers whose sole income came from wages and salaries.

At the other extreme, the richest 2%, who make more than $25,000 a year, receive about 90% of their income from property in the form of rent, interest, or profit. The top one-tenth of one percent of all taxpayers, with incomes over $200,000 a year, receive 23% of all dividends and 37% of all capital gains. The top two-tenths of one percent of all taxpayers own 65% to 71% of all stock.[13]

MORE PROFITS AND
MORE UNEMPLOYMENT

If the economy is to thrive, millions and millions of cars and refrigerators and TV sets must be sold. The rich can buy only a few, no matter how extravagant they are. Most consumer buying must come from wage and salary incomes, which are the main components of consumer demand. Therefore, *if wages and salaries are held down, while the share of profits rises, there is insufficient consumer demand.* Lack of consumer demand means that goods pile up in dealers' inventories. Naturally, if goods cannot be sold, workers are fired, and unemployment grows. Thus high profits and low wages would seem to lead to *less* consumer demand and more unemployment.

To avoid confusion, some elementary distinctions must be made here. An absolute increase in profits (and, of course, an increase in the increase in profits) *will* lead to more investment and more employ-

---

[12] See extensive data and discussion in Sherman, *Radical Political Economy, op. cit.*, pp. 49–50 ff.
[13] *Ibid.*

ment, *all other things being equal*—this is the kernel of truth in the cyclical version of the trickle-down theory. But all other things are not equal. Limited consumer demand reduces profit expectations, which leads to less investment.

We also concede, as Marx emphasized in criticizing naive underconsumption theory, that in the expansion phase of the cycle the increase in employment means greater wages and an important absolute improvement in the workers' standard of living. It is *not* that wages fall in the cyclical expansion, but that the *share* of wages falls while the *share* of profits rises. This is what limits consumer demand. In Keynesian terminology, the marginal propensity to consume of workers is much, much higher than that of capitalists. (Even Friedman finds an average propensity to consume of 96% for workers.)[14] Therefore, a shift in income distribution toward profits and away from wages (in shares) means a lower marginal propensity to consume out of all income. Since the share of the working class in income declines in the expansion, its brief improvement in employment and absolute amount of wages is always followed by a recession and absolute decline of employment and wages (even though its share of income again rises).

Nixon's NEP does provide a very small amount of tax relief (in higher exemptions and deductions) that will put a few more dollars into consumer demand. The main thrust of his tax program, however, is relief for the poor suffering corporations. He (and the Democratic Congress) are giving many billions of subsidies in the form of tax credits for new investment.

It is true that total demand includes not only consumption spending, but investment in new machinery and factories. So Mr. Nixon's ghost writers might answer that tax credits and higher profits after taxes will result in more investment in machinery and factories, and surely more workers will be employed in this work. That is true, but unfortunately it runs into a problem.

If more machines and factories are built, they have to produce something, and it has to be sold! In reality, the U.S. economy not only has "too many goods" relative to the low incomes of workers and consumers, it also has too many machines and factories for the present production level. In fact, some 27% of all capital goods are now lying idle. To make more machines and factories, while leaving workers' incomes too low to buy the new flood of goods (or even the present flood), is surely not the answer. In other words, a few more workers might be put to work immediately by Nixon's investment credits, but soon the problem will become worse as a result of this temporary "cure."

[14] Milton Friedman, *A Theory of the Consumption Function* (Princeton: Princeton University Press, 1957), pp. 69–79.

Unemployment involves a dilemma that cannot be solved by wage-price controls. From the viewpoint of the businessman, there is *both* a lack of demand *and* high costs, which make for low profit expectations, so less investment. The Nixon program would hold costs down by restricting wages and cutting corporate taxes. *If* demand were constant, this would produce more profits and, hence, more investment. But this only leads to the other side of the dilemma: low wages mean less consumer demand, while more investment leads to a greater flood of (unsold) consumer goods. So the Nixon program raises immediate profits rates, but may lead eventually to more economic depression and mass unemployment.

> . . . *let us recognize an unassailable fact of economic life. All Americans will benefit from more profits. More profits fuel the expansion that generates more jobs. More profits means more investment, which will make our goods more competitive in America and in the world. And more profits means there will be more tax revenues to pay for the programs that help people in needs. That's why higher profits in the American economy would be good for every person in America.*

> RICHARD NIXON
> October 7, 1971

III

Programs for the poor

> . . . *human nature is so constituted that no man can receive as a gift what he should earn by his own labor without a moral deterioration.*
>
> JOSEPHINE SHAW LOWELL*

> . . . *honest employment, the work that God means every man to do, is the truest basis of relief for every person with physical ability to work. . . . the help which needlessly releases the poor from the necessity of providing for themselves is in violation of divine law and incurs the penalties which follow any infraction of that law.***

In this section, Sol Stern, a New York based freelance writer, and David Wellman, Assistant Professor of Sociology at the University of Oregon, describe two government programs for the poor. The first program, welfare, dates back to the 1930s. The other, a manpower training program for low-income youth, was a creation of the 1960s.

Both chapters show clearly that not only the poor who are "served" by the programs but the low- and middle-level officials who work within the programs are powerless within the present system. Most of the government workers described by Stern and Wellman began their jobs committed to helping other people. Once in their positions they found that they and their clients are cogs in an assembly-line process; that they lack the resources —welfare funds and decent jobs—to significantly improve the lot of even a few low-income individuals; and that rather than helping low-income persons, they are forced to act as a buffer for the system, absorbing the anger engendered in the poor by its injustices.

The welfare program and the training program portrayed in these chapters illustrate the futility of reform policies. Inequality cannot be eradicated by computerizing the distribution of scanty welfare funds or by attempting to make low-income youth

* *Public Relief and Private Charity* (New York: 1884), p. 66.
** Charity Organization Society of New York, *Fifth Annual Report*, p. 29.

look middle class. Poverty and inequality can be eliminated
only by changing the basic structure through which income and
other resources are distributed in this nation. The poor know
this.

c h a p t e r   5

Welfare cops, computer cards, and chaos: making the poor pay

SOL STERN

The agency that dispenses welfare in New York City is called,
somewhat pretentiously, the Department of Social Services, and that at
least conjures up visions less depressing than the reality of the plain
old relief line that clutters up the sidewalk on 14th Street every week-
day morning. Sometimes it isn't long past dawn when the clients begin
queuing up outside the locked doors of the Waverly and Gramercy
welfare centers in an office building on the south side of the street,
near Fifth Avenue. Waiting are mothers with little children in hand,
old people in their 70's, 20-year-old narcotics addicts with that washed-
out look on their faces. They try to get there early because the word
is out that unless you have a spot up front you're likely to get turned
away, or spend the better part of the day getting your problems taken
care of.

And their problems almost exclusively involve money. This was true
of the white-haired lady in a long black coat, leaning on a cane near
the front of the line. She lived alone in a rooming house on upper
Broadway, and had to take the subway at 6:30 A.M. to get her spot in
line. Her Social Security payments are inadequate for her subsistence,
and the welfare department gives her about $50 per month to make up
the deficit. Last year she lost about $5 a month when the New York
State Legislature voted across-the-board cuts in welfare payments. That
hurt, she said, but not as much as all the problems she has been having

"Welfare Cops, Computer Cards, and Chaos: Making the Poor Pay" (editors title).
From Sol Stern, "The Screws Are on the Welfare System," *The New York Times
Magazine,* October 22, 1972. Copyright © The New York Times, 1972.

in the Waverly center during the past year. The workers used to give her money for a taxi to get to her doctor on the other side of town, she said, but now she has to take two buses even when it rains. "It's really terrible what's happening now," she said. "The social workers used to visit me. Now I have to come here by subway every time I need something. I wait around for hours and then I talk to a new worker who doesn't even know me. Sometimes they ask me to come back the next day. But I'm afraid to come here now. There are so many drug addicts around."

The Waverly center's disproportionately high percentage of addicts makes it somewhat unusual among the 47 centers carrying a case load of more than 1.25 million. But otherwise the center is typical of the others—and so is the turmoil that has been going on inside. No one likes it very much. Not the clients who wait inside on rows of plastic chairs, grumbling about the run-around they are getting. Not the shop-keepers on 14th Street who complain about the long lines interfering with their businesses. Not the special policemen who have been hired recently to keep order. Least of all, the caseworkers who arrive every morning for another day of insults, threats of violence and tedious paper shuffling.

The administrator responsible for the day-to-day functioning of the centers is a bright young appointee named Charles Morris. He has spent much of his six months on the job just dealing with crises created by the overcrowding and the security problems at the centers. Though he is hopeful that new management reforms will start paying off soon, he admits that "conditions in the centers verge on the near-danger level. Staff morale has been battered. We can't operate like this."

A similarly depressing picture was painted by Mrs. Janet Stackhouse, a pleasant white-haired lady who has been with the department for 33 years and is now a field manager in charge of four welfare centers. She identified the major problem as a staff shortage created by the Mayor's budget freeze. "We are in as bad a shape as we have ever been in," she said. "The absentee rate is terrific. It's unbelievable. On check days it's as high as 30 percent."

The "check days" Mrs. Stackhouse was referring to were not for the workers but for the clients. Welfare checks are sent out to the entire citywide case load on the same two days every month, through a centralized computer. Inevitably, thousands of checks are lost, stolen, mutilated or incorrectly computed. (Last year 45,000 checks that had been reported lost were fraudulently cashed.) On the two or three days after the checks go out, the centers are besieged by long lines of desperate clients whose requests for duplicate or corrected checks have to be processed by caseworkers.

Mrs. Fay Ruggiero, the director of the Lower Manhattan center, offered other salient facts which explain low staff morale. She said that now up to 33 different forms are required to open a new case. She also showed me a 4-inch-thick file of memos and directives that had come down from central offices since the beginning of the year. Most of them required other memos going out from her desk to the caseworkers, detailing new procedures to be followed. The paper explosion isn't very funny; but later, one of the caseworkers joked, "This department used to use up the equivalent of Sweden's paper pulp output. Now you can probably throw in Canada's as well."

Centers like Waverly and Gramercy are simply reeling under the accumulated pressures of the welfare explosion during the last decade. The mid-sixties were the years of "long hot summers," ghetto rebellions and community organizing. Welfare-rights groups were proliferating, organizing those already on the rolls and, indirectly, encouraging others to get on. In the centers, the social workers themselves were reflecting more liberal and radical attitudes.

In 1965, when Mayor Lindsay started his first term in office, the city's welfare case load was less than a half million. In the next three years it more than doubled. All together, in the seven-year period since 1965, the rolls grew by more than 770,000 cases. There are now whole neighborhoods in Bedford Stuyvesant, in the South Bronx, in East Harlem, where more than 50 percent of the residents are on welfare. One out of every six New Yorkers is on the rolls.

One case supervisor, not particularly happy with the way it all happened, said: "The feeling during that period was definitely one of 'don't let a riot start.' Lindsay wanted to keep the city cool and we were told to avoid trouble in the centers. Clients came in droves, sat in the centers and demanded to get on the rolls, or they would stay all night. You couldn't arrest them. You had to let them stay all night or give them money. We gave them money."

Unquestionably, those permissive days are over. The pressure is on to pare the rolls, and the word is out to center directors to call the Tactical Police Force at any sign of disorder. Mass protest has been superseded by random and individual acts of violence by angry clients frustrated by their encounters with a staff working under stringent and complicated new guidelines. Despite the recently announced decrease in the welfare case load for the month of July, the city may find it much harder to restrict the rolls than it was to let them grow, especially when the growth in staff has lagged far behind the increase in the case load. The city's budget crisis, and the Mayor's freeze on new hiring, have hit the centers particularly hard.

The quantitative increase in the case load was further complicated a year ago by the adoption of a whole new concept of welfare case-work. Under the old system, each caseworker (who tended to be a college graduate and in some cases a professionally trained social worker) had a stable case load of recipients to whom he was responsible for almost all the welfare functions: checking eligibility, determining payment levels, making referrals for employment. Under the new system, installed from the top by a team of management experts, the income-maintenance functions have been separated from social services. The former clerks of the system (usually women with high-school diplomas) have been upgraded to "income-maintenance specialists"; they take care of all the departmental dealings with the clients involving money. The former caseworkers, in theory, are now supposed to do pure social work. The new system was calculated to streamline operations at the centers along functional lines, and thus bring some relief from the back-breaking case loads.

At any rate, that was the way it looked on the organization charts. Instead, it is the almost unanimous opinion of workers and supervisors that the chaos and paper work have gotten worse. The new income-maintenance workers haven't been properly trained. Case files are passed around from one functional unit to the other and are often lost. Frustrated clients can't turn to the single responsible caseworker who used to answer their problems.

The unhappiest people of all are the veteran caseworkers. Through their union and professional organizations, they had always lobbied to be allowed to do more social work and less paper pushing. That was what the city promised would happen when the new system became fully operational. But because of the budget freeze, and the shortage in clerical staff, many of them have been left behind in units doing pure income maintenance. Others are in specialized units working on things like employment. Almost no one is out in the field doing pure social work.

The city's reform projects are simply being mangled by the sheer size of the case load. Those bearing the brunt of the reform failures are caseworkers like those I spoke to in a special unit that processes applications by narcotics addicts in the Waverly center. They work at 12 desks crammed into a small area sealed off from other units by a partition. Their job is tedious and dehumanizing, and they are constantly in hostile confrontations with the applicants—a situation symbolized by the two-foot-high barrier that keeps the clients from getting too close to them.

The workers laughingly called their working area the "narco pit," and referred to their clients as "our nodding acquaintances." A narcotics unit is, of course, one of the more unpalatable assignments in welfare, but the workers' cynicism extends to the entire system. They were more than eager to get in a blast at the top administrators down at Church Street. They are angry and disillusioned because they were promised a year ago that they would eventually be transferred to a social-services unit. "Nobody in his right mind around here believes it any more," said Allen Morris, a young, prematurely graying case supervisor, who led a general bitching session among about half a dozen workers. "This city just isn't going to spend any money on pure social services," said another worker. "We are worried about being phased out. We think they want to clericalize the whole system and have no social services." The consensus is that the new system has merely accomplished an increase in paper work and has made the security problem in the center more difficult.

The basic problem, as one of them put it, is that "you can't separate money problems from social problems." For those downtown administrators who had erected a whole system on the premise that you *could* do it, they had nothing but contempt. "They are ridiculous," said Morris. "They come in here and try to devise these new methods, but they can't even read a case record. They want to run an efficient business but we aren't a business. This isn't an assembly line. We aren't putting together a car. We are dealing with people." As for welfare reform, most of the workers seemed to think it was a joke. About the best reform they can think of is simply to go back to the old caseworker system, improving it with more, and better, staff. They also know this isn't about to happen.

Actually, most serious welfare reformers are pretty despondent these days. With an antiwelfare mood running very strong in the country, with the poverty program in disarray, and with welfare-rights groups in retreat, welfare reform has come to mean restrictive measures to get people off the rolls. Welfare cuts have been voted by 19 state legislatures. In New York, the 10 percent across-the-board cut was accompanied by tough new residency requirements—subsequently ruled unconstitutional—and restrictive work regulations. A spokesman for Governor Rockefeller revealed the new political consensus behind it all when he said: "We're no longer talking in terms of money with this bill. But as part of a package of welfare bills it sets a psychological tone. If people get the idea it's tougher, less of them will try to get on welfare."

. . . By May of this year even Mayor Lindsay, forced to respond to strong antiwelfare currents, was promising zero growth in the welfare rolls—a promise he seems to be trying to keep with a vengeance. The city would accomplish this unprecedented feat, he said, by cutting people off the rolls as new cases were being opened. "I am going to force the welfare system to back up in such a fashion that they are going to hold the line," he was quoted by a Daily News reporter. "We are going to cut services, check cases and get the cheats off the rolls— and the only way to do it is with a fine-ground filter in H.R.A. [Human Resources Administration]. Jule Sugarman has a tough team to do it."

Jule M. Sugarman is Lindsay's welfare commissioner (officially he holds two titles—Commissioner of Social Services and Human Resources Administrator). He was appointed early in 1971, in a clear break with the tradition of having a social worker head the department. Sugarman's forte was pure administration. He had built a career in the Federal bureaucracy with service in such agencies as the State Department, the Office of Economic Opportunity and the Federal Bureau of Prisons. Sugarman brought in a whole platoon of young Ivy-League-educated administrators and managers. They were ballyhooed as "whiz kids" who would overhaul and reform the welfare system. They were, boasted David A. Grossman, Lindsay's Budget Director, "a management team that is one of the best in the country and that I would put up against any welfare agency in the country."

Considering the continuing chaos in the welfare centers, that seems to be a somewhat premature celebration. Nevertheless the mood at central welfare headquarters at 250 Church Street seems to be a breezy confidence that modern management techniques will yet pay big dividends. There are over 200 new employees in top-level administrative and systems-engineering jobs, and many of them have rather unusual backgrounds. There is, for example, a former corporate planner from Allied Chemical Corporation, a former Air Force colonel who worked on the ABM system and a former assistant vice president of the American Stock Exchange. Sugarman, their boss, doesn't think there is anything strange in that—in fact he rather likes it. The Commissioner, a short, unemotional man, doesn't even resent that "whiz kid" label. "I don't object to the term as long as it's put in perspective. I believe in the managerial approach that is tempered by an awareness of social problems," he said.

In fact Sugarman is apt to compare the task ahead of him with the administrative challenges faced at agencies such as the Atomic Energy Commission and NASA. It is a concrete, limited and objectifiable problem which he hopes to solve by the installation of a workable system that will dispense welfare services. Having solved the problem, he will be ready to move on. "I would be surprised if three or four years from now there were more than 25 percent of us around here," he says. "We ought to work ourselves out of the job by solving the problem."

If Sugarman is a management enthusiast, his euphoria is nothing compared to the self-admitted "highs" that administration brings to 32-year-old Arthur Spiegel, the man who actually does most of the systems designs. Spiegel had established himself as an imaginative program manager in the city's Housing and Development Administration; he then moved into private business, where Sugarman's recruiters found him and lured him back into city service as Sugarman's deputy. With its enormous case load and its 15,000 employees, the scope of the management and systems problems simply "turned him on," says the tanned, athletic Spiegel.

To interview Spiegel is a little like getting a briefing from a Pentagon strategic planner. His carpeted office is lined with yellow, blue and orange charts giving a graphic overview of the massive new management innovations already in operation or planned for the future. Spiegel paces the office nervously as he outlines the master plan for a continuing "top-to-bottom overhaul of the city's welfare system." The separation of income maintenance and social services is just the beginning, he says. Soon there will be separate employment centers, a whole new operation for drug addicts, new training programs . . . and the list goes on and on. "I'm convinced the old system was unmanageable," says Spiegel. "Structurally, the old system was bankrupt. When I came in here, we had a backlog of 160,000 pieces of paper. We were sending out thousands of checks to people whose cases should have been closed for weeks. We were running the biggest manual paper mill in the country."

I remind him of the complaints in the centers that there is more paper work than ever before. "The process of separation of services was precipitous," he says confidently. "A lot of people were doing new things. We had a lot of temporary chaos which you would have under any rapid transition."

Spiegel is pinning a lot of his hopes on computer technology. He was appalled, he says, by the primitive state of the computer section in the department when he came in. He has now brought in scores of top computer specialists and expensive new hardware. Ultimately he hopes to have a large computer bank with "on-line" applications at the individual centers. In simple language, this will mean that, for example, anyone who makes an application for assistance will have his application punched into a terminal at the center that is plugged into a central data bank. This will immediately tell the worker all sorts of things, such as whether the prospective client has ever applied before, or if he is registered at any other center. That is just the beginning. In principle the computer could be plugged into an interdepartmental data bank containing income-tax, Social Security and police records. The staff has explored some of these possibilities but, says Spiegel, "it is not so much a technological problem as a legal and civil-liberties one."

The "whiz kids" believe that the systems-engineering approach will not only benefit the department and save money for the public treasury, but are also convinced that it will help the client. And here is where they begin to sound more like behavioral engineers. Spiegel talks a lot about "processing" clients, and his model seems to be a conveyor belt. He uses terms such as "tracking" and "pipelines," and it is clear that it is the clients who will be moved down tracks and into pipelines. And he also believes that all of this will make the clients more aware of the "consequences" of their actions. The idea seems to be that a scientifically constructed income-maintenance system will prod the clients into more rational (i.e., more economically prudent) behavior. It is as if some Pavlovian therapy were to occur during the clients' encounters with the tough, consistent, but fatherly welfare system. That such an interpretation is not all that far-fetched is indicated by the fact that the state has already mandated a system of "brownie points" in which the clients get monetary rewards for doing things like reporting to employment centers.

To the complaint that there might be something dehumanizing or Orwellian in this approach, Spiegel sticks confidently to his guns: "I believe that we are going to design a system that will do a better job of delivering tangbile services to people. My instinct is that if you have an administration that delivers the services, that is what the community wants."

The "whiz kids" haven't exactly been free to tinker with their new managerial approaches in a politically neutral atmosphere. There has been a little pressure from the caseworkers and the welfare-rights groups, but the real crunch has come from conservative antiwelfare forces in the state government. The major vehicle for attacks on the city welfare department has been the newly created office of State Welfare Inspector General, headed by a retired millionaire and professional philanthropist named George Berlinger. The state office, with its staff of 65 and its budget during the current fiscal year of $1.3-million, was given broad powers by the Republican Legislature to investigate abuses in the welfare system throughout the state. To date, they have directed their scrutiny almost exclusively at the city. Berlinger is a tall, youthful 64, elegant in dress and manner, who starts sounding off like Archie Bunker when he gets on the subject of Mayor Lindsay or Jule Sugarman or the welfare-rights groups. It was the rights groups, and Frances Piven and Richard Cloward, he says, who "went out and padded the rolls in order to bring the city to its knees. The Lindsay Administration let it happen. It was done for votes and to keep the city quiet—but we are paying a hell of a price for keeping the city quiet."

Berlinger's investigators have done studies of newly opened cases in three New York City welfare centers (one of them was the Waverly center). They claimed that 25 to 30 percent of the cases opened were actually ineligible. From this, and other data, Berlinger launched a press campaign charging that 30 percent of the city's case load was ineligible. In what quickly became a press-relations war fought with numbers and statistics, Commissioner Sugarman's office countered with studies showing an ineligibility rate of no more than 6 percent.

In fact, there are officials high up in the department who will privately concede that the truth may be close to Berlinger's figures in a purely technical sense; it all depends upon how one defines eligibility. One high-ranking supervisor told me, "Hell, it all depends on just how tough you want to be. If we wanted to, we could probably find more than Berlinger's 30 percent who we could technically call ineligible— that is, if we wanted to act like the Gestapo, following people around, checking up who they are sleeping with. But then what would we have? The people we knocked off the rolls, for this or that technicality, wouldn't be productively at work. They would still be in need."

It is an objective standard of need that is supposed to be the guiding principle for granting assistance, but in fact there is a morass of ambiguous state, Federal and city regulations on eligibility. For example, just what constitutes proof of need has been changing according to the vagaries of the political climate. Under the old caseworker system, the worker had to make a home visit to every applicant for assistance and conduct a thorough investigation of his income and family situation before the application could be approved. But then, at the crest of the liberal wave a few years ago, the Federal Government mandated local welfare departments to drop this "means test" and accept a simple affidavit from the applicant as proof of need. Now, under pressure from state welfare hawks, the city is requiring extensive additional documentation from clients. And in each relief category there are innumerable regulations for maintaining eligibility. Drug addicts must be registered in treatment programs. Home-relief recipients must report to employment centers. Mothers with dependent children must not have a man in the house. Two workers can look at the same case file and simply disagree, on the basis of the available information, as to whether it satisfies the eligibility requirements.

Berlinger insists, however, that up to 30 percent of the case load can actually be pared, with savings of billions of dollars to the city over the years. Behind Berlinger's numbers, there is, in fact, a philosophical premise—one which he alluded to in an address last December (even before he launched his attacks on the city welfare department) before a group of Long Island businessmen. "Assistance," he said, "is essential for those who cannot work because of age, physical disability or family circumstances. But we must help the employable person break the cycle of dependency and aid him in restoring his self-respect and personal pride through constructive work. Only in this way can the role of the family unit be strengthened, family discipline be re-established and the social ills associated with poverty be diminished."

This distinction between the "deserving poor" (comprising the aged, the blind and mothers with very small children) and the "able-bodied" (who presumably ought to be able to find work) is *the* conventional political wisdom during this season of welfare backlash. When Governors Rockefeller and Reagan put that concept into welfare law last year by making all the presumptive employables in their states register for work, President Nixon praised them lavishly for "biting the bullet the entire country is going to have to bite." Of the Nixon welfare-reform package introduced in 1969, with its provisions for a $2,400-per-year minimum for a family of four, only a restrictive make-work bill has been signed into law. The rest of the reform program was killed in the Senate early this month.

There isn't much of a political counterweight against this trend these days. But the radical truth about welfare reform was perhaps best summarized by sociologist Herbert Gans ("Three Ways to Solve the Welfare Problem," *New York Times* Magazine Section, March 7, 1971, p. 26): "None of the programs . . . can do much about the welfare problem itself. That problem is really in the heart of the American economy, which simply does not need all the unemployed looking for work at a living wage, and which cannot provide for all the working poor who require higher wages to support their families. Ultimately, therefore, an end to the welfare problem requires either remaking the economy so that it produces full employment at a living wage, or altering public beliefs about welfare so that the Government will provide the unneeded and underpaid with a decent income."

Occasionally even the "whiz kids" have spoken similar truths, as when Arthur Spiegel testified in the state legislative hearings on the Rockefeller make-work bill. Spiegel opposed the legislation because, he said, "the decreasing demand for labor renders impossible the operation of a program which relies heavily on private-sector demand, and renders unjustifiable a continued focus on efforts to adapt the individual to a labor market that does not exist."

If that perspective on the welfare problem has not been heard much in the recent numbers controversy between Sugarman and Berlinger, it is partly because the voices that might have generated it have been turning their attention elsewhere. Welfare-rights partisan Frances Piven concedes that the Berlinger-Sugarman debate lacked a little leavening from the other side. "The Welfare Rights Organization could have answered Berlinger," she says. "W.R.O. could have had access to the media and defined this whole ineligibility numbers game as fundamentally a class issue. Sugarman was just defending his agency."

That assessment is accepted by Hulbert James, the young man who led the New York Welfare Rights Organization through its most militant phase from 1967–1969. James, now a consultant to the National Council of Churches, but still deeply involved in the National Welfare Rights Organization, says that the movement made a tactical decision to shift its focus to the national scene, lobbying at the conventions and in Congress for its national legislative proposals. All this was done at the expense of local organizing.

Without the welfare-rights input, it is no wonder that the recent City Council hearings on welfare, starring both Sugarman and Berlinger, turned into a tedious marathon involving eligibility numbers and statistics, with almost no serious discussion of social policy. For the "whiz kids" it was more of the same. Impressive lists of managerial innovations were exhibited to convince the Council members that the problem of ineligibility would be handled systematically, without fanfare, and without press campaigns about fraud. It was all cut and dried. What they were going to do, said Mr. Sugarman to the Council, was to develop "sound programs for systematic renovation of the welfare system backed up by sound technology and sound management engineering."

It is not the first time that New York has had a group of "whiz kids" who promised systematic reform of the welfare system through efficient management. Once before there was a welfare crisis in the city, caused by an indiscriminate rise in the rolls. A new organization came into being called the New York Charity Organization Society which proclaimed strict new principles of "scientific philanthropy" that would rationalize and systematize the dispensing of relief. One ranking member of the organization, Robert Treat Paine Jr., denounced charity "which claims to do its work by going out of an afternoon, seeing a family and relieving its needs at once, and sneers at organization and methods and deliberations." The Charity Organization Society believed it was reforming the welfare system for good, and it attracted bright young graduates from the best colleges by offering them the challenge of really systematic reform work.

That was in 1888. Since then America has gone through depressions and recessions, and the relief rolls have expanded and contracted. And, like the poor themselves, welfare reform is still with us.

This is not to say that the "whiz kids" of today will not make a considerable dent in the operations of New York's welfare centers. They may indeed save the city some money. They may even succeed in bringing those long lines of clients in out of the cold this winter—and that would be of considerable benefit. It is just good to keep the history of welfare reform in mind as an antidote to the inevitable euphoria emanating from City Hall when those computers start punching out their IBM cards at the welfare centers next year.

chapter 6

Manpower training for low wage work

DAVID WELLMAN

"I guess these kids just don't want jobs. They're unwilling to try and help themselves. The clothes they wear are loud; they won't talk decent English; they're boisterous; and they constantly fool around. They refuse to take this program seriously."

"But isn't there a job shortage in Oakland?" I asked. "Does it really matter how they act?"

"There's plenty of jobs. They're just not interested."

It was the summer of 1966. The man with whom I was speaking was a counsellor for the Youth Opportunities Center in West Oakland. At the time, he was working on a federally sponsored program known as TIDE. I was observing the program for some graduate research that I was conducting. The purpose of TIDE was to help lower class youth become employable on the job market. The program ran for four weeks. I observed two four-week sessions. Youth from the ages of 16 to 22 were selected by local poverty program workers in the Bay Area. To make the program attractive for unemployed ghetto youth, the government paid participants five dollars a day. Two groups were involved: twenty-five young men and twenty-five young women. These groups met separately, only coming together periodically on common projects. I worked exclusively with the male group.

The young men who participated in the program had a distinctive style. They were "cool." Their hair was characteristically "processed" in one form or another. All sported a kind of sun glasses which they called "pimp's glasses." (These are very lightly tinted glasses, with small frames, which look like "granny glasses.") Their clothes, while usually inexpensive, were "loud" and ingeniously altered to express style and individuality. They spoke in a "hip" vernacular. Their vocabulary was small, yet very expressive. These young men are part of

"Manpower Training for Low Wage Work" (editor's title). From David Wellman, "Putting-On the Poverty Program," which originally appeared in *Steps*, published by the (now non-existent) Free University, Berkeley, California, 1967. Reprinted here by permission of the author.

a "cool world" in the ghetto. They represent a distinctively black, working-class culture.

To most liberals these men are "culturally deprived" or "social drop-outs." Most of them had flunked out of or been kicked out of school. Few had any intention of getting a high school degree. They had long and serious arrest and prison records. They seemed uninterested in "making it" in terms of majority social values and norms. They were skeptical, critical, and hostile toward both the TIDE program [and] white society in general.

The TIDE workers were liberals: sincere, well-meaning people. Those things which, for the young men, defined their own special culture were, for the TIDE workers, symptoms of cultural deprivation. They assumed that if the young men would only act a little less "cool" and learn to smooth over some of their unfortunate encounters with white authorities, they too could become full-fledged working members of society and find their place in the sun. The men were told that the aim of the program was to help them get jobs. TIDE would not train them for jobs. Instead it would train them to *apply* for jobs. They were going to learn how to take tests, how to make a good impression during a job interview, how to speak well, and how to fill out an application form properly. To accomplish these things, they would play games like dominoes to ease the pain associated with numbers and arithmetic; they would conduct mock interviews, take mock tests, meet with management representatives, and go on tours of places where employment was a good possibility for them. They were told to consider the TIDE program as a "job." That is, they were to be at the YOC office on time, dressed as if they were at a job, and be docked if they were late or made trouble. If they took the program seriously and did well, they were told, they stood a pretty good chance of getting a job at the end of four weeks. The unexpressed aim of TIDE then, was to prepare Negro youth for white society. Public government would serve as an employment agency for white, private enterprise.

It was obvious from the outset that the program was aimed at changing the youth by making them more acceptable to employers. Their grammar and pronunciation were constantly corrected. They were subtly told that their appearance would have to be altered for them to get a job. "Don't you think you could shine your shoes?" "Haven't you got trousers that are pressed better?" "It's not a good idea to wear tee-shirts and jeans to a job interview." Promptness, a virtue few of them possessed, was lauded. The penalty for tardiness was being put on a "clean-up committee" of being docked.

For the liberal white TIDE workers the program became a four-week exercise in futility. They seemed to feel that they weren't asking very much of the men. All they really asked was that they learn to make a good impression on white society. This "simply" entailed dressing a little better, increasing one's vocabulary, learning the art of taking tests, and broadly speaking, accepting the "rules of the game." This was "all" they demanded. And yet the men were uncooperative. They fooled around, often refused to take the program seriously, and insisted upon having a "good time." The only conclusion TIDE workers could arrive at was "they just don't want jobs."

What belies this proposition is the seriousness with which most of the men took *actual and distinct job possibilities*. For example, when told there was a job at such-and-such a factory and that a particular test was required, the men studied hard and earnestly applied for the job. The TIDE program *itself*, however, seemed to be viewed as only distantly related to getting a job. The men wanted jobs, but indicated that they felt their inability to take tests and fill out forms was not the problem. They talked about the shortage of jobs available to people without skills. They would pump the YOC people daily about job openings. Their desire for work was obviously not the problem.

Yet, one could hardly deny that the young men fooled around and refused to meet the program on its own terms. If ambition was not the problem, how then do we understand the fact that the men rarely took TIDE seriously?

To one way of thinking, TIDE really didn't demand much of the men. It simply asked that they change certain outward appearances. From the perspective of the men, however, the program seemed to demand a great deal. It asked that they change their manner of speech and dress. It asked that they ignore their lack of skills and society's lack of jobs. It asked that they act as if their arrest records were of consequence in obtaining a job. It asked, most importantly, that they pretend *they*, and not society, bore the responsibility for unemployment. TIDE didn't demand much of the men: only that they become white.

What took place during the four-week program, then, was a daily struggle between white, middle-class ideals of conduct and behavior, and the mores and folkways of the black community. The men were handling TIDE in the same manner that the black community has *always* treated white invasions and threats to its self-respect. They were using subtle forms of subversion and deception.

Confronted by a hostile society and lacking the social tools necessary for material well-being, members of the Negro community have devised ingenious mechanisms for coping with this hostility and simultaneously maintaining their self-respect and human dignity. Historians and sociologists alike have pointed to subtle forms of slave subversion, the content and ritual of Negro spirituals, and recently to the meaning of the Blues as means by which the black man in America has struggled to preserve his integrity as a human being. Many of these devices have persisted until today. They are currently to be found within the structure and culture of the black community. Some of the devices are new. They reflect new forms of struggle with current problems.

"Putting someone on" ("putting the 'hype' on someone," or "running a 'game' on a cat") seems to be an important device used by Negroes to maintain their personal integrity. "Putting someone on" is used as much in relations with black people as it is in relations with members of the white community. In both instances it allows one to maintain personal integrity in the face of a hostile or threatening situation. To "put someone on" is to publicly lead him to believe that one is "going along with" what he has to offer or say, while at the same time privately rejecting the offer, and subtly subverting it. "Putting someone on" may or may not be malicious, but this is not a defining characteristic. "Putting someone on" fails if the other person catches on: he is no longer "put-on." This allows the individual who is "putting someone on" to take pride in the feeling that he has "put something over on" the other person, often at his expense. It thereby allows each party to feel that it has been "successful." "Putting someone on" is to be contrasted with "putting someone down." This is an active and public process involving both defiance and confrontation.

TIDE was evidently interpreted by the men as a threat to their self-respect, as being defeating, useless, and humiliating. They responded to it in much the same way as they would to people inside and outside the ghetto who seemed to threaten their concept of dignity. Sometimes TIDE was "put on." Sometimes it was "put down." It was only taken seriously when it met the needs of the men. And then, only on *their* terms—without a loss of human dignity.

PUTTING-ON THE YOC

There was almost no open defiance or hostility toward those in charge of TIDE. It seemed as if the men were going along with the program. Two things, however, first led me to believe that if the men "accepted" the program, they did so only on their *own* terms.

They all appeared to have a "tuning out" mechanism. They just didn't "hear" certain things. For example, one young man was a constant joker and spoke incessantly. It mattered little to him whether or not someone else was speaking or if the group was supposed to be working on something. When he was told to "knock it off" (which was always) he simply never "heard" the command. On the other hand, when he was involved with the program and interested, he could hear just fine and responded to speakers quite adequately. "Tuning out" was, moreover, often a collective phenomenon. For instance, there was a radio in the room where the men worked. They would play it during lunch and coffee breaks. When the instructor would enter and tell them that work was to begin, they all seemed to be on a wave length frequency that differed from their instructor's. He would tell them that time was up, but they would continue listening and dancing to the music as if there were no one else in the room. However, without so much as acknowledging the instructor and without a word to each other or to him, when *they* were finished listening the radio went off and the session began. . . . It is important to note that this "deafness" was *systematic*. When they were interested or wanted to participate in the program, the men were no longer "deaf." They "tuned out" and "turned on" when *they* saw fit and at no other time. In this respect, there was little authority or control that instructors could exert over the young men: authority was undercut by deafness. The men were "going along with" the program—in a way. They weren't challenging it. But they were undermining its purpose: putting it on.

The second technique which I found the men using as a means of selectively accepting the program was "playing stupid." When they wanted to they could be incredibly "stupid." A major part of the program, for instance, was devoted to teaching them how to fill out employment applications properly. They were given lengthy lectures on the importance of neatness and lettering on these forms. They were expected to fill out such forms at least two or three times a week. After having filled them out a number of times, some of the men suddenly didn't know their mother's name, the school they last attended or their telephone numbers.

This "forgetfulness" or "stupidity" was sometimes duplicated during mock job interviews, which were conducted almost daily. Five or more of the men would serve as "employers" and interview their fellow trainees for an imaginary job. The "interviewers" usually took their job seriously. But after it became apparent that the interview was a game, many of the interviewees developed into hopelessly incapable job applicants. They didn't have social security numbers, they could not remember their last job, they didn't know what school they had gone to, and they didn't know if they really wanted the "job." To the absolute frustration of the interviewers and instructors alike, the "prospective workers" simply behaved like incompetents. Interestingly enough, when the instructor told them one morning that this time the interview was "for real" and that those who did well would actually be sent out on a job interview with a "real" firm, the "stupid" and "incompetent" transformed literally overnight into model job applicants.

These two mechanisms for dealing with the TIDE program were used differently and at different times by many TIDE participants.

Some men "tuned out" and "played stupid" more consistently than others. These men were usually less interested than others in being acceptable to white society. Overall, however, there was little variation in behavior. "Stupidity" occurred when jobs were unavailable.

PUTTING-DOWN THE YOC

"Putting something down" is almost the reverse of "putting someone on." It is a more active and public process. It involves, among other things, confrontation and defiance. When someone is "put-down" he knows it. The success of a "put-down" depends on his knowing it, whereas a "put-on" is only successful when its victim is unaware of what is happening. There were many aspects of the TIDE program which were actively "put-down" by the young men involved.

Among the most glaring "put-downs" were those aimed at the kinds of jobs for which the men were learning to apply. These jobs usually involved unskilled labor: post office work, warehouse and longshore jobs, truck driving, and assembly-line work. Some work was also to be had in the service industry, while some was outright menial labor: chauffeurs, janitors, bus boys, and so on. The reaction of most of the men to this limited prospect was best expressed by a question asked of the instructor by one young man:

"How about some tests for IBM?" he inquired with a straight face.

The room was in an uproar. They thought that was a great question. Many of them were hysterical with laughter. They seemed to feel they had really put this cat down hard. His response was typically bureaucratic, yet very disarming.

"Say, that's a good suggestion. Why don't you put it in the suggestion box?"

They didn't seem able to cope with that retort and so things got somewhat back to normal.

However, when employers came to the TIDE sessions to show the men how an interview should be conducted, they were treated in similar fashion. These employers usually represented companies which hired men for unskilled labor. They came to illustrate good interview technique. They did *not* come to interview men for real jobs. Their visits were sort of helpful-hints-for-successful-interviews sessions. One of the more socially mobile men was usually chosen to play the role of job applicant. The entire interview situation was played through. Some employers even went so far as to have the "applicant" go outside and knock on the door to begin the interview. The men thought this was both odd and funny, commenting to the employer:

"Man, you've already seen the cat. How come you making him walk out and *then* walk back in?"

The employer responded with a look of incredulity: "But that's how you get a job. You have to sell yourself from the moment you walk in that door."

The men seemed unimpressed and continued to crack jokes among themselves about the scene. The interview continued. The employer would put on a real act, beginning the interview with all the usual small talk he'd normally use to draw people out and put them at ease.

"I see from your application that you played football in high school."

"Yeah."

"Did you like it?"

"Yeah."

"Football really makes men and teaches you teamwork."

At about this point the men would get impatient.

"Man, the cat's here to get a job, not talk about football!"

"When are you going to tell him about the job?"

A wise-cracker chimed in: "Maybe he's interviewing him for a job with the Oakland Raiders."

The point of all this was usually well taken by the employer, and he would begin to ask questions more germane to the particular job. He would ask about the "applicant's" job experience, his draft status, school record, interests, skills and so on. The young man being interviewed usually took the questions seriously and answered frankly. But after awhile, the rest of the group would tire of playing this game and begin to ask (unrecognized, from the floor) about the specifics of a "real" job.

"Say man, how much does this job pay?"

"What kind of experience do you need?"

"What if you got a record?"

"How many days off do you get?"

The employer would politely remind them that this wasn't a "real" interview. But this would only satisfy the young men for a short while, and they would soon resume their questions. It didn't take long to rattle the interviewer completely. Sometimes the instructor would intervene and tell the men that the gentleman was there to help them, and would request that they treat him more gently. Again, this would stifle revolt for only a short while. Then, in a mood of outright defiance, they might begin playing dominoes while the interview went on. If this didn't evoke an irritated response, they might begin to play the game rather enthusiastically by loudly slapping down the dominoes each time they scored a point. In one instance, several of the men began slapping the tables rhythmically with dominoes, during the interview. That got the response they were looking for.

"Look!" said the employer, who had completely lost control of the situation. "If you're not interested in learning how to sell yourself why don't you just leave the room so that others who are interested can benefit from this?"

"Oh no!" was the response of the ringleaders, "We work here. If you don't dig us, then *you* leave!"

It wasn't too much later that he did.

Sometimes during these interviews the very nature of the work being considered was "put down." During an "interview" for a truck driving job, some of the men began to ask the employer about salesman jobs. Others asked him about executive staff positions. They weren't very interested in talking about a job driving a truck. They continually interrupted the interview with "irrelevant" questions about the role of an executive. They wanted to know how much executives were paid and what they did to get their jobs. At one point the employer himself was asked point-blank how much he was paid, what his experience was, and what he did. To some extent they had turned the tables and were enjoying the opportunity to interview the interviewer. He finally told them, in fact:

"I'm here to *do* the interviewing, not to *be* interviewed."

In spite of this they managed to return to interviewing him. And when they weren't doing that, they were asking him about the qualifications necessary for other, more skilled jobs. In most such situations it became quite clear that they were not interested in the kinds of jobs most employers had to offer—not interested enough, that is, to participate seriously in a mock interview for an imaginary job.

The young TIDE participants were remarkably unimpressed, moreover, by the status of an employer. Regardless of his rank, the men treated their visitors as they would their peers. Sometimes visiting employers were treated more harshly and with genuine, open defiance. On one tour of a factory the men were escorted by the vice-president in charge of hiring. To some people this might have been considered an honor, and the man would have been treated with an extra ounce of deference. To the TIDE participants, however, he was just another guide. And after informing the men of the large number of unskilled positions available, he was asked about hiring some of them, on the spot. He responded by saying that this was just a tour and that he was in no position to hire anyone immediately. Some of the men were noticeably irritated at this answer. One looked at him and said:

"Then you're just wasting our time, aren't you?"

Although shaken, the executive persisted, telling the men about technical operations at the plant. Throughout his talk he referred to his audience as "boys."

"Now, when you boys come to apply for a job you will need proof of a high school education."

"If you boys want to work here you will need to join the union."

This constant reference to "boys" was obviously bothering the men. Each time the word would crop up, they squirmed in their seats, snickered, or whispered angrily to each other. The vice-president seemed unaware of the hostility he aroused. But finally, one of the bolder men spoke up firmly.

"We are young mens, not boys!"

The speaker blushed nervously and apologized. He made a brave attempt to avoid repeating the phrase. Habit, however, was victorious and the word slipped in again and again. Each time he said "you boys" he was corrected, aloud, and with increasing hostility. For a while it seemed as though the young men were more interested in catching him saying "you boys" than in anything else he said. . . .

Throughout the entire TIDE program the young men had been "putting-down" people and projects. The men used the context of a government training program as a protective device which enabled them to "put down" institutions and individuals otherwise impervious to attack. TIDE provided insulation for them. And it offered an opportunity for meeting with people otherwise unavailable to them. In addition, the men rapidly developed a high degree of group consciousness upon which they could fall back for protection and inspiration. Armed in this manner, they then went out to "get" or "put down" normally inaccessible institutions. When consulted about whom they wanted to come and speak to them (which the men seemed to interpret as "come be put down by them"), they called for the police, a city councilman, state assemblymen, businessmen, and officials of the poverty program. Almost all these people were "put down" in one way or another when they appeared at the YOC. The TIDE people were anxious to have these visitors. TIDE workers thought it was a good idea for the young men to meet with community leaders and officials, in order to show them that these leaders were interested in their problems and would help if the men would show a little initiative. The men "showed initiative" by inviting important people to speak with them: to be "put down" by them. They "put on" the YOC in order to "put down" this array of visitors. The "put-downs," then, were also a "put-on" of the YOC. By using the program as a cover for airing their grievances, the men were, in effect, altering TIDE to meet their needs.

As the program was conceived by the government, TIDE did not meet the needs of the young men. Indeed, it wasn't meant to. The Great Society was trying to run a game on black youth. It wanted them to cease being what they were. It wanted to lead them into white middle-class America. It tried to trick them by leading them to believe that America was interested in getting them jobs.

But there aren't many jobs in America for young men who have arrest records, who lack skills, and who are black. There aren't jobs for black youth who refuse to accept white America's definition of self-respect and integrity. The young men knew that. TIDE knew it too. The very jobs over which TIDE had some control (that is, government jobs) are rarely filled by people with the backgrounds of ghetto youth. But TIDE didn't train the youth to work. It attempted to train them to pretend that there was no problem.

The men saw through it. They diagnosed it as a sham. They rejected its invitation into white America.

When a "put-on" is detected, it fails.

TIDE was more than a "put-on" of black youth. It was also an attempt to persuade the youth to "put on" potential employers. By training men to speak well, dress well, fill out application forms properly, and to take tests easily, TIDE evidently sought to "fool" employers into hiring these young men. But this was never made explicit to the men. Why, then, didn't TIDE workers just come right out and say it: "Look men. What we're suggesting is that you put on your employers; make them believe you're someone you're not."

The suggestion is absurd. The reasons for its absurdity are revealing.

It wouldn't work. This "new" approach would really not be new. It would only assert more openly that black culture is not acceptable to white society. It would still be asking the men to pretend they were someone else. It would still imply that there is something wrong with who they are. Finally, it would assume that there is work for those who want it. The young men knew there wasn't.

It could never happen. To suggest that the young men had to "put on" employers in order to win jobs implies that the employers have some responsibility for unemployment and racial exclusion. But the TIDE program, indeed much of the Great Society, assumes that the door to happiness—to America—is open if people will seek to enter on middle-class terms. "Teaching" the TIDE participants to "put on" the interviewer runs counter to the assumptions which are held dear by the poverty program and the nation. It would be impossible for government representatives even to entertain such a step.

Our hypothetical proposition would also threaten the morale of the TIDE workers. I'm sure that most of them were well-intentioned, good, liberal people. They are also human beings. And as human beings they must strive for personal integrity in their work situation. Their job is not an enviable one. Facing fantastic barriers, they must try to get work for people. Their success is limited. But for them to recognize that society bears most of the responsibility for inequality would be to render their work worthless. To ask them to admit that their work is a "put-on" is to threaten their concept of self-worth. The institutional framework of the TIDE worker, like that of most welfare workers, therefore calls forth an orientation which holds the client, and not society, responsible for his situation.

The TIDE worker, then, would never consider asking the men to "put on" employers. Faced with defeat and frustration, as they were, they responded predictably: "they just don't want jobs." Ironically enough, the institutional requirements of northern liberalism have called forth a response very similar to the familiar line of southern racism. Wasn't it the "old fashioned" southern bigot who used to say: "Negroes don't have jobs because they are lazy and shiftless"? There is a difference to be sure. The southerner felt that black people are inherently shiftless and lazy. Thus, they are destined to be without jobs of consequence. Most modern liberals seem to view black people as temporarily hindered by psychological and cultural impediments. Inequities in the employment and opportunity structure of America, they seem to suggest, are minor in comparison with the deficiencies of black people themselves. What black people need, according to the liberals, is cultural enrichment and the ability to "sell themselves" to white society. In the end, northern liberals and southern racists agree: the problem is mainly with Negroes.

IV

Poverty and profits

In this nation I see tens of millions of its citizens—a substantial part of its whole population—who at this very moment are denied the greater part of what the very lowest standards of today call the necessities of life.

I see millions of families trying to live on incomes so meagre that the pall of family disaster hangs over them day by day. . . .

It is not in despair that I paint you that picture. I paint it for you in hope —because the Nation, seeing and understanding the injustice in it, proposes to paint it out. We are determined to make every American citizen the subject of his country's interest and concern. . . . The test of our progress is not whether we add more to the abundance of those who have much; it is whether we provide enough for those who have too little.

FRANKLIN D. ROOSEVELT[*]

President Nixon has adopted a responsible common-sense approach to our urban problems. His answer is jobs and job training. The accent is on the solid American ethic of working for a living. . . . Workfare instead of welfare. That is the American way. . . . That's the only way to bridge the gap between the Haves and the Have-Nots in America.

GERALD R. FORD[**]

Chapters seven and eight treat two different aspects of the relationship between poverty and profits. The first, by David Horowitz with Reese Erlich, examines a new facet in the already intimate relationship between business and government—the 1960s corporate management of Job Corps camps, a multimillion-dollar portion of the federal poverty programs. This chapter not only illustrates how business has capitalized on poverty programs and has dehumanized their operation, but also substantiates the great extent to which large interlocked corporations shape and control all federal social programs at home and abroad.

[*] Second Inaugural Address, January 20, 1937.
[**] United States Representative from Michigan, Before the National Federation of Republican Women, Washington, D.C., September 27, 1969.

Hundreds of corporations, in addition to the Litton Industries described by Horowitz, have profited from federal poverty
programs. In 1970, the *New York Times* reported that over the
preceding seven years at least 254 companies had each obtained
$100,000 or more in contracts from the U.S. Office of Economic
Opportunity.[1] At the end of fiscal 1970, OEO was channeling
$11,507,978 through thirty-two technical assistance, consulting,
evaluation, and support contracts to sixteen companies that together employed thirty-five former antipoverty officials.[2]

Roy Ash, formerly Litton's number-two man, has been in the
business-government spotlight frequently since 1968 when Horowitz wrote his article. First, Litton's disasterous "shipyard of
the future" involved $100 million plus cost overruns and long
delays for the Navy leading to questions concerning Ash's managerial skill.[3] Then, despite Ash's recent threats to go over the
heads of Navy officials to obtain approximately $400 million in
bailout funds for Litton, President Nixon in late 1972 appointed Ash director of the U.S. Office of Management and
Budget.[4] Allegations of scandalous business conduct when he
was building his fortune were made at the time of Ash's ap-
pointment.[5] The most serious of the charges, which were part
of the record of two jury trials held during the 1960s, was that
as top financial officer of the Hughes Aircraft Company in 1949–
53, he forced accountants to make bookkeeping entries that they
testified were false and that caused the Air Force to be over-
billed by forty-three million dollars. That amount was repaid
to the government less than four months after Ash left the company.[6]

The Senate, wishing to question the newly appointed director
of the Office of Management and Budget on his past business
dealings, passed a bill to require for the first time Senate con-
firmation of the person to fill the important post. The bill,
passed by the House, was vetoed by President Nixon.[7] The

---

[1] *The New York Times,* November 8, 1970, Sec. 1, p. 1: column 4; p. 54, column 2.

[2] Ibid.; also see Milwaukee Welfare Rights Organization, *Welfare Mothers Speak
Out* (New York: Norton Publishing Company, 1972), chap. 3; and James A. Kalish,
"The Urban-Problems Industry," *Washington Monthly* 1, no. 10 (November, 1969):
6–16.

[3] Rep. Les Aspin, "The Litton Ship Fiasco," *The Nation,* 215 (December 11, 1972).

[4] Rep. Les Aspin, "The Case Against Roy Ash," *The Nation* 216, no. 9 (February
26, 1973): 265.

[5] Wallace Turner, "Allegations Against Ash Center on Bookkeeping for Hughes
and Origin of Litton Industries," *New York Times, January* 28, 1973, 42: column 1.

[6] *Ibid.*

[7] *New York Times,* May 19, 1973, sec. 1, p. 4.

President's veto was overriden by the Senate and sustained by the House.[8] By mid-1973, after the Watergate disclosures had removed many of President Nixon's advisors from their posts, Ash sat in the President's three-man "super cabinet" with Henry A. Kissinger and Secretary of the Treasury George P. Shultz.[9]

Chapter eight by Barry Bluestone, assistant professor of economics at Boston College and an active member of the Union of Radical Political Economists, deals not with the rich who have already made their way through and continue to profit from the capitalist system, but with the poor who are trying to obtain a foothold in the system. Bluestone's chapter examines several forms of black capitalism and suggests a context in which black economic self-determination might be successful.

chapter   seven

Proving poverty pays:
big brother as a holding company

DAVID HOROWITZ WITH REESE ERLICH

"According to our computer," says Robert Allan Jr., head of Litton Industries' Greek project, "there's less than 800 weeks before the present trend will be irreversible. . . . The need for food and the lack of capacity of technology in . . . underdeveloped nations will be overwhelming. . . . It's time that we got to work on it." To listen to Litton executives and to read their annual reports, one might suppose that Litton was some enormous social welfare agency rather than a multibillion-dollar defense contractor. In reality, it is both of these and more.

Litton Industries produces S&H Green Stamps and Stouffer Foods,

"Proving Poverty Pays: Big Brother as a Holding Company" (editor's title). From David Horowitz with Reese Erlich, "The Rise of Conglomerate Corporations," *Ramparts*, November 30 and December 14–28, 1968. Reprinted here by permission of Noah's Ark, Inc.

8 *New York Times*, May 23, 1973, sec. 1, p. 5; May 24, 1973, sec. 1, p. 4.

9 John Herbus, "White House Staff Seeks to Carry On During Crisis," *New York Times*, May 29, 1973, p. 20: column 3.

missile guidance systems and nuclear attack submarines. It runs important programs of the War on Poverty at home. And abroad it recently secured an $800 million contract—to which Mr. Allan's statement referred—with the Greek military junta for the economic development of the whole geographical region of Western Peloponnesus and Crete. Litton is the perfect example of the new corporation extending itself beyond the limits that have divided the private oligarchies of business from the realms of responsibility traditionally reserved to government.

Among the corporate bearers of this brave new American future, Litton stands out as something of a paradigm and archetype foreshadowing the shape of things to come. It has gathered about itself the full mystique of modernity: advanced technology, the "systems engineering" approach (a product of military contracting), electronics and space.

In 1953, when a group headed by Charles "Tex" Thornton bought Litton, then a small electronics firm, for $1.5 million, the company showed $3 million in sales. This year its worth has grown to a fantastic $1.8 *billion* level, making it the 44th largest industrial corporation in the U.S., ranking ahead of such traditional giants as Alcoa Aluminum, Coca-Cola and Dow Chemical.

It is perhaps natural that the guiding forces of American society, frustrated by the nation's stubborn social ills which appear to be insoluble by traditional means, should turn to the methodology of military-space development as the Way to Get Things Done. Unable to confront the real moral and political dimensions of its economic and social crisis, the American leadership defines the crisis as basically a technical problem and is immensely comforted thereby: the technical problem is large, to be sure, but it is one that can be handled without any serious reassessment of American values and institutions—and without the social upheaval that might be necessary to restructure them.

The social engineering approach to race and poverty is merely the logical extension of the pervasive liberal doctrine of pragmatic America and the "end of ideology." As John F. Kennedy, whom many look on as the last national statesman to bear the torch of idealism, affirmed in his famous Yale address in 1962: "What is at stake is not some grand warfare of rival ideologies which will sweep the country with passion, but the practical management of a modern economy. What we need is . . . more basic discussion of the sophisticated and technical issues involved in keeping a great economic machinery moving ahead."

The domestic upheavals in the years following President Kennedy's address have torn to shreds the mythology of the crisis-free welfare state. But the mythology of salvation through the application of technology by the Great Partnership between government and the private corporations has not only survived, it has risen to a new intensity of apocalyptic promise. The theme recurs across the political spectrum, though Democrats may call it a domestic Marshall Plan while Republicans and Wallacites more candidly emphasize Incentives to Business.

Litton industries was the first corporation to take over one of the poverty program's multimillion-dollar Job Corps camps—whose large urban centers are now run completely by private enterprise—and was an early promoter of the "military systems" approach for other areas of national policy. As the idea has caught on, proposals have proliferated. General Bernard Adolph Schriever, special Administration consultant on housing and urban development programs, has already suggested that aerospace's management process be applied to these programs, and aerospace industrial teams have begun pushing for contracts in such areas as urban traffic management and water conservation.

While the notion of a military-industrial complex has gained currency in recent years, the *technological* underpinning of the new intimacy between government and business has gone largely unnoticed. Yet full 70 percent of all research and development being done in the United States today (about $16 billion worth), is paid for by the federal government, whereas a little more than 20 years ago it supported almost none at all. The significance of this for the civilian economy was spelled out recently by Litton's number two man, Roy Ash, in explaining his company's relation to the military sector. Since "almost all new products have their first application in military uses," said Ash, "we always want at least 25 percent of our business in defense and space."

Ash's statement and the facts behind it reflect the final collapse of the cornerstone of old-fashioned capitalism. In the old days private corporations would develop technological innovations at their own expense, risking the outlay with a view to being rewarded by future returns from the competitive marketplace. This was the very essence of entrepreneurship. However, technical research has now become extremely expensive, and because of the gentlemanly pace of competition among the monopolistic giants of the American economy, these corporations are no longer forced by fear of rivals to risk such investments. So they have become accustomed to getting the government to pick up the tab before they move. These corporations have grown economically lazy, in part because *they* really *can* live better on the largess of the so-called welfare state. One of the factors that has made it possible for them to pry such huge sums of research money out of the government has been the unprecedented increase in the concentration of economic—and with it, political—power in the last decade.

This tremendous concentration movement in the economy has been spearheaded by the advance of the "conglomerate" corporations, formed by the acquisition of companies operating in diverse markets. Litton is the star of this movement, with enterprises in 18 distinct industrial categories.

Tex Thornton is the paradigm new corporate manager of the paradigm new corporation. His career follows the now well trodden path from civilian Washington to the military to the corporate elite.

Thirty years ago Tex Thornton was a $1400-a-year clerk in Washington; today he is a university trustee, a member of the President's Advisory Commission on Civil Disorders (the Kerner Commission) and head of its special Advisory Panel on Private Enterprise. He was one of a handful of nominees considered to succeed Robert McNamara as Secretary of Defense. He has already achieved the coveted seat next to President Nixon at White House business meetings. In addition to being chairman of the board of Litton, he is an "interlocking director" of such giants as TWA, Lehman Corporation, General Mills, the Western Bancorporation (a bank holding company for the Bank of America interests) and Union Oil. Needless to say, in Thornton's new circles being a millionaire is not at all unusual, but he has already made $80 million and is aiming for the status of centimillionaire. If the market for Litton stock holds up, he will soon make it.

NUMBERS GAMES

The traditional conception of the growth of a business brings to mind images of the firm selling more of its products, creating new ones, and building new plants to produce more to sell. Only a fraction of Litton's growth, in fact, was achieved in this way. Of the $97 million increase during Tex's first four years, for example, sales from Charlie Litton's original firm accounted for only $11 million. The rest of the increase in sales resulted from the acquisition of some 17 previously existing companies and their incorporation into a new overall financial superstructure: "Litton Industries, Inc." As Thornton explains, "We had to grow fast. There wasn't time to learn a business, train people, develop markets. . . . We bought time, a market, a product line, plant, research team, sales force. It would have taken years to duplicate this from scratch."

Buying, not building, was the formula of Litton's growth. To understand how a small firm with limited resources *can* buy itself into bigness, one must understand how corporate growth can feed on itself. For the very act of merger creates new power to merge on an even larger scale through its effect on the value of the corporation's stock.

The value of the stock and therefore of the corporation is not determined by adding up the values of tangible assets: cash reserves, inventories, equipment, plant and so forth. The value of the stock is determined by what people are willing to pay for it, and they will pay more now if they expect its value to rise in the future.

The key to conglomerate growth is the fact that a company's stock can be—and ordinarily is—the "money" that is used to purchase another corporation. So a smart businessman can make the process come full circle. By successfully creating a glamorous "growth image" on the stock market that excites expectations of real future growth, he can drive the value of his stock up. This then gives him new "money" with which to buy *real* assets in the form of another corporation: in other words, his business can grow in fact and not just on paper, thereby confirming the expectations he aroused and further strengthening the image. And so the circle becomes a spiral of increasing growth.

Conglomerates are so obviously based on highly speculative, not to say shady, principles that even the Wall Street Journal has been prompted to ask a few probing questions about them: how much of their growth is based on improved products and efficiencies and how much reflects the attractive arithmetic of acquisition and the temptations of empire building? . . . Can they be managed efficiently?

This last question has an especially poignant ring for Litton's supermanagers. In 1968, Litton's second quarter report admitted a disastrous 30 percent earnings drop (Litton's stock price plummeted nearly 50 percent at the news), reflecting managerial errors so gross that not even the most creative accounting techniques could cover them up.

The mistakes affected several of Litton's divisions, including its business furniture, Royfax duplicators, Monroe calculators, and its Royal typewriter line. But the biggest error of all provided the clue to the overall pattern of Litton's debacle. The Litton shipyard, which had been accustomed to a rich diet of cost-plus contracts at the government trough ("Your chances of losing money" under such contracts, admits a Litton executive, "are not too great"), had for the first time bid competitively on a package basis for the construction of automated merchant vessels—a *civilian* contract under which you don't get to come back for more money if you can't make it at the agreed-upon price. The result of this market test was that Litton underestimated the costs, submitted a bid that was too low, and instead of netting a profit, had to write off a loss of $8 million.

In what must rank as the understatement of the year, Fortune, after noting that the key to Litton's setback was its inability to stand the test of the relatively competitive civilian market, observed: "The requirements for profitability in government work are less exacting than those of the private marketplace."

Under government contracts there is a decided lack of competitive strictures. Little or no capital is risked by the corporation. If it makes errors of judgment, timing, cost analysis and so forth, there are no competitors to take advantage of its mistakes. And it has an enormously understanding buyer. If costs are underestimated, they can always be adjusted up through contract renegotiation. One former Litton executive with responsibilities in this area estimated that as a matter of *normal* practice, Litton in the course of production and development renegotiated its contracts to one and a half times the original price—a nice margin for inept planning and mismanagement.

In short, its vulnerable growth strategy could never have carried Litton so far had it not possessed the ability, though a small firm at the outset, to get a front-line position in the prime military contract game and latch on to that secret fuel which alone can launch space age corporations towards the moon: the financial largess of the state.

CONTRACTING NATIONAL SECURITY

. . . the creation of the U.S. Air Force as a separate military service . . . may have had more important consequences for U.S. industry than any other event in recent decades."

—FORTUNE, SEPTEMBER 1968

The high point of Litton's close connections in Washington was reached during the reign of Tex Thornton's one time subordinate, Robert McNamara, as secretary of Defense. Thornton, who was often a breakfast guest at the Pentagon, claims never to have talked business with the secretary during those visits. But, as the executive of another corporation in the contract field observed in a *Ramparts* interview, "A clever man would merely let it be known that he was having breakfast with McNamara every other morning. When talking to procurement officers and the like, he wouldn't even have to mention McNamara's name."

The subtle but far-reaching significance of good connections was pointed out by the leading student of the military-industrial complex, Professor H. L. Nieburg: "Officials in the lower reaches of the government bureaucracy (both civilian and military) charged with administration of contracts, find themselves dealing with private corporate officials who often were their own former bosses and continue as companions of present bosses and congressional leaders who watchdog the agencies. A contract negotiator or supervisor must deal with men who can determine his career prospects; through contacts, these industrial contractors may cause him to be passed over or transferred to a minor position in some remote bureaucratic corner, sometimes with a ceremonial drumming before a congressional committee."

Among Litton's vice presidents are Joseph Imirie, a former under-secretary of the Air Force, and John H. Rubel, a former assistant secretary of Defense (a key member of the McNamara team). But what may be Litton's most important connection is Tex's close friendship with George Mahon, chairman of the vital House Appropriations Committee.

But political strings are only half the story. More than anything else, it is the defense contracting system itself, as it evolved after World War II, which has created the new and sinister relationship between the giant corporations and the state.

Following the profiteering scandals of World War I, which revealed that American business had milked the American taxpayer by "sliding" price policies on military contracts, and had spent the lives of many American soldiers by producing cheap, shoddy equipment, the practice of competitive bidding on government contracts was instituted to simulate the open market. The two armed services developed their own "in-house" design and production capabilities which served to measure and check outside performances. Under the pressures of the Second World War, contracting procedures on aircraft, ordnance and ammunition reverted to the cost-plus basis which had inspired the earlier scandals. Then a series of developments after the war produced the current unprecedented state of affairs.

First, as part of a movement heralded as a return to "free enterprise," plants, factories and facilities built by the government during the war were either sold to private corporations, usually at a fraction of their original cost, or were leased at nominal fees to contractors, to use for military contracts. This largely deprived the government of the performance "yardstick" of its in-house facilities.

Second, the Air Force was established as an independent military service. Naturally, it did not have the already built in-house capabilities of the other two services, so it hired out the entire process of designing, producing and even maintaining weapons systems, instead of presenting its own designs to contractors for production. This necessitated a cost-plus contractual basis, since no prearranged price could be fixed for so indeterminate a process. In addition, the Air Force's prime contracting corporations, now responsible for complete weapons systems, had to establish, in the words of one Congressional Report, "procurement organizations and methods which proximate those of the government." These prime contractors were thus in a position to force subcontracting small companies out of business, acquire their proprietary information, make or break geographical regions and decide a host of other critical issues of national import, without even the quasi-democratic checks imposed on the federal bureaucracy.

Once established, prime systems contracting quickly spread to the other services. A losing battle with the Air Force for responsibility for missile program development taught the Army that its extensive in-house capabilities and technical independence were a distinct disadvantage. For in the political struggle over missile development, the Air Force's corporate prime contractors constituted a powerful lobby in Congress against which all the in-house expertise of the Army was of no avail. A quick learner when the future of its bureaucracy is at stake, the Army began to disband its in-house facilities and to surrender its jurisdictional and discretionary capacities to private industry and the latter's impressive political power. For any corporation in advanced technologies on the way up, prime contracting soon became the indispensable order of the day.

THE TECHNOLOGY OF PROFIT

The vast accretion of power in the last decade to military-based conglomerates like Litton and Ling-Temco-Vought has caused remarkably little public concern, considering the implications for an ostensibly free society. There are many factors behind this default, but probably the most important one is the least conspicuous. It is the universal conviction that bigness and even monopolistic concentration are inevitable, being the natural and necessary consequences of technological modernity. To protest therefore seems merely to stand in the way of progress, mindlessly repudiating the bounty of the age in favor of nostalgic illusions. Yet the actual empirical studies that have been made provide no substantive basis for the thesis that technology requires monopoly—indeed they point strongly in the opposite direction.

Thus, the authoritative study in the field (Joe S. Bain's *Industrial Organization*) concludes that for 80 to 90 percent of the industries investigated, there is no need for high concentration to make production and distribution efficient. On the other hand, many of the new technologies have a decidedly decentralizing thrust, and as Dr. John M. Blair, chief economist for the Senate antitrust subcommittee, has pointed out, highly monopolistic industries like steel have been decentralizing their assembly plants at the same time that another model of monopolistic concentration, General Electric, has "shut down its huge Schenectady factory while making a veritable religion of decentralization."

If relatively high concentration is not technologically justified for single industry firms, it is hardly justified for the conglomerates, which are made up of randomly acquired companies encompassing diverse product lines and categories.

For that reason among others, the heads of Litton, like all conglomerate managements, don't like to admit that they are such an enterprise (although their more than 80 companies operate in 18 distinct industrial categories). According to number two man, Roy Ash, Litton's acquisitions have been in fields where its technological capabilities give it a competitive edge. "In truth," comments Fortune, "considerable mental agility is required to perceive an impending technological revolution in some of the businesses Litton has bought—e.g., office furniture."

Litton Industries cannot in fact seriously claim to provide any benefits of integrated production to its jumble of subunits. And if they are sometimes inclined to invoke the salutary but mysterious influence of their mode of central management, when they get down to it the feature of their organization about which they are proudest is just how decentralized it is—with acquired companies remaining autonomous and even rivals of their sibling subunits.

Office furniture aside, Ash's claim that Litton's size facilitates technological innovation reflects another major technological myth of our age: that the giant corporation is a necessary agent for *creating* new technologies.

Yet in an authoritative study of 61 "major contemporary inventions," it was found that only of 12 of these could be attributed to the laboratories of large corporations.

Can it be that the supercorporation of the space age is really all that shortsighted and tightfisted about seeking new technologies? Private industry does after all spend $9 billion a year on research and development (four percent on basic research, the rest largely on altering, refining, packaging and marketing existing technologies). And of that, the larger firms, those with more than 5000 employees, certainly carry their share. Though they make up only three percent of the companies doing research, they spend 85 percent of the total. That looks like pretty extravagant entrepreneurial daring. Of course this investment in the future is made considerably easier for them by the fact that the government puts up 60 cents of every R&D dollar that private industry spends. Moreover, two-thirds of the rest is ultimately charged off as overhead on government contracts.

So it seems that the real entrepreneur is the government, who is not only extraordinarily openhanded about putting up the investment, but agreeably lighthearted about not reaping the profits on it. So agreeable, in fact, that it goes on to buy the product that it financed, at a healthy profit to the surrogate developer. Like buying the Brooklyn Bridge, this must be looked on as an act of peculiar generosity. It is a game where the roles of politician, general, corporate manager and government official are shifted around so rapidly that an embarrassed player can even forget if he is to be the donor or the recipient.

But then again it's not their money. If the corporation is spending the government's money, the government is spending the taxpayer's. If he had a very clear idea of it, the taxpayer might frown on this happy arrangement and spoil all the fun, but his attention is turned toward the welfare pennies allegedly squandered on people who don't work. Whereas the men on the board at Litton have very good jobs indeed.

With an eye to the immense dominions of largess still to be granted by the sovereign power, Litton has been careful to keep its representatives at court and to keep a foot in every available political door. Among its executives and directors are Defense Department secretaries and military generals, highly influential Democrats and equally important Republicans, liberal Humphrey supporters and the chief financial backer of Ronald Reagan—in short, the whole spectrum of legitimized political power (and potential contract dispensation). With its expansive political network as a foundation, Litton has been in the forefront of the move to extend systems contracting to nonmilitary fields. Litton was the first private contractor to take over responsibility for a War on Poverty Job Corps project and the first corporation to apply the systems approach to the economic development program of an entire geographical region (in Greece), and its distinctive mode of operation in these instances provides an ominous portent of things to come.

CONTRACTING POVERTY

"The input—the raw material—that is fed into this machine is people. The output is people. It is the function of this machine to transform these people." That is the philosophy of "education" held by John H. Rubel, vice president of Litton's Economic Development Division, as expressed in a letter to Sargent Shriver. Rubel, formerly assistant secretary of Defense under RobertMcNamara, is credited with having convinced Shriver to award Job Corps contracts to private enterprise rather than strictly to educational institutions. Of course, it was only fair that Litton should get one of the first contracts: the Parks Job Corps Center in Pleasanton, California.

Litton's predictably titled Educational Systems Division includes many valuable properties, such as the American Book, D. Van Nostrand and Chapman-Reinhold publishing companies. They also serve as program administrators for Oakland Community College in Bloomfield Hills, Michigan. Its most important enterprise, however, is the Parks Center, because the Job Corps is the opening wedge for Litton's entrance into social welfare and education.

Litton's public relations department celebrates the Parks Job Corps camp as a free enterprise success story. Recently, Parks placed its 5000th "graduate" in a job; the center has thus placed more of its graduates than any other Job Corps camp in the country. Of course, the PR men neglect to mention that the number one "employer," accounting for roughly 40 percent of Parks' graduates, is the U.S. military.

The waiting room of the placement office, where each graduate of the nine-month course goes to inquire about future employment, is plastered with posters urging, nondenominationally, enlistment in the Army, Navy, Air Force or Marines. A life-size cardboard cutout of a sharp looking black soldier salutes the graduate as he steps in the door. Piles of brochures invite him to learn "The Secret of Getting Ahead in Today's Action Army." And lest the message be forgotten, on the way out a flashing sign reminds him: DESIRABLE LOCATION—YOUR U.S. ARMY —TRAINING GUARANTEED WITH BIG BUSINESS—YOUR CHOICE OF SCHOOLS— STEADY ADVANCEMENT.

Of course where enticement fails, there is always induction. Every week an IBM print-out announces the names of those at the Parks Center who have turned eighteen. Each one must then register for the draft with a Litton employee, conveniently certified by the local Hayward board. Upon graduation, Litton notifies the corpsman's draft board of his new educational achievements. (Litton arranges for the majority of its enrollees at Parks to receive a high school equivalency diploma, which makes those who had been deferred due to low scores on the Army mental aptitude exam eligible for retesting.) Al Cassell, the head of placement at the Parks Center, explained: "We get draft notices by the hundreds every day. We furnish the draft board with information relative to the training level achieved by the young man. . . . We take him to Hayward and have him retested. . . . If he passes . . . the Hayward testing center notifies his local board, and they in turn will usually draft him."

Even if the corpsman does not improve his score on the test, his new high school diploma might well make him eligible for induction. At one time, in a kind of reciprocal trade arrangement, Litton kept a Job Corps recruiter at the frequently embattled Oakland Induction Center in California. Many ineligible draftees, led to believe that they would become qualified for a high paying job in industry, enrolled in the program only to find themselves returned full circle at the end of the course. Two sergeants from Hayward go out to the Parks Job Corps Center every day. No other prospective employers have permanent recruiters there.

Vernon Alden, president of Ohio University, envisioned the Job Corps as a place that would "offer a new environment where hopes can be lifted and skills developed free from the shackles of oppressive and antagonistic surroundings." So much for visions.

Litton's Job Corps center, located on an unused Navy base, is sur-
rounded by a barbed wire fence with checkpoints manned by Litton-
employed guards. The 2000 corpsmen sleep in open bay Army barracks,
wear green uniforms, march to their meals at the mess hall, and are
hauled off to the brig when they misbehave. The young men arriving
at Parks are not exactly prepared for such an environment. Most of
them have been signed up by the Litton recruiters who are stationed
throughout the poverty areas of the nation advertising the wealth of
opportunity in California. Since Litton's contract with the Office of
Economic Opportunity (OEO) depends on a sufficient number of enrollees, the recruiters use every possible means to lure them. Of course,
they give the standard come-on: training for a good-paying job, the
equivalent of a high school diploma, $30-a-month spending money, a
$50-a-month bonus upon graduation for time completed, and a chance
to get away from home. There is also exotic talk of pools and girls,
private rooms with TV's—even draft deferments!

If getting them there is half the battle for Litton, keeping them
there is the other half. When a new enrollee decides that life was better
back home, even though home may have been a decaying urban slum,
his request to leave is met with hostility by Litton officials. He is told
that he cannot leave for at least 90 days for any reason other than a
death in the immediate family. Moreover, if he wants to quit at any
time prior to the end of his nine-month course, he must pay his own
way home, often halfway across the country.

Those who protest this policy too loudly are "quieted" by muscular
counselors or hauled off to the brig. Some become desperate. A psy-
chiatric social worker at Parks reported that he had been assigned to
work with a young boy from Dallas, Texas, who had sliced his arm
open in an attempt to get out. But even with all of Litton's tenacity,
55 percent drop out before the end of the course.

Justice at Camp Parks is supposed to be administered by a Center
Review Board (CRB) comprised of corpsmen and Litton people. But
by disciplinary counselor Lindsay Johnson's own admission, the board
is his rubber stamp: "I have a good working relationship with the
CRB," he notes. "They do whatever I tell them to."

While Job Corps discipline is harsh, it is not really like the Army's.
As one Parks teacher told *Ramparts*, "It isn't feasible to take these kids
off the streets . . . and put them in the equivalent of boot camp, especially since the counselors aren't armed." Rather, Litton does try, in
its own words, to "rehabilitate the entire social perspective" of the
corpsmen, including particularly their work ethics and attitude toward authority. As Pat Coughlin, Parks' program coordinator for occupational training told us. "If the boss tells [the corpsman] to pick up a

broom and sweep the floor, he's got to learn not to tell the boss what to do with the broom."

If the physical surroundings at the Parks Center are grim and the general atmosphere intimidating, the educational operation is laughable. The Basic Education program is intended to bring the corpsman's reading and arithmetic skills up to a level appropriate to the specific job skills in which he is to be trained. The curriculum materials for the reading course, developed by Litton, are somewhat unusual. The pretest, which determines the student's reading level before he takes the course, and the post-test, which determines his level upon completion of the course, are identical. In addition, the actual teaching materials used during the course and those used to measure any improvement contain the same text and exercises as do the pre-test and post-test. Of course, this setup merely passes off the repeatedly coached memorization of a particular passage as the ability to read. But schemes like this enable Litton to present impressive statistical evidence "documenting" their expertise in educating underprivileged youth—a cruel but profitable joke. When a Parks teacher complained that all the enrollees were only learning how to improve their scores on one particular test, the head of Litton's curriculum development at Parks replied, "We're not doing anything here that college fraternities don't do for their members." True enough. Still, no college fraternity has yet been awarded a $25 million government contract to educate ghetto youth.

Aside from such relatively subtle deceptions, there is doubt about the simple veracity of the figures used in the statistics Litton has put out about Parks. According to Professor William Austin, former president of the Parks Federation of Teachers and Counselors, "Public relations officers kept putting out fake figures. . . . One would hear about this number of corpsmen being placed in job positions and this number of corpsmen demonstrating academic success by various grade levels. . . . All of it was nonsense. . . . There was so much pressure on supervisors to produce figures that in general people just faked them. . . . Fifty percent or more of the corpsmen didn't make it to class . . . if a corpsman quit after having completed just one module out of 15 in the total training, he would be considered a 'graduate.' "

Austin feels that educating the corpsmen is not Litton's primary concern. "The corpsmen didn't mean a damn thing," Austin reported. "There was a lot of very expensive equipment around which nobody had any idea how to use. . . ."

Along with its display of educational ingenuity in the management of the Job Corps Center, Litton has exhibited those lucrative skills which have made it a leader among defense contractors. It subcontracts to its own divisions as a means of maximizing profits while minimizing service. Litton originally received from OEO a $12.8 million cost-plus contract with a fixed but redeterminable fee for running the Job Corps Center. It then decided to buy unnecessary textbooks from the American Book Publishing Company, a member of Litton Educational Systems. A General Accounting Office (GAO) investigation later showed that $337,000 worth of American Book Publishing Company textbooks lined closet shelves at Parks. According to a copyrighted story in the Denver Post, "Among the books it bought for Job Corpsmen, many of whom could barely read, were textbooks on the theory of relativity, the stock market and the slide rule."

The same GAO report noted that there was, in the words of the San Francisco Chronicle, "a devastating picture of high costs, waste and disciplinary problems at a Job Corps Center [Parks] in California. After two years of operation the estimated cost of the Center had jumped from $12.8 million to $25.5 million, the dropout rate was 55 per cent and only eight percent of the enrollees were placed in jobs related to their training."

Given what is known about Parks, it is not surprising that a great deal of racism is exhibited there. One new employee, upon arriving at the gate, was met by a guard who hailed him with, "So you're another one coming out here to help these dumb niggers." But far more unnerving was the surrealistic scene when a Litton executive flew over Parks in his private plane dropping dollar bills to the corpsmen assembled below. Litton officials amused themselves by watching the young men trample each other in a frantic effort to grab the money. A former Litton employee remarked that the object of the "airlift" was to "see how fast the niggers could run."

Litton, in keeping with a gentleman's agreement with officials of the semi-suburban towns near Camp Parks, has forbidden corpsmen to enter them. Young men from the Parks Center have reported that whenever they ventured into one of the neighboring communities, they were returned to Parks by local police, although they had created no disturbances. Litton's idea of community relations is to keep the cages locked during the week and to bus the corpsmen on weekends to "hospitality houses" in the nearby cities of San Francisco and Oakland.

According to Professor Austin, living conditions and sanitary facilities at Parks were at times worse than those in the big city ghettos the corpsmen came from. At one point, hygiene conditions in the dormitories were so bad that Austin approached public health people at the University of California to ask what could be done. The answer seemed to be "nothing," because the center was located on a military base leased to a private company, and no one knew if county health officials had any right to enter the base.

If Litton was running Parks so poorly, why didn't the government step in and enforce its contract? The answer is that in the spring of 1967, the OEO did try to enforce part of its contract with Litton. The teachers union at Parks had been refused a room to meet in at the center after working hours, a denial which violated both the National Labor Relations Act and Job Corps bulletin 67–12. Despite the intervention of W. P. Kelly, a director of the Job Corps; Richard Groulx, an executive of the Alameda County Central Labor Council; and several arbitrators from the OEO office in Washington, Litton was able not only to refuse to meet with anyone, but also to fire the president, two vice presidents and the secretary-treasurer of the teachers union for "disloyalty to the company." The last OEO arbitrator, Hyman Bookbinder, commented to Groulx and union officials that the OEO was unable to enforce the terms of its contract with Litton.

During the teachers' strike at Parks that resulted from Litton's action, Senators Robert Kennedy, Joseph Clark and George Murphy of the Senate Subcommittee on Employment, Manpower and Poverty, were in San Francisco on a nationwide tour of the Poverty Program. The senators curiously reversed their original plan to visit Parks, and showed no interest in discussing the situation there with Parks teachers and corpsmen. Cynics said it was possibly because Litton was one of the largest contributors to the Democratic Party, of which Kennedy and Clark were members.

In a recent paper, Professor Austin observed, "Job Corps facilities have been a popular form of educational experimentation for these companies, allowing them to train their staffs and develop materials on taxpayers' dollars." The real profits will come, it is hoped, from supplying the physical plant, audio-visual equipment, curriculum materials and "experts" to educational programs in large cities.

CONCLUSION

[Government] exhaustion with social problems is by no means the only thing that the process of business supplanting government has going for it. Government agencies depend on the political influence of business to help them compete for funds and authority. Those which engage in lucrative contracting methods naturally receive the most enthusiastic support, while recalcitrant agencies and programs suffer. This was the pattern in military contracting in the '50s, when prime contracting started with the Air Force and spread to the Army, and later to the Navy. The Air Force was contracting out whole weapons systems, and the contractors, naturally, became a powerful lobby for that service. Thus the Army found itself losing valuable missiles appropriations in Congress to its rival. The Air Force had upped the ante, and the Army was forced to meet the price. Like a protection syndicate, business gives security to those who cooperate with it.

Now, as government social agencies struggle for funds, the Wall Street Journal reports that, "Business is turning into an important force for pushing embattled domestic proposals through Congress." And an executive of the Department of Housing and Urban Development—whose special advisor, General Bernard Adolph Schriever, is called the "space general" for his role in NASA—is quoted as saying: "Each agency has gradually developed a list of firms interested in its field . . . we don't keep them turned on all the time, but we know how to turn them on. . . ."

Among the businessmen who are throwing their support behind constructive social welfare programs is James J. Ling, mastermind of Ling-Temco-Vought, which ranks 38th in Fortune magazine's 1968 listings, six notches ahead of Litton. A recent interview with Ling in the Chicago Tribune indicates the perspective of one of the most important new men of conglomerate power. When L-T-V reaches a point where it absorbs the competition or where it is number one on Fortune's list, reports the Tribune, Ling would be willing to consider a political role for himself.

Ling usually votes Republican, though he contributed to the Kennedy, Johnson and Humphrey campaigns and was a delegate to this year's Democratic convention. He doubts that he has the temperament to obtain elective office, but he might accept a cabinet post, preferably as secretary of Defense or secretary of Health, Education and Welfare. . . .

Corporations like L-T-V and Litton Industries are feeding the whole range of social problems into their computers. Will they be the ones called upon to solve them? It may be that there are just enough people who will take comfort in the idea that however bad things look, Big Brother is already there extending a helping hand.

chapter eight

Black capitalists and white capitalism

BARRY BLUESTONE

"Black economic self-determination," entails black ownership, operation, and control of business enterprise. Ironically, this scheme developed by black militants appears to have caught the fancy of government officials on both sides of the aisle as well as won the enthusiastic support of a previously disinterested corporate "elite." Under the rubric of "black capitalism"—a term coined by the mass media—the illusion has been generated that such diverse personages as Roy Innis of CORE and Arjay Miller of Ford share the same political-economic perspective. The fact behind the illusion, however, is that "black economic self-determination" and " black capitalism" are potentially very different games played under vastly different rules. Indeed, one set of rules may portend a viable inner-city political movement with some new jobs within an internally controlled inner city economic base while the other may lead to a few more jobs for the black community, but inevitably at the expense of greater inner city subservience to the white economic structure.

THE GHETTO ECONOMY

According to recent estimates, blacks constitute over 11% of the population, yet own or operate less than 1% of the nation's five million private businesses.[1] Fewer than $3\frac{1}{2}\%$ of the non-white labor force are managers, officials, or proprietors, while 14.2% of white employment is found in such occupations. And while one in forty whites is a proprietor of some sort, only one in a thousand Negroes is so situ-

---

"Black Capitalists and White Capitalism" (editor's title). From Barry Bluestone, "Black Capitalism: The Path to Black Liberation," *Review of Radical Political Economics* 1, no. 1 (May, 1969). Reprinted by permission of *Review of Radical Political Economics*.

[1] Sar Levitan, "Community Self-Determination and Entrepreneurship: Their Promises and Limitations," *Poverty and Human Resources Abstracts*, Vol. 4, No. 1, January–February, 1969, p. 18.

ated. The distribution of business enterprises is, indeed, even more dismal than these statistics imply, for an overwhelming proportion of Negro-owned business is extremely small-scale and marginal, lying at the periphery of the American economic structure. It should come as no surprise, then, that the black customer, even in his own neighborhood, inevitably faces a white man when he buys his furniture, his clothing, or his vegetables. . . .

The call has gone out to expropriate the company store and develop it to meet the needs of the community, and not the pocketbooks of absentee landlords and shopowners. The initial demand calls for blacks to take over or buy out ghetto shops and then not only manage them, but reap the profits that might accrue from such enterprise. More far-reaching, however, is the expressed desire to expand the ghetto's economic base. For it is clear that while the expropriation of retail shops, laundries, and small scale customer service industries will place black faces behind the counters, the misery of low incomes and constant subservience can never be overcome by small-scale superficial means. Development of a production as well as a distribution sector is necessary to generate a viable economy.

Such a development, however, necessarily requires tremendous capital and expertise, two "commodities" which are not native to the inner city and must be imported from White America. For this reason, many black communities are turning to the federal government and large-scale white enterprise for aid. The response from Washington and especially from the top men of the corporate sector, as we have indicated, has been more than mildly enthusiastic.

THE MANY FACES
OF BLACK CAPITALISM

In response to the call for black economic development, scores of "black capitalism" schemes have been unveiled, each with its own particular ideology and structure. Strategies range from large established corporations entering the ghetto to establish centrally controlled subsidiaries which capitalize on surplus labor and low wages to perspectives which foresee community ownership and control of large-scale production and distribution centers, a form of "black socialism."

The simplest case is the traditional one. With a small amount of acquired capital, either saved or borrowed, private black entrepreneurs buy out individual white stores and manage them according to time-honored custom. Drugstores, grocery markets, and clothing outlets remain traditionally marginal, reaping small profit, adding only slight employment opportunity and little income to the community. The only critical difference is the black face behind the counter and the fact that the small trials and tribulations of capitalist ownership now accrue to a black rather than white soul. To be sure, external direct control is minimized under this plan (although the competitive marketplace continues to call the tune). But to see in this strategy a means to economic development indicates a serious myopia, for almost by definition, the traditional scheme fails to aggregate enough capital for investment in profitable large-scale enterprise.

A significant alternative to "corner store" capitalism is posed by white corporate intervention in the ghetto economy. Having already cashed in on over $13 million worth of on-the-job training programs financed from tax dollars, firms like AVCO, Raytheon, Fairchild-Hiller, Lockheed, Ling-Temco-Vought, and Aerojet-General are turning their attention to government subsidized black enterprise. In fact as early as 1966, following the Watts riot, Aerojet-General developed the Watts Manufacturing Company and placed a Negro business leader in the president's chair.

While Aerojet's philanthropy created several hundred new jobs in a riot-torn city thereby providing some marginal improvement in a post-marginal condition, it has done little to realign the relationship of the black community to the white power structure. For the control of the Watts subsidiary does not emanate from the ghetto; rather the "black" company remains the child of Aerojet and it is to the father firm that WMC, Inc. pays deference, and in the long-run, possibly profits.

Beyond direct corporate intervention in the ghetto are concerted efforts to develop black corporations from within the inner city. The most famous and successful of these efforts remains the Opportunities Industrialization Center program pioneered by the Rev. Leon H. Sullivan of Philadelphia.

Beginning with a quarter million dollars raised from his church, Sullivan invested in a million dollar apartment complex. Later "Progress Plaza," the largest black-owned shopping center in the world was established with 16 privately-owned shops on 4½ acres. Not content, Sullivan's acquired business sense directed him into the aerospace industry where he created Progress Aerospace Enterprises with management borrowed from the General Electric Corporation and a G.E. subcontract for $2.5 million of component production for the U.S. moon mission. In addition, Sullivan's Zion Investment Corporation has established the Progress Garment Manufacturing Company in Philadelphia which employs seventy-five workers. Management responsibility of the Investment Corporation rests in a Board of Directors selected by its 3,500 shareholders. The waiting list for stock ownership is in excess of 2,000 families. Philadelphia has over half a million Negroes.

The Opportunities Industrialization Center program has now spread to over 70 cities and $5 million has been raised from the private sector to initiate local projects. Even Puerto Rico, Kenya, Senegal and Nigeria are experimenting with the OIC training program, a program aimed at creating skills for use in private enterprise both in and outside the ghetto. In the United States, the OIC National Industrial Advisory Council, composed of 25 "influential" business leaders has been created by Sullivan to help sell the program to corporate heads who conceivably might give aid to newly developing black business. George Champion, chairman of the board of the Chase Manhattan Bank heads up the Advisory Council.

How evenly spread the benefits from Sullivan's efforts will be is yet to be seen. Whether capitalism can work for the black working-class as well as the bourgeousie remains a moot point. Nevertheless, it appears evident that the OIC program has gained the support of white business and thus the scarce resources of capital and technical expertise seem assured at least in the short-run. But inherent in such a strategy lingers the potential for external domination and control by an "amiable" white power structure. And thus how much of the black community can escape poverty and powerlessness in this way cannot be exactly determined, but surely the rosy beginning need not point ineluctibly to a rosy future.

Yet a fourth strategy is now being developed by a small group of black businessmen, economists, and accountants in Detroit. The Inner City Business Improvement Forum (ICBIF) was established immediately after the 1967 Detroit riot.[2] With an inventory showing less than 35% of the ghetto economic base owned by blacks, and a $50,000 gift "bribed" from Henry Ford II, ICBIF set out to build a black infrastructure within the inner city to stem the outward flow of black-earned dollars. Over the past eighteen months ICBIF's leadership has evolved a "community concept of comprehensive inner city development" which stresses the need to develop not only retail outlets controlled by the black community, but the absolute necessity of establishing a production sector and black banking system to accumulate internally generated investment funds. Shying away from the paternalistic New Detroit Committee, created even before the 1967 conflagration cooled, ICBIF has turned to individual white investors and increasingly to the government for seed capital. In 1968 *"Our" Supermarket* was established on Detroit's East side to serve a large part of the surrounding black community. ICBIF provided 10% of the funds, while a leading city bank and the Small Business Administration picked up the first

[2] Information on the Inner City Business Improvement Forum (ICBIF) was obtained from an oral interview with the organization's Executive Secretary, Walter McMurtry.

and second mortgages to supply the rest of the initial capital outlay. Now one-dollar shares are being sold in the community so as to assure that profit from the supermarket goes to the community consumer rather than suburban interests. The board of directors for this supermarket and similar ventures created by ICBIF is chosen by the "block" clubs in the serviced area. This, along with a strict limit on an individual's stockholdings, ensures democratic control of each enterprise.

ICBIF has also aided traditional black retail businesses, supplying them with technical aid and seed capital in some cases. Unlike the major enterprises of ICBIF, these are left in private control along the lines of "corner store" black capitalism. With a combination of community owned and operated supermarkets and privately owned and operated small-scale retail shops, the black community in Detroit is beginning to gain some control over the estimated $750 million worth of consumer dollars which annually pass over inner city store counters.

ICBIF's comprehensive development scheme has already transcended its humble beginning. Between July and December, 1968, $850,000 was committed to ICBIF which was used to establish a dozen new black business enterprises ranging from privately controlled clothing stores to a small community controlled iron foundry which supplies parts to the auto industry.

Evidence from ICBIF's first year and a half of operation, indicates that Detroit appears to possess the potential for developing a semi-autonomous viable inner city economy, one which could provide thousands of jobs and a large number of investment outlets. Aided initially by white business, fearing the chaos of the black ghetto, the plan envisioned by ICBIF foresees a cutting of the umbilical cord to the white community. Free of external manipulation, black control is gained over an independent economic structure which can interact with the white-controlled economy from a position of comparative advantage rather than subservience. But whether even this scale of independent black enterprise is sufficient for economic viability, free of white support, is questionable.

To complete a typology of black business strategies, we should add those schemes which are avowedly political and only secondarily economic in nature. The economic development strategy, in essence, is no more than an organizational tool for building an indigenous inner city political base. By investing small amounts of capital, either generated internally or "hustled" from guilt-ridden whites, a nascent community-controlled black economic sector is launched, providing some new employment opportunities, but more importantly, a rallying point for community action. Profits from the enterprise are plowed back into the organization both for further business expansion and for political action. In this manner, the community organization becomes self-sufficient and free from external control. As the economic substructure expands, the political organization matures, benefitting from a well-financed base. Educational and cultural activities can be added to the political thrust of such a movement, thus creating an integrated program of community action.

By now it should be patently clear that each of the strategies outlined above can be evaluated upon two potentially conflicting criteria: first, the speed with which the plan leads to economic development as measured by rising employment, incomes, and capital outlay; and second, whether the scheme possesses a structure and dynamic conducive to economic and political liberation as measured by economic self-sufficiency and political influence. The conflict between the pace of development and self-determination arises from the scarcity of capital and expertise in the ghetto. For the inner city community to develop economically over a short period of time, much capital and talent must be imported from the white community. Inevitably, large-scale importation leads to surrendering some control over the direction of development.

Thus, while one scheme leads rapidly to investment in the ghetto by white business, it almost assuredly fails to promise radical change in the structure of power relations between white and black. On the other hand, development carried on solely by the black community may contribute some political freedom, but at the cost of continued economic stagnation. A conscious decision must then be made by the black community as to which road it chooses to travel, and indeed, how much "liberty" should be surrendered to hasten the development process. For the black community, to have their cake and eat it too will seldom be a permissible choice.

In understanding the corporate manager's positive attitude toward black ghetto enterprise, one must realize that corporate profits will not be endangered by the introduction of the black capitalism strategy envisioned by the corporate establishment. The reason is simple: This strategy foresees the black community providing only two generalized products: (1) Retail services to fill the community's need for vegetables, meats, drugstore products, and television repair, etc., and (2) Small-scale manufacture of intermediate goods used in the industrial sector to produce automobiles, washing machines, and computers. In the first case, the corporate sector is left unharmed by black capitalism because the corporate sector sells very little at the retail level and when it does, it usually does not do it in the ghetto. The squeeze here will be on the small-time white shopkeeper; the corner grocer and the local repair shop owner.

Ghetto manufacturing firms, examples of the second case, will not only fail to deplete corporate profits, but actually will contribute to them. It is for this reason that corporations like Aerojet have spread their "philanthropy" into the ghetto. Excess profits of the largest industrial giants can be invested in the inner city (without fear of retaliation from the government anti-trust division) to establish subsidiaries which provide them with cheap parts and labor hired at less than union scale.

Sidestepping unions in the already organized parts supply industry is a difficult, if not risky practice. Since the 1950's, such attempts have been rare by large corporations. But now the opportunity for circumventing union power by means of coalition with the federal government and the black community has emerged. The small plant can pay half the going wage of the unionized vendor operation thereby ensuring a competitive edge over union plants, and yet still pay above the wage scale normally offered low-skilled workers in the ghetto. In this way both the ghetto and the corporation benefit. Such a symbiotic relationship between the corporate elite and the community poor at the expense of the unionized workingclass has the potential for evolving as the most exotic in a long line of techniques aimed at curbing union strength. Ford hired blacks to break unions in the twenties and now Ford has a better idea. It, like other modern corporations, has found a new, almost socially acceptable way to do the same thing in the sixties and seventies. Little wonder the AFL-CIO has vigorously attacked all black capitalism plans.

Last, but not least, mention must be made again of the profits which can be gleaned from government subsidy programs designed to induce big business participation in inner city development. With such subsidies or tax incentives as specified in the Community Self-Determination Bill, for example, little effort is required on behalf of the corporate structure to create a "ghetto-industrial" complex including cost-plus contracts and the profits they imply. We may not be very far off in concluding that it appears the corporate establishment is more than happy to help the black community—especially if it gets a little helping itself!

"BLACK CAPITALISM" RECONSIDERED

Business brought into the ghetto by the white corporate establishment may very well add something to the inner city environment. Some new jobs will be created, the average wage in the core city may rise a bit, and a few enterprising Negroes will no doubt reap the ability to escape the ghetto altogether. For some a new sense of pride may even develop. But what is equally true is that no black capitalism scheme which relies on the white establishment for sustenance will lead to a form of inner city economic development which in turn can lead to black socio-political liberation. To put it plainly, it is not in the interest of big business to develop a viable black economic sector, competitive in the newly evolving growth industries. At best the black community will vie with the blue collar union sector for a share of the intermediate goods market.

But if corporate intervention in the inner city will not create a viable economy, can independent private black capitalism, unaided, but also unencumbered by the mixed blessing of corporate involvement, lead the black community to freedom? The answer is probably no. Independent private black enterprise cannot serve as the catalyst for economic development and political power.

It is a sad fact that private small-scale enterprise pays extremely low wages, reaps little profit for its owner, and consequently contributes little to economic development *per se*. While black retail capitalism will boost the inner city multiplier by some small amount, the additional income thus generated will fail to raise a significant number from poverty. Consider, for instance, the average hourly wage rates paid in retail trade across the nation in the mid-1960's:[3]

Limited price variety stores	$1.31
Eating and drinking places	1.14
Drug and proprietary stores	1.56
Gasoline service stations	1.52
Apparel and accessory stores	1.70
Retail food stores	1.91

These were average rates; the inner city wage levels helped to keep them this low. In addition statistics on low-wage industry profits show that there is little room to raise these wage rates much beyond such low levels.[4] All of this is due to the high degree of business competition in the retail field, which subjects the small-scale firm to a profit and wage squeeze. Add to this the additional costs which small-scale business in the inner city must bear because of higher insurance costs, uninsured losses due to crime, and the higher cost of inner city transportation, and the picture of low wages and low profits comes sharply into focus. Hence, while the sight of black faces behind ghetto drugstore counters may be comforting psychologically, it is not economically.

A small private production sector will also fail to add much viability to the inner city economy. In the first place it is highly unlikely that

[3] Barry Bluestone, "Lower-Wage Workers and Marginal Industries," in Ferman, Kornbluh, and Haber, *Poverty in America*, second edition, University of Michigan Press, Ann Arbor, 1968.

[4] George Delehanty and Robert Evans, Jr., "Low-Wage Employment: An Inventory and an Assessment," Northwestern University, mimeo., no date.

individuals from the black community will have the ability to raise sufficient capital, independent of white business and government, to initiate enterprise especially in the fastest growing sectors of the economy: electronics, computers, automation equipment design, etc. To be successful in these industries requires enough capital to keep pace with rapid technological change. In addition the efficient size of manufacturing firms is usually beyond the capacity of ghetto residents with their present inadequate resources. Finally, even if the capital could be raised to develop one or two competitive production centers, the marginal addition to the welfare of a ghetto the size of Detroit's, Chicago's, New York's, Los Angeles', or even Cleveland's would be insignificant in terms of producing a catalyst for full-scale economic development.

The result, inevitably, of black entrepreneur capitalism is not the creation of an inner city economic infrastructure, but the development of a larger black bourgeoisie, which given rising income, will quickly emigrate from the ghetto taking along both a large part of the wage bill and all of the profit. The tendency toward a black class society is thereby reinforced, with continued low wages and welfare programs in the inner city and a richer, only slightly more numerous, black middle class community on the outside. Again income will flow outward in great quantity, leaving the bulk of the ghetto residents no better off, save for a few more low-wage jobs and a few more black faces across the drugstore counter. Profits are reaped by an enlarged black middle class, while the losses continue to be borne by the poor.

AN ALTERNATIVE . . .

The alternative to both white dominated ghetto intervention and small-scale private black capitalism is community-owned enterprise. Inner city residents can pool both the capital they own and that which can be bribed from the government or other sources on a "no-strings" basis, and under democratic rule, invest in cooperative industry on a relatively large scale. As the black community "owns" the industry, the wages and dividends from such enterprise remain within the inner city. Those who choose to leave the ghetto should not be allowed to take more capital out of the community than the small amount they originally contributed (with some interest) nor should they be permitted to take part of the wage bill with them. As long as there remains unemployment in the inner city, residents who choose to emigrate must relinquish the jobs they hold in community enterprise. Escape from the ghetto remains open, but not at the expense of the majority of the ghetto community. In order to maximize reinvestment so as to build as viable and diversified an inner city economy as possible, leakages of capital and income must be kept to a minimum. Community ownership and control ensures that the route from poverty is provided the entire black underclass, not merely a chosen few. Furthermore, if a good part of black community development is to be financed by federal funds—through low-interest loans or seed grants— justice is only done if the whole community benefits and not merely a relatively small number of private entrepreneurs. Both on efficiency and equity grounds, then, black cooperative enterprise is preferable to "traditional" corner store capitalism.

. . . AND A REALISTIC PERSPECTIVE

Here we must add a word of caution. Despite grandiose plans and even federal support, the black community should not be hoodwinked by either the corporate establishment nor many of its own ebullient leaders into believing that "black capitalism" in any of its forms including black "socialism" can automatically lead to economic and political freedom. For no matter how important a goal, black economic self-determination will ultimately be largely an illusion. To be sure, hundreds, possibly even thousands of jobs will be created and many businesses may end up under black control; but in the final analysis, the market will determine which businesses succeed and which fail. Unlike the textbook model, the American market, manipulated in good part by the already existing corporate structure, allows few new small independent enterprises to reach the strata of "big business." The inner city, starved for capital and expertise—even with federal aid—begins far back in the field of potential money-winners. Thus mythologizing about the possibility of the black community creating through its own industry the route to equal affluence will be in vain or worse, a practice conducive to self-destructive frustration. In the context that the *goal* of economic development is the answer *per se,* the trap of "black capitalism" is laid.

Yet there exists another context in which to place black economic self-determination, and it is in this context that we find the genius of the black economic development strategy. While the creation of a black economy in the ghetto may not lead inexorably to a viable economic base—competitive with the staunchest of "white" enterprise— the act of striving toward an inner city economy yields a powerful tool for organizing the black community into a coherent political force capable of extracting concessions on jobs, housing, income, and dignity from the government and from the corporate establishment. While "black socialism" alone may not be capable of rooting out poverty, it may root out powerlessness and thus gain for the black community the indirect means to freedom from poverty and the manifestations of racism. In the striving for economic independence, not only is dependence on the white power structure for jobs and poverty incomes reduced, but the economic incentive to coalesce within the black community increases as well. Jobs and income are created within the community and it is from such a base that political and social power are born.

Black community enterprise will, in addition, have a considerable impact on the whole economy, not because it can successfully compete with white enterprise directly, but because income generated from community enterprise can be used to develop well-financed political organization, capable of confronting City Hall and Congress with a united front. If in the past, the black movement has been stifled by a lack of financial support, especially once it diverged from the strict integrationist political line, the community movement will now have a self-financed base. For while a large part of the "profit" from black community enterprise can be reinvested in expanded business projects, a part can also be earmarked specifically for political activity.

Taken in this context, black community enterprise not only places black faces behind drugstore counters, and allows a moderate scale production sector, but more importantly, it facilitates the creation of an indigenously financed, strictly independent, political force within the ghetto. Unlike "corner store" black capitalism which fails on two accounts: (1) to create an economic infrastructure capable of pulling the black community out of poverty, and (2) to create a meaningful community controlled power base; and unlike corporate intervention in the ghetto which adds longevity to white economic and political dominance over the black community, black community enterprise, or what we have called "black socialism" promises a new hope for political liberation.

While as a "goal," the black economic development strategy may be an utter failure in any of its forms, as a "means" one of its forms, "black socialism," may be judged in the future an unqualified success. The real question of black enterprise then must not be whether it succeeds on the accountant's balance sheet, but whether it succeeds ultimately in the struggle to redistribute a just share of political and social power toward the black community.

V

Causes of poverty: establishment and nonestablishment perspectives

Look abroad over our own city, over every large city of the country, and is there not a "wound" (and oh! how deep and ghastly) visible on every hand. There is the wound of idleness and improvidence—the indisposition to do manfully our appointed task in life, and leading by a direct path to poverty, destitution and want.

S. HUMPHREYS GURTEEN*

*Official data show . . . how large a part of the pauperism of this city and State is occasioned by indolence, intemperance, and other vices . . . There is little pauperism among us not directly or indirectly traceable to these and kindred sources.***

Ideological hegemony, the preponderant authority of a given ideology throughout a nation which is supportive of the nation, is necessary for the survival of the government and economy of any national state. Ideological hegemony is constructed and maintained partially through childhood and adult socialization processes—overt and covert indoctrination by the schools and the media, and speeches by government and corporate representatives—and partially by individual social psychological processes necessitated by the structure of the social system itself. Persons whose income, assets, and status fall below those of most others in the nation must, for example, psychologically adjust to that system and their position in it *if* they have no reason to hope that it will change.[1] They will adjust by rationalizing their

* Buffalo English Episcopal clergyman and charity organization spokesman, *Provident Schemes* (Buffalo: Charity Organization Society of Buffalo, 1879), p. 16.

** New York Association for Improving the Condition of the Poor, *Thirteenth Annual Report* (New York: 1856), pp. 36–37.

[1] Cf. Ely Chinoy, *Automobile Workers and the American Dream* (Boston: Beacon Press, 1955); Robert E. Lane, *Political Ideology* (New York: The Free Press, 1962);

169

position to themselves through various means: e.g., they *chose* to drop out of school and therefore they are poor, but their son or daughter by staying in school need not be poor. Those who are well-placed in society and see others living miserably around them also need to relieve their discomfort at the sight of poverty. They may do so by attempting to isolate themselves from the poor, one function of suburbia; by giving a portion of their wealth to charity; and/or by "blaming the victim" (as described by William Ryan, a Boston College Professor of Psychology, in chapter nine).

Social science and other intellectual work has also generally fallen within the boundaries of national ideologies.[2] In chapter ten, Howard Wachtel examines three different economic perspectives on poverty and three theories of the state. The liberal and conservative theories discussed in his paper buttress the present political economy of the United States. Even the rivalry between the conservative and liberal perspectives is useful to the establishment for it gives citizens the feeling that they have alternatives, when in fact both perspectives fully support the state. The radical perspective, on the other hand, suggests that poverty is the "result of the normal functioning of the principal institutions of capitalism" and that only by turning to a different economic structure can the eradication of poverty and considerable reductions in inequality be achieved. Barry Bluestone,

---

Lewis Lipsitz, "Work Life and Political Attitudes: A Study of Manual Workers," *American Political Science Review* 58, no. 4, (1964); Lewis Lipsitz, "On Political Beliefs: The Grievances of the Poor," in Phillip Green and Sanford Levinson, eds., *Power and Community: Dissenting Essays in Political Science* (New York: Pantheon, 1970); and Joan Huber, William H. Form, and John Pease, "Income and Stratification Ideology," *American Journal of Sociology* 75, no. 4, part 2 (January, 1970): 703–16. Chinoy and Lane found that low-income individuals in their samples did not question the existence of equality of opportunity or admit to feeling exploited, but psychologically adjusted to their economic and status positions by rationalizing their positions in various ways. Lipsetz, Huber, and Form found, on the other hand, that low-income individuals in their samples perceived that equal opportunity did not exist in the United States and questioned governmental and corporate actions affecting the distribution of resources in the U.S. The discrepancy between the two sets of findings may perhaps be explained by the poor and working classes' lack of hope during the mid-nineteen-forties and mid-fifties (the times of the Chinoy and Lane studies) that their relative economic and status positions might be improved, and their hope during the sixties (the time of the Lipsetz, Huber, and Form studies), spawned by the Civil Rights Movement and the War on Poverty, that their positions might indeed be improved.

2 Cf. John Pease, Joan Huber, and William Form, "Ideological Currents in American Stratification Literature," *The American Sociologist* 5, no. 3 (May, 1970): 127–37; and Martin J. Sklar, "On the Proletarian Revolution and the End of Political-Economic Society," *Radical America* 3, no. 3: 1–41.

in chapter eleven, analyses aspects of the American industrial structure that have been neglected by conservative and liberal economists, and explains the important ways in which the U.S. government intervenes in the market place and determines in part the distribution of wages within the nation. The neglect by conservative and liberal economists of the impact of the defense department's eighty billion dollars plus in yearly purchases and other government actions on the wages of American citizens has supported the myth that America offers equal opportunity for all.

c h a p t e r   9

Blaming the victum:
ideology serves the establishment

WILLIAM RYAN

Twenty years ago, Zero Mostel used to do a sketch in which he impersonated a Dixiecrat Senator conducting an investigation of the origins of World War II. At the climax of the sketch, the Senator boomed out, in an excruciating mixture of triumph and suspicion, "What was Pearl Harbor *doing* in the Pacific?" This is an extreme example of Blaming the Victim.

Twenty years ago, we could laugh at Zero Mostel's caricature. In recent years, however, the same process has been going on every day in the arena of social problems, public health, anti-poverty programs, and social welfare. A philosopher might analyze this process and prove that, technically, it is comic. But it is hardly ever funny.

Consider some victims. One is the miseducated child in the slum school. He is blamed for his own miseducation. He is said to contain within himself the causes of his inability to read and write well. The shorthand phrase is "cultural deprivation," which, to those in the know, conveys what they allege to be inside information: that the poor child carries a scanty pack of cultural baggage as he enters school. He doesn't know about books and magazines and newspapers, they say. (No books in the home: the mother fails to subscribe to *Reader's Digest*.) They say that if he talks at all—an unlikely event since slum parents don't talk to their children—he certainly doesn't talk correctly. (Lower-class dialect spoken here, or even—God forbid!—Southern Negro (*Ici on parle nigra*.) If you can manage to get him to sit in a chair, they say, he squirms and looks out the window. (Impulse-ridden, these kids, motoric rather than verbal.) In a word he is "disadvantaged" and "socially deprived," they say, and this, of course, accounts for his failure (*his* failure, they say) to learn much in school.

Note the similarity to the logic of Zero Mostel's Dixiecrat Senator. What is the culturally deprived child *doing* in the school? What is wrong with the victim? In pursuing this logic, no one remembers to ask questions about the collapsing buildings and torn textbooks, the frightened, insensitive teachers, the six additional desks in the room, the blustering, frightened principals, the relentless segregation, the callous administrator, the irrelevant curriculum, the bigoted or cowardly members of the school board, the insulting history book, the stingy taxpayers, the fairy-tale readers, or the self-serving faculty of the local teachers' college. We are encouraged to confine our attention to the child and to dwell on all his alleged defects. Cultural deprivation becomes an omnibus explanation for the educational disaster area known as the inner-city school. This is Blaming the Victim.

Pointing to the supposedly deviant Negro family as the "fundamental weakness of the Negro community" is another way to blame the victim. Like "cultural deprivation," "Negro family" has become a shorthand phrase with stereotyped connotations of matriarchy, fatherlessness, and pervasive illegitimacy. Growing up in the "crumbling" Negro family is supposed to account for most of the racial evils in America. Insiders have the word, of course, and know that this phrase is supposed to evoke images of growing up with a long-absent or never-present father (replaced from time to time perhaps by a series of transient lovers) and with bossy women ruling the roost, so that the children are irreparably damaged. This refers particularly to the poor, bewildered male children, whose psyches are fatally wounded and who are never, alas, to learn the trick of becoming upright, downright, forthright all-American boys. Is it any wonder the Negroes cannot achieve equality? From such families! And, again, by focusing our attention on the Negro family as the apparent *cause* of racial inequality our eye is diverted. Racism, discrimination, segregation, and the powerlessness of the ghetto are subtly, but thoroughly, downgraded in importance.

The generic process of Blaming the Victim is applied to almost every American problem. The miserable health care of the poor is explained away on the grounds that the victim has poor motivation and lacks health information. The problems of slum housing are traced to the characteristics of tenants who are labeled as "Southern rural migrants" not yet "acculturated" to life in the big city. The "multiproblem" poor, it is claimed, suffer the psychological effects of impoverishment, the "culture of poverty," and the deviant value system of the lower classes; consequently, though unwittingly, they cause their own troubles. From such a viewpoint, the obvious fact that poverty is primarily an absence of money is easily overlooked or set aside.

The growing number of families receiving welfare are fallaciously linked together with the increased number of illegitimate children as twin results of promiscuity and sexual abandon among members of the lower orders. Every important social problem—crime, mental illness, civil disorder, unemployment—has been analyzed within the framework of the victim-blaming ideology.

I have been listening to the victim-blamers and pondering their thought processes for a number of years. That process is often very subtle. Victim-blaming is cloaked in kindness and concern, and bears all the trappings and statistical furbelows of scientism; it is obscured by a perfumed haze of humanitarianism. In observing the process of Blaming the Victim, one tends to be confused and disoriented because those who practice this art display a deep concern for the victims that is quite genuine. In this way, the new ideology is very different from the open prejudice and reactionary tactics of the old days. Its adherents include sympathetic social scientists with social consciences in good working order, and liberal politicians with a genuine commitment to reform. They are very careful to dissociate themselves from vulgar Calvinism or crude racism; they indignantly condemn any notions of innate wickedness or genetic defect. "The Negro is *not born* inferior," they shout apoplectically. "Force of circumstance," they explain in reasonable tones, "has *made* him inferior." And they dismiss with self-righteous contempt any claims that the poor man in America is plainly unworthy or shiftless or enamored of idleness. No, they say, he is "caught in the cycle of poverty." He is trained to be poor by his culture and his family life, endowed by his environment (perhaps by his ignorant mother's outdated style of toilet training) with those unfortunately unpleasant characteristics that make him ineligible for a passport into the affluent society.

Blaming the Victim is, of course, quite different from old-fashioned conservative ideologies. The latter simply dismissed victims as inferior, genetically defective, or morally unfit; the emphasis is on the intrinsic, even hereditary, defect. The former shifts its emphasis to the environmental causation. The old-fashioned conservative could hold firmly to the belief that the oppressed and the victimized were born that way— "that way" being defective or inadequate in character or ability. The new ideology attributes defect and inadequacy to the malignant nature of poverty, injustice, slum life, and racial difficulties. The stigma that marks the victim and accounts for his victimization is an acquired stigma, a stigma of social, rather than genetic, origin. But the stigma, the defect, the fatal difference—though derived in the past from environmental forces—is still located *within* the victim, inside his skin. With such an elegant formulation, the humanitarian can have it both ways. He can, all at the same time, concentrate his charitable interest on the defects of the victim, condemn the vague social and environmental stresses that produced the defect (some time ago), and ignore the continuing effect of victimizing social forces (right now). It is a brilliant ideology for justifying a perverse form of social action designed to change, not society, as one might expect, but rather society's victim.

As a result, there is a terrifying sameness in the programs that arise from this kind of analysis. In education, we have programs of "compensatory education" to build up the skills and attitudes of the ghetto child, rather than structural changes in the schools. In race relations, we have social engineers who think up ways of "strengthening" the Negro family, rather than methods of eradicating racism. In health care, we develop new programs to provide health information (to correct the supposed ignorance of the poor) and to reach out and discover cases of untreated illness and disability (to compensate for their supposed unwillingness to seek treatment). Meanwhile, the gross inequities of our medical care delivery systems are left completely unchanged. As we might expect, the logical outcome of analyzing social problems in terms of the deficiencies of the victim is the development of programs aimed at correcting those deficiencies. The formula for action becomes extraordinarily simple: change the victim.

All of this happens so smoothly that it seems downright rational. First, identify a social problem. Second, study those affected by the problem and discover in what ways they are different from the rest of us as a consequence of deprivation and injustice. Third, define the differences as the cause of the social problem itself. Finally, of course, assign a government bureaucrat to invent a humanitarian action program to correct the differences.

Blaming the Victim is an ideological process, which is to say that it is a set of ideas and concepts deriving from systematically motivated, but *unintended,* distortions of reality. In the sense that Karl Mannheim[1] used the term, an ideology develops from the "collective unconscious" of a group or class and is rooted in a class-based interest in maintaining the *status quo* (as contrasted with what he calls a *utopia,* a set of ideas rooted in a class-based interest in *changing* the *status quo*). An ideology, then, has several components: First, there is the belief system itself, the way of looking at the world, the set of ideas and concepts. Second, there is the systematic distortion of reality reflected in those ideas. Third is the condition that the distortion must not be a conscious, intentional process. Finally, though they are not intentional, the ideas must serve a specific function: maintaining the *status quo* in the interest of a specific group. Blaming the Victim fits this definition on all counts. Most particularly, it is important to realize that Blaming the Victim is not a process of *intentional* distortion although it does serve the class interests of those who practice it. And it has a rich ancestry in American thought about social problems and how to deal with them.

Thinking about social problems is especially susceptible to ideological influences since, as John Seeley has pointed out,[2] defining a social problem is not so simple. "What is a social problem?" may seem an ingenuous question until one turns to confront its opposite: "What human problem is *not* a social problem?" Since any problem in which people are involved is social, why do we reserve the label for some problems in which people are involved and withhold it from others? To use Seeley's example, why is crime called a social problem when university administration is not? The phenomena we look at are bounded by the act of definition. They become social problems only by being so considered. In Seeley's words, *"naming* it as a problem, after naming it as a *problem."*

We must particularly ask, "To whom are social problems a problem?" And usually, if truth were to be told, we would have to admit that we mean they are a problem to those of us who are outside the boundaries of what we have defined as the problem. Negroes are a problem to racist whites, welfare is a problem to stingy taxpayers, delinquency is a problem to nervous property owners.

Now, if this is the quality of our assumptions about social problems, we are led unerringly to certain beliefs about the causes of these problems. We cannot comfortably believe that *we* are the cause of that

[1] Karl Mannheim, *Ideology and Utopia,* trans. Louis Wirth and Edward Shils. (New York: Harcourt, Brace & World, Inc., A Harvest Book, 1936). First published in German in 1929.

[2] John Seeley, "The Problem of Social Problems," *Indian Sociological Bulletin,* II, No. 3 (April, 1965). Reprinted as Chapter Ten in *The Americanization of the Unconscious* (New York: International Science Press, 1967), pp. 142–48.

which is problematic to us; therefore, we are almost compelled to believe that *they*—the problematic ones—are the cause and this immediately prompts us to search for deviance. Identification of the deviance as the cause of the problem is a simple step that ordinarily does not even require evidence.

This has been the dominant style in American social welfare and health activities, then: to treat what we call social problems, such as poverty, disease, and mental illness, in terms of the individual deviance of the special, unusual groups of persons who had those problems. There has also been a competing style, however—much less common, not at all congruent with the prevalent ideology, but continually developing parallel to the dominant style.

Adherents of this approach tended to search for defects in the community and the environment rather than in the individual; to emphasize predictability and usualness rather than random deviance; they tried to think about preventing rather than merely repairing or treating—to see social problems, in a word, as social. In the field of disease, this approach was termed public health, and its practitioners sought the cause of disease in such things as the water supply, the sewage system, the density and quality of housing conditions. They set out to prevent disease, not in individuals, but in the total population, through improved sanitation, inoculation against communicable disease, and the policing of housing conditions. In the field of income maintenance, this secondary style of solving social problems focused on poverty as a predictable event, on the regularities of income deficiency. And it concentrated on the development of standard, generalized programs affecting total groups. Rather than trying to fit the aged worker ending his career into some kind of category of special cases, it assumed all sixty-five-year-old men should expect to retire from the world of work and have the security of an old age pension, to be arranged through public social activity.

These two approaches to the solution of social problems have existed side by side, the former always dominant, but the latter gradually expanding, slowly becoming more and more prevalent.

Elsewhere[3] I have proposed the dimension of *exceptionalism-universalism* as the ideological underpinning for these two contrasting approaches to the analysis and solution of social problems. The *excep-*

[3] William Ryan, "Community Care in Historical Perspective: Implications for Mental Health Services and Professionals," *Canada's Mental Health*, supplement No. 60, March–April, 1969. This formulation draws on, and is developed from, the *residual-institutional* dimension outlined in H. L. Wilensky and C. N Lebeaux, *Industrial Society and Social Welfare* (paperback ed.; New York: The Free Press, 1965). Originally published by Russell Sage Foundation, 1958.

tionalist viewpoint is reflected in arrangements that are private, voluntary, remedial, special, local, and exclusive. Such arrangements imply that problems occur to specially-defined categories of persons in an unpredictable manner. The problems are unusual, even unique, they are exceptions to the rule, they occur as a result of individual defect, accident, or unfortunate circumstance and must be remedied by means that are particular and, as it were, tailored to the individual case.

The universalistic viewpoint, on the other hand, is reflected in arrangements that are public, legislated, promotive or preventive, general, national, and inclusive. Inherent in such a viewpoint is the idea that social problems are a function of the social arrangements of the community or the society and that, since these social arrangements are quite imperfect and inequitable, such problems are both predictable and, more important, preventable through public action. They are not unique to the individual, and the fact that they encompass individual persons does not imply that those persons are themselves defective or abnormal.

The danger in the exceptionalistic viewpoint is in its impact on social policy when it becomes the dominant component in social analysis. Blaming the Victim occurs exclusively within an exceptionalistic framework, and it consists of applying exceptionalistic explanations to universalistic problems. This represents an illogical departure from fact, a method, in Mannheim's words, of systematically distorting reality, of developing an ideology.

Blaming the Victim can take its place in a long series of American ideologies that have rationalized cruelty and injustice.

Slavery, for example, was justified—even praised—on the basis of a complex ideology that showed quite conclusively how useful slavery was to society and how uplifting it was for the slaves.[4] Eminent physicians could be relied upon to provide the biological justification for slavery since after all, they said, the slaves were a separate species—as, for example, cattle are a separate species. No one in his right mind would dream of freeing the cows and fighting to abolish the ownership of cattle. In the view of the average American of 1825, it was important to preserve slavery, not simply because it was in accord with his own group interests (he was not fully aware of that), but because reason and logic showed clearly to the reasonable and intelligent man that slavery was good. In order to persuade a good and moral man to *do* evil, then, it is not necessary first to persuade him to *become* evil.

---

[4] For a good review of this general ideology, see I. A. Newby, *Jim Crow's Defense* (Baton Rouge: Louisiana State University Press, 1965).

It is only necessary to teach him that he is doing good. No one, in the words of a legendary newspaperman, thinks of himself as a son of a bitch.

In late-nineteenth-century America there flowered another ideology of injustice that seemed rational and just to the decent, progressive person. But Richard Hofstadter's analysis of the phenomenon of Social Darwinism[5] shows clearly its functional role in the preservation of the *status quo*. One can scarcely imagine a better fit than the one between this ideology and the purposes and actions of the robber barons, who descended like piranha fish on the America of this era and picked its bones clean. Their extraordinarily unethical operations netted them not only hundreds of millions of dollars but also, perversely, the adoration of the nation. Behavior that would be, in any more rational land (including today's America), more than enough to have landed them all in jail, was praised as the very model of a captain of modern industry. And the philosophy that justified their thievery was such that John D. Rockefeller could actually stand up and preach it in church. Listen as he speaks in, of all places, Sunday school:

> The growth of a large business is merely a survival of the fittest. . . . The American Beauty rose can be produced in the splendor and fragrance which bring cheer to its beholder only by sacrificing the early buds which grow up around it. This is not an evil tendency in business. It is merely the working-out of a law of nature and a law of God.[6]

This was the core of the gospel, adapted analogically from Darwin's writings on evolution. Herbert Spencer and, later, William Graham Sumner and other beginners in the social sciences considered Darwin's work to be directly applicable to social processes: ultimately as a guarantee that life was progressing toward perfection but, in the short run, as a justification for an absolutely uncontrolled laissez-faire economic system. The central concepts of "survival of the fittest," "natural selection," and "gradualism" were exalted in Rockefeller's preaching to the status of laws of God and Nature. Not only did this ideology justify the criminal rapacity of those who rose to the top of the industrial heap, defining them automatically as naturally superior (this was bad enough), but at the same time it also required that those at the bottom of the heap be labeled as patently *unfit*—a label based solely on their position in society. According to the law of natural selection, they should be, in Spencer's judgment, eliminated. "The whole effort

---

[5] Richard Hofstadter, *Social Darwinism in American Thought* (revised ed.; Boston: Beacon Press, 1955).

[6] William J. Ghent, *Our Benevolent Feudalism* (New York: The Macmillan Co., 1902), p. 29.

of nature is to get rid of such, to clear the world of them and make room for better."

For a generation, Social Darwinism was the orthodox doctrine in the social sciences, such as they were at that time. Opponents of this ideology were shut out of respectable intellectual life. The philosophy that enabled John D. Rockefeller to justify himself self-righteously in front of a class of Sunday school children was not the product of an academic quack or a marginal crackpot philosopher. It came directly from the lectures and books of leading intellectual figures of the time, occupants of professorial chairs at Harvard and Yale. Such is the power of an ideology that so neatly fits the needs of the dominant interests of society.

If one is to think about ideologies in America in 1970, one must be prepared to consider the possibility that a body of ideas that might seem almost self-evident is, in fact, highly distorted and highly selective; one must allow that the inclusion of a specific formulation in every freshman sociology text does not guarantee that the particular formulation represents abstract Truth rather than group interest. It is important not to delude ourselves into thinking that ideological monstrosities were constructed by monsters. They were not; they are not. They are developed through a process that shows every sign of being valid scholarship, complete with tables of numbers, copious footnotes, and scientific terminology. Ideologies are quite often academically and socially respectable and in many instances hold positions of exclusive validity, so that disagreement is considered unrespectable or radical and risks being labeled as irresponsible, unenlightened, or trashy.

Blaming the Victim holds such a position. It is central in the mainstream of contemporary American social thought, and its ideas pervade our most crucial assumptions so thoroughly that they are hardly noticed. Moreover, the fruits of this ideology appear to be fraught with altruism and humanitarianism, so it is hard to believe that it has principally functioned to block social change.

c h a p t e r   t e n

Looking at poverty
from radical, conservative,
and liberal perspectives

HOWARD M. WACHTEL*

Poverty is a condition of society, not a consequence of individual characteristics. If poverty is a condition of society, then we must look to societal institutions to discover the cause of poverty rather than to the particular individual characteristics of the poor. The societal institutions which have been of particular importance for western industrialized countries are the institutions of capitalism—markets in labor and capital, social stratification and class, and the state.

The interaction of these institutions of capitalism manifest themselves in a set of attributes and problems that we normally associate with the condition of poverty in society. These *attributes* of poverty, however, are incorrectly viewed as the causes of poverty. For example, income distribution, the living conditions of the poor, education, health, and the personal characteristics of the poor are merely surface manifestations (the superstructure) of a systemically caused problem. It is important to differentiate between these manifestations of poverty —normally called "the poverty problem"—and their underlying causes. We return to this theme later, but first let us contrast this formulation with the orthodox view of poverty and its causes.

Since the industrial revolution commenced in Great Britain and spread to other western nations, the poor have been blamed for their own poverty. The causes of poverty have been assigned to the characteristics of the individual rather than to societal institutions. In nine-

"Looking at Poverty from Radical, Conservative, and Liberal Perspectives" (editor's title). From "Looking at Poverty From a Radical Perspective," *Review of Radical Political Economics* 3, no. 3 (Summer, 1971): 1–18. Reprinted by permission of *Review of Radical Political Economics*.

* For their help in preparing this paper, I thank: David Gordon, Richard Edwards, James Weaver, Jim Campen, Stephan Michelson, Frank Ackerman, and Dawn Wachtel. Many of the ideas in this paper have grown out of conversations with Mary Stevenson and Barry Bluestone.

teenth century America this was given a crude formulation within the industrializing ideology of individualism. The New Deal provided a temporary break from this tradition. However, this ideology has re-appeared in the more sophisticated mid-twentieth century liberalism in which we now reside. Public policy has mirrored these trends in social ideology, starting with the Elizabethan Poor Laws and their American counterparts down to the Great Society's poor laws.

Social science research has mirrored our social ideology. Virtually all of the past and contemporary social science research has concentrated on the characteristics of individuals who are defined as poor by the federal government. Being poor is associated with a set of individual characteristics: age, sex, race, education, marital status, etc. But these are not *causes* of poverty. There have been dozens of studies of the so-called "causes of poverty"; not surprisingly, these studies merely associate the "cause" of poverty with a particular set of individual characteristics. For example, if you are poor and have low levels of education, it does not *necessarily* follow that low levels of education are a cause of poverty since education itself is endogeneous to the system. The causes of inequality in education and their impact on incomes must be analyzed by examining social class, the role of the state, and the way in which educational markets function.[1]

There has been essentially no social science research in the last ten years on the question of poverty which has gone beyond a mere cataloging of the characteristics of the poor.[2] A proper formulation of the problem would start with poverty as a result of the normal functioning of societal institutions in a capitalist economy. Given the existence of poverty as a result of the functioning of societal institutions, the next question is: who is poor? Is poverty randomly distributed across the population with respect to various individual characteristics or is it nonrandomly distributed? Poverty research has demonstrated that the incidence of poverty is *nonrandomly* distributed in America. Blacks, Mexican-Americans, Indians, women, the old, etc., have a higher probability of becoming poor than do individuals without these characteristics. The so-called studies of the "causes" of poverty have simply estimated the differential importance of the individual characteristics associated with the poor. The research has only demonstrated which groups of people are affected most adversely by capitalist institutions.

[1] This question is examined in Sam Bowles, "Contradictions in U.S. Higher Education" (mimeographed, January, 1971).

[2] Even some of the more "sophisticated" statistical work has merely *measured* the differential importance of various personal characteristics while providing minimal insights into the *causes* of poverty. For example, see Lester C. Thurow, *Poverty and Discrimination* (Washington: The Brookings Institution, 1969), Chapter 3.

The orientation of this poverty research has not been accidental, and it reveals some interesting insights into the sociology of knowledge. Since the industrial revolution, the poor have been blamed for their own condition. They have been charged with causing squalor. Hence, the research of the 1960's has been rendered compatible with the prevailing ideology of capitalist countries with only a few minor modifications of the crude formulations of earlier centuries to make the ideology more palatable to a supposedly more enlightened populace. In this context, the research has performed an important stabilizing and obfuscating function; it has received wide acceptance precisely because it has been conveniently supportive of existing social arrangements and our prevailing social ideology.

THEORIES OF POVERTY

Examined from a perspective of radical political economics, poverty is the result of the normal functioning of the principal institutions of capitalism—specifically, labor markets, social class divisions and the state.

An individual's class status—his or her relationship to the means of production—provides the point of departure for an analysis of income inequalities and low incomes in an absolute sense. If an individual possesses both labor and capital, his chances of being poor or in a low income percentile are substantially less than if only labor is possessed. For individuals earning incomes under $10,000, nearly all income comes from labor. However, for individuals earning between $20,000 and $50,000 (in 1966), only slightly more than half comes from labor; while for individuals with incomes between $50,000 and $100,000 only a third comes from labor. And if you are rich—earning in excess of $100,000—only 15 percent comes from wage and salary earnings while two-thirds comes from capital returns (the balance is composed of "small business" income).[3]

More important than the magnitude of capital income is its unequal distribution in our economy. Were we to redistribute this income, we could alleviate the purely financial aspects of low incomes. A direct transfer of income that would bring every family up to the Bureau of Labor Statistics' "Moderate but Adequate" living standard in 1966 (roughly $9,100) would have required $119 billion.[4] This comes to about 20 percent of total personal income, slightly *less* than the proportion of personal income derived from ownership of capital.

[3] Frank Ackerman, Howard Birnbaum, James Wetzler, and Andrew Zimbalist, "Income Distribution in the United States" (mimeographed, 1970), pp. 14–16.

[4] Donald Light, "Income Distribution: The First Stage in the Consideration of Poverty," *Review of Radical Political Economics* 3, no. 3 (Summer, 1971).

Consequently, any meaningful discussion of the causes of income inequalities or low incomes must start with a discussion of Marx's class categories. The plain fact is that the probabilities of being both a capitalist and poor are slim compared with the opportunities for poverty if labor forms the principal means of acquiring income. And under capitalism, there is no mechanism for sharing the returns from capital—it all goes to the private owners of capital.

The individual's relationship to the means of production is only the starting point in the analysis. The labor market is the next institution of capitalism which must be analyzed to understand the causes of poverty. Given the fact that workers have no capital income, the chances of becoming poor are increased. However, not all workers are poor in any sense of that ambiguous term. This leads us to our next concept in the analysis—*social stratification*. Social stratification refers to the divisions within a social class as distinct from the class itself. In this context, the divisions among workers in the labor market lead to social stratification among the class of workers which has had important implications for the cyclical and secular movements in class consciousness.

The functioning of labor markets, interacting with individual characteristics of workers, determines the wage status of any particular individual in stratified labor markets. The labor market causes poverty in several important ways. Contrary to conventional wisdom, nearly every poor person is or has been connected with the labor market in some way. Poor individuals sift into several categories. First, there are enormous numbers of *working poor*—individuals who work fulltime and full year, yet earn less than even the government's parsimonious poverty income. These people earn their poverty. Of all poor families attached to the labor force in 1968, about one-third (1.4 million) were fully employed workers. Of the more than 11 million families with incomes under $5,000 in 1968, nearly *30 percent* were headed by a fulltime wage earner. The incidence of the working poor is greater among black poor families and families with female heads. About *22 percent* of all black poor families were headed by an individual working fulltime in 1968. And a *third* of all black families with incomes under $5,000 worked fulltime. The Department of Labor reports that 10 million workers in 1968 (nearly 20 percent of the private nonsupervisory employees) were earning less than $1.60 per hour —the wage rate that yields a poverty income if fully employed.[5]

---

[5] A few lone researchers have been trying to alert us to the plight of the working poor. The most comprehensive studies are: Barry Bluestone, "The Tripartite Economy: Labor Markets and the Working Class," *Poverty and Human Resources* (July–August, 1970), pp. 15–35, and Barry Bluestone, "Lower-Income Workers and Marginal Industries," in Louis A. Ferman, Joyce L. Kornbluh, and Alan Haber (eds.),

A second significant proportion of the poor are attached to the labor force but are not employed fulltime. Some of these individuals suffer intermittent periods of employment and unemployment, while others work for substantial periods of time and then suffer severe periods of long-term unemployment.

A third significant portion of the poor are handicapped in the labor market as a result of an occupational disability or poor health. However, these occupational disabilities are themselves related to a person's earlier status in the labor force. There are greater occupational hazards and opportunities for poor health in low wage jobs. Low incomes can contribute significantly to poor health, especially in the American markets for health care where enormous incomes or proper health insurance are an absolutely essential precondition for the receipt of medical care. Disabilities are widespread throughout the economy. In 1966, nearly *one-sixth* of the labor force was disabled for a period longer than *six months*. Only 48 percent of the disabled worked at all in 1966, while 12 percent of the employed disabled workers were employed only part-time. As a consequence of disability, many households with disabled heads are poor—about 50 percent.[6]

Thus we see that nearly all of these poverty phenomena are endogenous to the system—they are a consequence of the functioning of labor markets in the economy. This argument can be extended to birth defects as well. There is a growing body of evidence which suggests that many forms of birth defects are related to the nutrition of the mother which, in turn, is related to family income (itself dependent upon the class status of the family and the labor market status of the family wage earners). Even with the evidence as tentative as it is, we can say that the probability of birth defects is greater in families with low incomes and the resultant poor nutritional opportunities.[7]

Another category of the poor are not presently attached to the labor market—the aged, the prison population, members of the military, the fully handicapped, and those on other forms of public assistance (principally women with dependent children). Though these individuals are not presently attached to the labor force, in many instances their low income is determined by past participation in the labor force.

For example, the ability of aged persons to cope with their non-

---

Poverty in America (Ann Arbor: University of Michigan Press, 1968), revised edition, pp. 273–302.

[6] The President's Commission on Income Maintenance Programs, *Background Papers* (Washington: Government Printing Office, 1970), pp. 139–142.

[7] See Leon Eisenberg, "Racism, the Family, and Society: A Crisis in Values," *Mental Hygiene* (October, 1968), p. 512; and R. L. Naeye, N. M. Diener, W. S. Dellinger, "Urban Poverty Effects on Prenatal Nutrition," *Science* (November 21, 1969), p. 1026.

employed status depends upon their wealth, private pension income, savings and public pension income (social security). Each of these, in turn, is related to the individual's status in the labor force during his working years. The one partial exception is social security which is typically cited as an income equalizing program where payments are only partially related to contributions. But even in this case, the redistributive effects of social security are not as great as they have been advertized, as we shall see later in this paper. This point aside, the payments for social security are so small that retired people, dependent solely on this source of income, end up in the government's poverty statistics.

The important elements of income for retirees are all associated with past labor force status and with the class status of the individual. High paid professional and blue-collar jobs typically provide private pension supplements to social security, while low paid jobs do not. Individuals with income from capital can continue to earn income from capital beyond the years they are attached to the labor force, while wage earners cannot. High income workers and owners of capital have vehicles for ensuring their security in old age, while medium and low wage earners have only social and financial insecurity to contemplate in their old age.

To a somewhat lesser extent other poor nonparticipants in the labor force attain their poverty as a result of their (or their spouse's) past association with the labor force. Even for the handicapped, the prisoner, or the welfare mother, the labor market is not a trivial determinant of their poverty status.

If labor force status provides such an important and inclusive explanation of poverty among individuals, the next question is: what determines an individual's status in the labor force? For simplicity, we will take occupation as an imperfect proxy for labor force status, bearing in mind that there is substantial variation in wage status within occupational categories as well as among occupational categories.

In broad terms, an individual's wage is dependent upon four types of variables:

1. Individual characteristics over which the individual exercises no control—age, race, sex, family class status, and region of socialization.
2. Individual characteristics over which the individual exercises degree of control—education, skill level, health, region of employment, and personal motivation.
3. Characteristics of the industry in which the individual is employed—profit rates, technology, product market concentration, relation of the industry to the government, and unionization.

4. Characteristics of the local labor market—structure of the labor demand, unemployment rate, and rate of growth.[8]

One observation is immediately apparent: there are very few variables that lie within the individual's control that affect his labor market status. Even the individual characteristics placed in category two are not completely within the control of the individual. For example, as Coleman, Bowles and others have shown, education is heavily dependent upon the socioeconomic status of the family, an attribute which lies outside of individual control.[9] Health is partially endogeneous to the system as discussed above. Geographic mobility depends upon income and wealth.

This classification scheme is a useful starting point, but a more formal analysis is needed to understand the way in which these several categories of variables interact in the labor market to yield low incomes.

The occupation an individual enters is *associated with* individual characteristics: educational quantity and quality, training, skills, and health. These attributes are normally defined as the *human capital* embodied in an individual. The differences in these variables among individuals, which influence their entry into occupations, are dependent upon race, sex, age and class status of the family. Although human capital is *defined* by the set of characteristics associated with the individual, the *determinants* of the differing levels of human capital among individuals are found in the set of individual characteristics that lie outside of the individual's control.[10]

The story does not end here; the wage is not solely dependent upon the occupation of an individual. The fact that one person is a janitor, another a skilled blue-collar worker, tells us something about the wage that each will receive but not everything. There is a substantial variation in wage within each of those occupations that is dependent upon the industry and the local labor market in which an individual works. There are a variety of industrial and local labor market characteristics which yield different wages for essentially the same occupation and

8 This classification of variables is used to analyze low-wage employment in Howard M. Wachtel and Charles Betsey, "Employment at Low Wages," (mimeographed, 1971). In this study, industrial attachment was the most important determinant of wage earnings.

9 See Bowle's, *op. cit.*, and James S. Coleman, et al., *Equality of Educational Opportunity* (Washington: Government Printing Office, 1968). Data pertaining to this is contained in David Gordon (ed.), *Problems in Political Economy: An Urban Perspective* (Lexington: D. C. Heath & Co., 1971), pp. 178–181.

10 This model is borrowed from the work in progress of Barry Bluestone and Mary Stevenson.

level of human capital. The wage will be higher for a given occupation in an industry with high profit rates, a strong union, highly productive technologies, a high degree of product market concentration, and a favorable status with the government.[11] A similar type of analysis holds for the impact of local market conditions.

In sum, the individual has very little control over his or her labor force status. If you are black, female, have parents with low socioeconomic status, and dependent upon labor income, there is a high probability that you will have relatively low levels of human capital which will slot you into low-paying jobs, in low wage industries, in low wage labor markets. With this initial placement, the individual is placed in a high risk category, destined to end up poor sometime during her working and nonworking years. She may earn her poverty by working fulltime. Or she may suffer either sporadic or long periods of unemployment. Or she may become disabled, thereby reducing her earning power even further. Or when she retires, social security payments will place her in poverty even if she escaped this fate throughout her working years. With little savings, wealth, or a private pension income, the retiree will be poor.

In contrast with this radical political-economic theory of the causes of poverty, both conservative and liberal political-economic theories look for the cause of poverty in terms of some individual characteristic over which the individual is presumed to exercise control. The conservative theory of poverty relies upon markets in labor and capital to provide sufficient mobility either within a generation or between generations to alleviate poverty. If one does not avail himself of the opportunities for social and economic mobility through the market, the individual is to blame. The poor cause their own poverty and its continuation. The individual is presumed to be master of his own destiny, and individualism will lead any deserving person out of poverty. (Of course, the people who posit these notions are the nonpoor.) For the undeserving poor, only institutionalization of one form or another will do.[12] These people are trapped by their lower class life styles which prevent them from escaping poverty. If the poor would only work, there would be no poverty. The Elizabethan poor laws and their American counterpart considered unemployment a crime for which the penalty was work. Gilbert and Sullivan were appropriate when they said "let the penalty fit the crime."

The liberal (and dominant) theory of poverty grants some recog-

---

11 Barry Bluestone, "Lower Income Workers and Marginal Industries," pp. 286–301.

12 Edward C. Banfield, *The Unheavenly City* (Boston: Little, Brown and Co., 1968).

nition to institutions as partial causes of poverty as well as social class as an intergenerational transmitter of poverty. But rather than seeking remedies by altering these social institutions or searching for ways to break class rigidities, liberals concentrate their energies on trying to find ways to use government either to ease the burden of poverty or assist the individual in adapting to prevailing institutions. The liberals reject exclusive reliance upon the market to foster social mobility and attempt to use government to equalize opportunities within the market or assist individuals in coping with their poverty status by direct income transfers. Nonetheless, their commitment to "alleviating" poverty without systemic changes is as deep as any conservative's. Manifestations of this orientation abound. The entire social work profession, borne out of liberal social reform, exists principally to help people cope with a rotten personal or family situation. Hungry people are given nutritional advice rather than access to food, which would involve structural changes in agricultural markets.

The objective of liberal social policy is equal opportunity—a random distribution of poverty—though we are far from that goal today. The radical challenge goes as follows: if you start from a position of inequality and treat everyone equally, you end up with continued inequality. Thus the need to create equality in fact rather than in opportunities.

Manpower programs, educational assistance, and the like are the principal policy results of the contemporary liberal human capital approach to social mobility. All of these programs are based on an essentially *untested* view of the labor market: namely, that personal characteristics over which the individual has control are the major causes of unequal and low incomes. These programs are quite similar in their ideological premise to virtually all the poor laws of capitalist society, starting with the Elizabethan poor laws. Poverty is associated with the absence of work for which work is the cure. The poor are incapable of managing their own affairs so they must be "social worked" to adapt to the rigor and needs of an industrialized and urbanized society.

This view of poverty is wrong in theory, in fact, and in social values. The causes of poverty lie outside the individuals' control in markets for labor and capital and class backgrounds. Equally important, something happens both to the people seeking to help the poor and to the poor themselves when we take as our starting point the premise that people are poor because of some manipulable attribute associated with the person.

THEORIES OF THE STATE
AND THE POOR

Corresponding to the several political-economic theories of poverty are *theories of the state,* i.e., theories which discuss the origins and the role of government in eliminating poverty.

The *conservative* theory of the state views the origins of government as emerging from the consent of the governed. The proper economic role of the state is to leave things alone—*laissez faire.* The state exists solely to protect the basic institutions of capitalism—private property, markets in labor and capital, and markets in goods and services. It does this by providing both a domestic and a foreign military and by providing a system of courts to protect property and adjudicate disputes arising out of private property conflicts. The deserving poor will attain social mobility in this generation or the next via the normal functioning of markets. Any efforts by the state to interfere in this process will only distort these opportunities for mobility. Hence, the role of the state is simple: do nothing about the poor but protect their means to social mobility—free markets and capitalism.[13]

Liberals view the state as a mediator between conflicting interest groups in a pluralistic society. Since market institutions work imperfectly at best, the role of the state vis-a-vis the poor is to compensate for these shortcomings of the market by providing the opportunities denied to individuals by markets. "Where *opportunities* are free, the poor will disappear," might be a good liberal slogan. While the conservative would retort: "where markets are free, the poor will disappear." Liberals also recognize the existence of a residual population for whom no amount of indirect compensation will prevent their poverty. For these people, public welfare—direct payments—is the only solution.[14]

Radicals view the origin of the state in terms of a class of people who exercise dominant decision-making power in state institutions and who transmit their class power intergenerationally.[15] One's relationship to the means of production is an essential, but not exclusive, de-

[13] A recent statement of this view is in Milton Friedman, *Capitalism and Freedom* (Chicago: University of Chicago Press, 1962), especially Chap. 2.

[14] For an exposition and critique of the pluralist theory, see Jack L. Walker, "A Critique of the Elitist Theory of Democracy," *The American Political Science Review,* Vol. LX, No. 2 (June, 1966), pp. 285–295 and the reply in the same issue of the APSR by Robert A. Dahl, "Further Reflections on the 'Elitist Theory of Democracy'," pp. 296–305. Democratic pluralism has been integrated into economic literature by John Kenneth Galbraith, *American Capitalism: The Concept of Countervailing Power* (Boston: Houghton Mifflin Co., 1952).

[15] For a recent exposition of this theory, see Ralph Milliband, *The State in Capitalist Society* (New York: Basic Books, 1969).

terminant of power, and the education system is an intergenerational transmitter and legitimator of this power. This is not the place to probe deeply into this complicated subject, but ask yourself this question: who is powerful in your local community? Are these people workers or owners (and managers) of capital?

Given this view of power in the state, as distinct from the liberal pluralist view or the conservative consent-of-the-governed view, the role of the state is to ensure the continued survival and perpetuation of its class of decision-makers. If this analysis is valid, then the state becomes part of the problem rather than part of the solution. This does not mean that the same individuals or their inheritors have power in perpetuity, though this occurs—merely ponder the name Lodge, Harriman, or Rockefeller for awhile. This is why the term class is used, analytically distinct from a ruling elite or conspiracy theory of the state. In fact, liberals rather than radicals are the major proponents of conspiracy theories—witness the interest among liberals in a "military-industrial complex" conspiracy rather than a class analysis of the power of the military and its camp followers.

Several hypotheses flow from the radical theory of the state. First, government as a totality will reinforce the disequalizing tendencies of the market through its support of basic capitalist institutions even though liberals for the past 40 years have been attempting to do precisely the opposite. Second, programs to assist the poor will perhaps have some impact in the short run, but in the long run will either atrophy, become anemic in their impact, or become distorted in their purpose. Third, only those public programs that are compatible with the basic institutions of monopoly capitalism will see the light of day in the first instance and will survive to suffer the fate outlined above in the second hypothesis.

In contrast, liberals assume that the state intervenes on behalf of the underclass to redistribute wealth, opportunity, and privilege. In fact, the term used to characterize collective decision-making in economics is the *social welfare function*. As chapter three, "Government Spending and the Distribution of Income," shows, however, the possibility that state intervention buttresses the status quo, or even increases inequality in the distribution of income, cannot be dismissed.

chapter eleven

Labor markets, defense subsidies and the working poor

BARRY BLUESTONE

Contemporary labor market analysis, steeped in the "human capital" school of orthodox economics, has unfortunately led to the widespread belief that the poor are poor primarily because they lack marketable skills. Based on this analysis, the federal government has stressed manpower programs as the main route to improving the status of low-paid workers and the underemployed. Yet, human resource development programs have not met with unqualified success. Many argue that this has occurred because the *specific* manpower programs have been misdirected or underfunded. The facts of the matter, however, suggest that the source of poverty may lie more in the weaknesses of the American industrial structure than in the weaknesses of the poor themselves. Attempts at reducing poverty by remaking the poor rather than restructuring the economy have met with limited success.

To develop an antipoverty strategy that has a greater chance of success requires a new labor market analysis. Such an analysis must seek to understand both the weaknesses of those who find themselves impoverished *and* the inadequacies of a market structure which make poverty wages and poor working conditions characteristic for a significant part of the workforce. A new labor market analysis, based on the tripartite nature of the American economy, is necessary to place the problem of the low-paid worker in proper perspective.

THE WAR ON POVERTY

The federal government directed between $140 and $170 billion in aid to the poor during the decade of the sixties.[1] State and local

"Labor Markets, Defence Subsidies, and the Working Poor" (editor's title). From Barry Bluestone, "The Tripartite Economy: Labor Markets and the Working Poor," in *Poverty and Human Resources Abstracts* 5, no. 4 (July–August 1970): 15–35. Reprinted by permission of Sage Publications, Inc.

[1] Estimated from *The Budget of the United States Government: Fiscal Year 1970* (Washington: U.S. Government Printing Office), p. 47.

governments may have added as much as an additional $100 billion to bring the total of publicly provided antipoverty funds to something in excess of a quarter of a trillion dollars during this period. Such an expenditure is not insignificant, even when measured against other federal programs, in particular those related to defense, which swamped this sum by a factor of at least three.

The progress made against poverty during the past decade is limited, but not insignificant. In 1959, there were 8.3 million families in the United States who were officially designated as "poor" according to the very low poverty standard established by the Social Security Administration.[2] Nearly one in five American families was regarded as impoverished under this standard. A decade later the poverty threshold, adjusted for increases in the cost of living, was surpassed by all but 10 percent of the families in this country.

Nonetheless, in 1968 there remained 22 million people living in 5 million families classified as poor by the SSA criterion. A more realistic poverty line developed by the Bureau of Labor Statistics more than doubles the number of poor families.[3] Data from the Current Population Report on family income in 1968 indicate that 22.4 percent of all families in the nation had a total money income of less than $5,000.[4] For urban families of four, a $5,000 annual income fell short of the "low" BLS budget by more than a thousand dollars in 1968.

The quarter of a trillion dollars has aided many families, but nevertheless has been inadequate to ameliorate, much less eliminate, the economic and social plight of all of the disadvantaged. However, the failure of the poverty program to do more for more of the poor, cannot be explained purely on the basis of inadequate funding. More poverty funds will inevitably improve the economic position of the poor, but the uses to which the funds are put determines how effective the total antipoverty strategy will be. During the sixties, there is good reason to believe that in addition to the unsatisfactory level of spending, the distribution of the poverty program dollar left something to be desired. Not enough went into income maintenance programs, not enough went into manpower programs; but even beyond this, *much* too little was

---

[2] U.S. Department of Labor, *Manpower Report of the President* (Washington: U.S. Government Printing Office, March 1970), p. 120.

[3] Bureau of Labor Statistics, *Three Standards of Living for an Urban Family of Four Persons* (Washington: U.S. Government Printing Office, March 1970), p. 7. The "lower" budget to maintain family health and well-being at a minimum adequate level was $5,915 in 1967. This budget allows an average urban family of four to purchase a nutritionally adequate diet, just adequate rental housing, and other requisites to exist in a reasonable, but unelaborate fashion.

[4] U.S. Department of Commerce, *Current Population Reports: Income in 1968 of Families and Persons in the United States* (Washington: U.S. Government Printing Office, December 1969), Table 24, p. 60.

directed toward expanding the number and quality of job opportunities for the poor and much too little for the economic expansion of the regions and industries where the poor are prevalent. In the seventies, more emphasis in these areas will be necessary if an antipoverty strategy is to be fully successful. Before this will occur, however, it will be necessary to reanalyze a good part of the theory underlying the antipoverty strategy of the last decade.

PROGRAMS IN AID OF THE POOR
IN THE 1960s

During the 1960s the federal government fought poverty with a diversified strategy. Nonetheless, the most powerful tactic used in the battle was not explicitly aimed at the poor. In 1961 the overall unemployment rate stood at 6.7 percent. For women the rate was 7.2 percent and for minority groups, especially among the young, the rate of unemployment exceeded 30 percent in some urban areas. By 1969 the overall unemployment rate had fallen to 3.5 percent, much of this reflecting the increased employment opportunities for nonwhites. Over this period the unemployment rate for nonwhite males, for instance, fell from 12.8 percent to 5.3 percent; for females from 11.8 percent to 7.8 percent.[5] Such employment gains played a crucial role in bringing many families above the poverty line during the sixties. This did not come about automatically, however. Unemployment remained above 5 percent until the 1964 tax cut and the growth of federal expenditures in the late sixties gave a needed boost to aggregate demand.

Three-fifths of the federal share of the $250 billion ten-year total and an even higher percentage of the state and local contribution to the eradication of poverty was directed into cash assistance for the poor.[6] In 1961 nearly seven-eighths of all federal funds directed toward the poor were in the form of cash assistance. By 1970, with the tremendous growth in poverty programs, cash assistance still accounted for nearly 50 percent of all federal outlays for the poor. If one includes federal provision for health programs, housing, basic education, and food programs aimed at the poor, more than *five-sixths* of total federal anti-poverty outlays are accounted for. *While absolutely needed to ensure even bare subsistence, these funds attack the effects of poverty, not the root causes.*

For the disabled, the aged, and for others who cannot work, cash and commodity assistance is the only solution to poverty. Many of these people remain poor for the simple reason that present levels of

---

[5] *Manpower Report of the President,* Table A-12, p. 229.
[6] *Budget of the U.S. Government,* p. 47.

maintenance are much too low. For those capable of work, however, income security programs, no matter how necessary for immediate relief, are no more than temporary palliatives. For these millions of people, an attack on the *causes* of poverty is necessary. It is therefore the remaining *one-sixth* of federal outlays for aiding the poor which is most in need of study.

THE MANPOWER
PROGRAMMING BIAS

By 1969, the federal government was spending over $2.1 billion a year in attempts to "upgrade," "rehabilitate," "train," "retrain," "integrate," "reintegrate," and "prepare" the poor for the prevailing job market. This was done through such programs as MDTA, the Job Corps, the Work Incentive program, and JOBS.

In contrast, little constructive thought, and even less money, was allocated to deal with the imperfections in the economic system itself, imperfections which force millions of Americans of adequate skill into poverty. While Congress added some teeth to equal employment opportunity legislation and raised the minimum wage from $1.00 to $1.60 during the decade, little was done to affect the structure of labor markets and the systemic immobilities of both labor and captial which account for a significant part of the continuing poverty problem. Funds for economic development—the creation of new jobs and new and expanded industries—were limited to a total of $508 million in 1969, less than a quarter of the budget for manpower programs.

Since 1964 the largest relative increases in poverty funds have been in basic education, job training, and other employment aids. Outlays for these purposes, plus those for health assistance, rose from 11 percent of total aid in 1964 to nearly 40 percent in 1970.[7] In contrast, the Area Redevelopment Act of 1961 was never well funded and its successor, the Public Works and Economic Development Act of 1965, with its emphasis on long-range economic-development for areas with persistent unemployment and low family income, has never had much money to loan or spend. In fiscal 1968, for instance, the Economic Development Administration, created under the 1965 Public Works Act, loaned only $52 million for business development and funded only $175 million in public facility projects. The total appropriated in 1969 was a meager $275 million.[8]

The bias toward refurbishing people and against refurbishing eco-

---

[7] *Ibid.,* p. 46.

[8] Sar A. Levitan, *Programs in Aid of the Poor in the 70's* (Baltimore: Johns Hopkins Press, 1969), p. 68.

nomic institutions was clearly exposed in a recent statement by former Secretary of Labor George Shultz in testimony before the Ways and Means Committee. With respect to the newest antipoverty design, the Family Assistance Program, Shultz told the committee:[9]

I hasten to add that the labor market itself must be recognized as a constraint on the full achievement of our expectations. It is a fact that our economy has a lot of jobs that pay low wages. We are not going to be remaking the encomy in this program. We have to relate to the labor market. We can only put people in the jobs that exist.

What this means is that we will have to thread our way between our goals of providing good jobs—after training when possible—and the realities of the kinds of jobs that are available.

The bias toward human resource development programs stems partly from the fear that technological progress is destroying all low-skill jobs. In turn, Congress tenaciously holds to the belief that the economic evolution experienced in the U.S. is self-generating and on balance good for society. Tampering with the evolutionary process through specialized incentives for economic expansion in low-wage industries and depressed regions is consequently considered unwise. Rather than government attempting to intervene in those industries where low wages prevail, Congress has been determined to emphasize the need for producing manpower which can meet the "challenge of future job markets." In the meantime, while federal outlays for manpower programs grow, millions of workers continue to toil at jobs which pay them no more than enough to ensure their poverty.

THE WORKING POOR

If all of the poor were incapable of work or so permanently unskilled that only the most menial jobs were available to them, the problem of poverty would be widespread, but the solution would be straight-forward: income maintenance. In fact, however, the majority of poor and near-poor families have heads of household who work for their poverty, often at jobs requiring sophisticated skills. In 1968, for instance, 50.2 percent of families with income below $3,500 were headed by persons who worked at least sometime during the year. Within this group of 3.4 million families, there were 1.4 million where the head of household worked full-time all year long. More than one in five families with income below this low standard had a fully employed head. For the more than 11 million families with income of

9 George Shultz, *The Family Assistance Act of 1969* (statement before the Committee on Ways and Means, House of Representatives, October 16, 1969).

less than $5,000 in 1968, almost 30 percent were headed by a person who worked full-time all year long. Black families were even more prone to work for their poverty. Of the 1.4 million black families with income less than $3,500, more than 6 out of 10 had a working head of household, and more than 22 percent worked full-time all year long. Almost a full third of all black families with incomes under $5,000 were headed by a person who worked full-time for 50 or more weeks during the year.

In many cases, low income among families is due either to involuntary part-time employment or to employment which is erratic or seasonal. Nevertheless, wage rates are so low in many industries that even full-time year-round employment results in a poverty income. In 1968, for instance, the Department of Labor reported over 10 million people in the labor force working at jobs which paid $1.60 or less per hour in cash wages, nearly a full fifth of the private nonsupervisory employees in the economy.[10] Of full-time year-round employees, nearly 2.8 million men representing 7.5 percent of the full-time male workforce earned less than $3,000 in 1968; one in five men working this much earned less than $5,000.[11] For women employed full-time year-round, over 20 percent earned under $3,000 and *three out of every five* had total money earnings of less than $5,000. While low wages can be found in virtually every industry and most occupations, poverty wages are concentrated in agriculture, nondurable goods manufacture, retail trade, and personal services. Operatives, laborers, sales clerks, and clerical workers are most prone to suffer low-wage employment.

Whether the government *can* influence the level of wages within any given industry or region is of great importance to the millions of low-wage workers in the economy. If government is powerless in this regard, or if the social costs of public intervention in the economy are prohibitive, then the human resource development strategy is the only one left for those poor, but capable of work. On the other hand, there is mounting evidence that government has had a profound influence on the present distribution of wage income in the economy. In this light explicit policies toward depressed economic sectors can indeed have an impact on the incomes of a sizable number of the working poor.

The debate over the best strategy for improving the economic standing of the poor must begin with a serious discussion of whether, and how, part of the economic structure of American society can be altered to the benefit of the disadvantaged. Labor economists have begun to

---

[10] U.S. Department of Labor, *Manpower Report of the President* (Washington: U.S. Government Printing Office, April 1968), Table 5, p. 27.

[11] *Current Population Reports*, Table 45, pp. 108, 110.

develop a meaningful framework within which the debate can be fruitfully joined.

POST-WAR LABOR ECONOMICS AND THE STUDY OF POVERTY

Labor market investigation in the 1950s was oriented toward the "demand" side, or industry side, of wage determination. During this period, labor economists concentrated on researching inter-industry and inter-regional wage differentials and developing models to measure the effects of unionization, profits, concentration, and capital intensity on industry wages.[12] Major stress was placed on explaining why the automobile industry pays so much more to its semiskilled workers than the textile industry.

In most of these early studies, differences in "human capital" between employees in different industries were either discounted or ignored altogether. Variation in wage rates and total remuneration among members of the working class was explained in terms of "demand" side variables alone, e.g., industry profits, capital intensity, unionization, and the characteristics of product demand. The implication of these studies, although not always explicitly stated, is that relative wage rates and therefore relative employee incomes can be affected through changes in the structural or institutional framework of an industry. Unionization, for example, can materially and substantially affect the incomes of the labor force in an industry. Increased capital investment can do likewise. If the results of these studies are correct, significant inroads against impoverishment can be made if structural factors affecting the low-wage sector of American industry can be altered.

The 1960s saw a major shift away from these industry studies to research on "human capital." Labor economists led by Gary Becker, Edward Denison, and Theodore Schultz began to focus on the supply side of wage and income determination.[13] Abstracting from, or often

---

[12] See Harold Levinson, *Unionism, Wage Trends, and Income Distribution* (School of Business Administration, University of Michigan, 1957); J. W. Garbarino, "A Theory of Inter-industry Wage Variation," *Quarterly Journal of Economics*, 64, 2 (May 1950); Lloyd Reynolds and Cynthia Taft, *The Evolution of the Wage Structure* (New Haven: Yale University Press, 1956); Lloyd Reynolds, *The Structure of Labor Markets* (New York: Harper and Row, 1951); Arthur M. Ross and William Gouldner, "Forces Affecting the Interindustry Wage Structure," *Quarterly Journal of Economics*, 64, 2 (May 1950); and Clark Kerr, "The Balkanization of Labor Markets," in E. Wight Bakke, *Labor Mobility and Economic Opportunity* (New York: Wiley, 1954).

[13] See Gary S. Becker, "Investment in Human Capital: A Theoretic Analysis," *Journal of Political Economy*, 70, 5, Part 2 (October 1962); Walter Y. Oi, "Labor

just overlooking, the effect of industry and institutional structure on wages and labor force participation, the human capital oriented social scientists concentrated on the education, skills, training, health, mobility, and attitudes of the labor force. It was the human capital approach which lent a theoretical base to the manpower development strategy for solving the problems of the poor. Differences in income among individuals were attributed almost solely to differences in the amount of human capital each worker has at his disposal. Those with more education, more training, better health, and greater mobility were found empirically to possess higher incomes.

To make this point clear, the human capital oriented economist often analyzes the whole spectrum of occupations from physician to janitor, correlating income with education and skill. The high correlation is said to indicate the importance of human capital elements in income determination. The implication from the whole spectrum is unfortunately often extrapolated to every segment of the range. According to the strict human capitalist, more education and skills for the working poor will inevitably lead to significantly higher incomes, as it has for professionals and other highly skilled workers. Unfortunately, this is not necessarily true. A cross-section analysis of the entire occupational structure often misrepresents the dynamics of any individual segment of the spectrum. Therefore, while the education/income correlation may be high for physicians measured against janitors, the human capital implication for those who do not aspire to a college degree may be misleading. For much of the working class, it may be more important to be in a high wage industry at any level of skill than to be adequately skilled and trapped in an industry which offers only low wages. For many of the working poor, the problem may lie in the industries in which they work, not in the skills they individually possess.

BILATERAL LABOR MARKET SEGMENTATION

In the 1950s too little attention was paid to differences in the inherent productivity of the workforce; in the 1960s, too little to the real economic and institutional differences among industries and firms. A revised labor market model is needed which pays proper attention to both sides of the wage nexus and, what is more, accounts for the

---

as a Quasi-fixed Factor," *Journal of Political Economy*, 70, 6 (December 1962); T. W. Schultz, "Investing in Poor People: An Economist's View," *American Economic Review*, 55, 2 (May 1965); and Edward Denison, *The Sources of Economic Growth in the United States and the Alternatives Before Us* (New York: Committee for Economic Development, 1962).

imperfections in mobility of both labor and capital. The model must posit "segmentation" on both sides of the market, for labor is not fully mobile between sectors of the economy and industries vary greatly in terms of their ability to pay high wages. The imperfections in labor mobility and the lack of competitiveness among industries and firms in the economy may be precisely what is responsible for the low income of many of the working poor.

In the formal model below, industries of diverse economic and institutional characteristics operating within product and labor markets characterized by chronic immobility are represented as I_1, I_2, and I_3. Segments of the labor force, each with a different level of human capital, are represented by H_1, H_2, and H_3. The curve H_1 represents individuals possessing a relatively small stock of human capital. These individuals have little formal education, few technical skills, and may be less then completely dependable as workers. H_2 and H_3 represent segments of the work force possessing more education, higher skills, possibly better health, greater on-the-job dependability, etc. One might view these individual segments of the labor force as possessing various degrees of *endogenous productivity.**

The professional economists must be cautioned immediately against interpreting the diagram in the conventional supply and demand framework. The curves, I_i ($i = 1,2,3$), are *not* conventional demand curves since they do not embody any information about the *total* marginal physical product of labor. On the other hand, these curves, unlike normal demand curves, embody information on the degree of unionization in the industry. In essence, the I_i curves indicate the relative state of an industry (or individual firm) in terms of profit, capital, unionization, and product elasticity. I_1, for instance, represents an industry characterized by low profits, low capital intensity, weak unionization, and highly elastic product demand.

This model has a number of interesting implications:

1. Differences in labor "quality" can account for a significant degree of wage inequality. For instance, a worker possessing the characteristics of H_3 labor in industry I_1 will earn a significantly higher wage than a worker in the

---

* The term "endogenous" productivity refers here to the productivity of an individual disregarding or holding constant the amount of physical capital at his disposal. We can take the example of two typists, who, given the same electric typewriter, could produce exactly the same output. These two typists have the same total productivity as well as equal endogenous productivities. However, if one of the typists was forced to work on an outdated portable while the other was permitted to use a modern electric, the former would have a total productivity well below the latter, although the two typists would still have equal endogenous productivities. In a world of barriers to mobility, this distinction becomes vital.

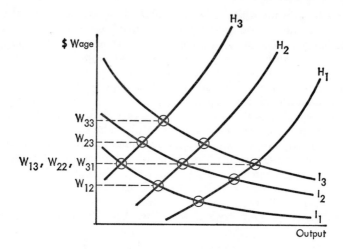

same industry with H_1 education, skills, etc. This accords well with the human capital school.

2. On the other hand, differences in the characteristics of industries can explain substantial differences in the wages of labor like quality. Two individuals, both with generally the same complement of human capital, say H_2, but employed in different industries, I_3 in one case, I_2 in the other, will earn significantly different amounts according to this model.

3. Furthermore, workers of different quality can earn roughly similar wages or the more "qualified" individual can earn less because of the industry attachment of each worker. A relatively low-skilled employee in industry I_3 can indeed earn more than a higher-skilled worker who becomes trapped in industry I_2 because of institutional barriers to mobility.

In case 1, a skilled machine operator in the automobile industry will probably earn more than an unskilled sweeper or semiskilled assembly line worker. In case 2, a semiskilled operative in the textile industry will earn less than an equally skilled operative in the fabricated steel industry. The worker in the textile firm may be trapped in that industry because of barriers to geographical mobility, because of racial or sexual discrimination, or because of the risk of moving from one industry to another after seniority has been accumulated in the low-wage industry. At any moment in time, high-wage industries may be laying off rather than hiring because of temporary recessions, thus limiting entrance into the high-wage sector. Trade unions, especially in the construction industry, may restrict entry into the high-wage sector through apprenticeship programs specifically designed to limit the size of the labor force. For these or other reasons, many qualified workers remain rooted in low-wage industries.

If labor mobility were perfect, the wage of each individual (after accounting for "equalizing" differences due to different working conditions, risks attendant to the job, etc.) would accurately reflect differing amounts of human capital. Although wage differentials would still exist, they would be solely a function of the endogenous productivity of each worker. *"From* each according to his ability; *to* each according to his skill" would prevail. The return on being the right color or the right sex at the right time and in the right place would be reduced to zero.

Unfortunately for a large segment of the working class, and especially the poor, labor mobility is far from perfect. The barriers to mobility can be classified into three groups:

Individual Barriers to Mobility

Insufficient education
Insufficient training and skills
History of unreliable job performance
Disutility of geographical mobility
Disutility of occupational mobility

Industrial Barriers to Mobility

Hiring and on-the-job racial discrimination
Hiring and on-the-job sexual discrimination
Trade union barriers to entry
Use of "education level" as a pure rationing device

Social Barriers to Mobility

High financial cost of geographic relocation
Personal risk attached to mobility
High levels of aggregate unemployment
Racism
Sexism
Lack of labor market information

Such a partial listing of the barriers to mobility indicates some of the difficulty of ensuring perfect labor force flexibility in the economy. What is even more crucial is that, except for the first three, the individual worker has virtually no control over these barriers to mobility. Hence, in the absence of extensive government involvement in the restructuring of labor markets, the individual is seldom in the position to do much in the way of increasing his own mobility.

A number of studies of labor mobility, including that of Parnes,[14] the Organisation for Economic Co-operation and Development

14 Herbert S. Parnes, *Research on Labor Mobility* (New York: Social Science Research Council, 1954).

(OECD),[15] and Lansing and Morgan,[16] have stressed the mobility problems of low-income classes. While mobility may be high for the labor force as a whole, the "vertical" mobility of the poor is considerably lower because of discrimination, extreme risk, and the high financial costs of interregional relocation. In addition, mobility may be increased in general because of a temporary or permanent buoyancy in the economy, yet fail to trickle down to the disadvantaged. Immobilities on the one hand and the segmented nature of the "demand" side on the other, in terms of the differential ability of industries to pay adequate wages, appear to force large numbers of adequately skilled workers, both white and black, male and female, to remain in low-wage industries.

It is important to note that programs designed merely to increase the mobility of the labor force will not be successful in eliminating poverty. While particular individuals now denied high-wage jobs may benefit from a removal of market barriers, low-wage jobs will still exist. At best, increased mobility will distribute workers more "fairly" over the existing set of jobs. The wage of each worker may now more accurately reflect his relative ability rather than his race, sex, class, or age. Some black workers will exchange places with some white workers in the occupational hierarchy and some women will replace men, but increased mobility alone will *not*, in general, increase the number of high-wage jobs or reduce the number of jobs at poverty wages.

THE TRIPARTITE ECONOMY

The formal segmented labor market model, with barriers to mobility of both labor and capital, provides a good theoretical framework for analyzing low-wage poverty. However, a more simple, more aggregative approach to market fragmentation will better identify the economic and institutional factors which differentiate industries from one another. Empirical observation of the American industrial structure suggests a tripartite organization within the economy as a whole. Such a schema includes a central or core economy, a peripheral sector,[17] and finally what Louis A Ferman has called an "irregular" economy.[18] Each segment of the overall economic structure can be

---

[15] Organisation for Economic Co-operation and Development, *Wages and Labour Mobility*, 1965.

[16] John B. Lansing and James N. Morgan, "The Effect of Geographical Mobility on Income," *Journal of Human Resources*, 2, 4 (Fall 1967).

[17] Robert T. Averitt, *The Dual Economy: The Dynamics of American Industry Structure* (New York: W. W. Norton and Co., 1968).

[18] Louis A. Ferman, "The Irregular Economy," (Institute of Labor and Industrial

described with a unique set of "demand" side or industry characteristics.

THE CORE ECONOMY

The core economy includes those industries which comprise the muscle of American economic and political power. The core economy is by far the largest sector of the three in terms of financial resources. Entrenched in durable manufacturing, the construction trades, and to a lesser extent, the extraction industries, the firms in the core economy are noted for high productivity, high profits, intensive utilization of capital, high incidence of monopoly elements, and a high degree of unionization. What follows normally from such characteristics are high wages. The automobile, steel, rubber, aluminum, aerospace, and petroleum industries are ranking members of this part of the economy. Workers who are able to secure employment in these industries are, in most cases, assured of relatively high wages and better than average working conditions and fringe benefits.

Robert R. Averitt has listed the economic advantages of the large core economy firm.[19] These include

1. extensive assets which allow center firms to outspend smaller peripheral firms;
2. better geographic and product diversification which allows center firms to withstand losses in one area or on one product almost indefinitely;
3. vertical integration which allows center firms to underbid free agent and forward satellite retailers for large contracts;
4. the ability of center firms to become their own suppliers and distributors, thus insuring low-cost inputs and a distribution network;
5. favored access to finance when credit is scarce or restricted; and
6. political advantage: center firms can maintain a staff in Washington to advise on the locus of critical decision making, what information to prepare, and who to see.

Such factors are often decisive in gaining favorable laws and administrative rulings on such matters as tariffs, taxes, and subsidies, as well as successful contract bids. In addition, the extensive resources available to the core economy firm allow such firms to spend the great amounts on research and development necessary for continued high profits in a dynamic economy.

Relations, Research Division, University of Michigan-Wayne State University, mimeo, 1969).

[19] Averitt, *The Dual Economy*, p. 70–71.

THE PERIPHERAL ECONOMY

Beyond the fringes of the core economy lies a set of industries which lack almost all of the advantages normally found in center firms. Concentrated in agriculture, nondurable manufacturing, retail trade, and subprofessional services, the peripheral industries are noted for their small firm size, labor intensity, low profits, low productivity, intensive product market competition, lack of unionization, and consequently low wages. Unlike core sector industries, the periphery lacks the assets, the sheer size, and the political power to take advantage of economies of scale or spend large sums on research and development. At the present rate, the peripheral industries are more than likely doomed to a continuation of the "repressive economic environment" they are accustomed to.

The workers who are trapped in the periphery become the working poor. In many of these industries, more than half the workforce was employed during the sixties at wage rates under the 1966 equivalent of $1.60 per hour.

THE IRREGULAR ECONOMY

The irregular economy, the third sector in the tripartite schema, includes the vast bulk of monetized economic activity which is not included in the national income accounts. The "industries" in this sector, mainly concentrated in the ghetto, have escaped the scrutiny of the Social Security Administration and the Internal Revenue Service by remaining informal and only loosely attached to the organized network of the regular economy. To a great extent, the irregular economy involves

1. informal work patterns that are frequently invisible to outside observers;
2. an organized set of occupational roles specific to ghetto life;
3. work skills and competencies that are a product of ghetto life; and
4. the acquisition of work skills and competencies through nontraditional channels.

Some of the work opportunities in the irregular economy are deviant by middle class moral and legal standards, but most are not. Job activities may range from daily contract work for gardening to plumbing, electrical work, and automobile repair. These job experiences allow the worker to engage in pseudoentrepreneurial activity that is closed to him in the other two sectors of the economy.

In a broader sense, the irregular economy provides the ghetto with a pattern of economic life that is largely nonconventional in its learning and opportunity structures. The ghetto is a market place for a wide range of occupational skills that do not fit neatly into the occupational skill categories and criteria operative within the conventional labor market. The nonunion or nonlicensed craftsman, the home appliance repairman, the "Mr. Fixit," the street or door-to-door hustler, all fall within the irregular ghetto economy. In addition, illegal activities—dope peddling, prostitution, gambling, etc.—are part of this economic sector.

For many full-time and part-time participants in the irregular economy, the only alternative open in the regular economy is work in the peripheral sector. Compared to the periphery, the irregular economy often offers higher wages, better working conditions, and a sense of independence. For this reason many ghetto residents choose to work in this sector of the economy.

There is good reason to believe that mobility from the irregular economy or the periphery to core sectors firms is severely limited for a significant segment of the working poor. While some of this immobility can probably be traced to a lack of skills, "improper" work attitudes, and other human capital factors, a good deal of it is due to institutional barriers erected either capriciously or purposefully by firms, by unions, and by the explicit or implicit action or inaction of government.

Mobility between sectors may be increased during periods of rapid economic growth, but significant structural changes in the underlying economy will be necessary if the inter-sectoral barriers to mobility are to be lowered. High levels of aggregate demand can be of only temporary help. Manpower programs, at the very best, might alter the composition of the working poor, but the number of jobs at poverty wages will not be reduced.

BEYOND MANPOWER PROGRAMMING

In a recent article, Michael Piore of MIT argued that:

The manpower problems of the urban ghetto appear best defined in terms of a dual labor market; a *primary* market offering relatively high-paying, stable employment, with good working conditions, chances of advancement and equitable administration or work rules; and a *secondary* market, to which the urban poor are confined, decidedly less attractive in all of these respects and in direct competition with welfare and crime for the attachment of the potential labor force.[20]

[20] Michael Piore, "On-the-Job Training in the Dual Labor Market," in Arnold R.

Piore defines the two markets according to the "stability" of the individuals within the labor force, rather than the characteristics of the industries, and thus is led to assume that individuals become low-wage workers because of unstable working habits. More simply, he argues that low wages in the secondary market (the periphery) are a function of an unstable work force. In fact, the direction of causation between instability and low wages may run precisely in the opposite direction: the ghetto labor force may be unstable because it is doomed to low wages. Under these conditions, losing one's job is not much more catastrophic than keeping it. If this is the case, higher wage rates in the ghetto may be sufficient to develop a better, "more stable" workforce.

In an empirical study of the ABCD manpower project in Boston, Peter B. Doeringer concludes that in fact low wages may be the cause of instability rather than the reverse.[21] The mean hourly rate on the last four jobs held by ABCD applicants before they joined the program was $1.83. The Doeringer study went on to report that:

When asked why they left the ABCD jobs, many applicants mentioned the low wage, the poor working conditions and lack of advancement opportunities. *These workers knew that such menial jobs are always available and that the accumulation of an erratic work history would not be a barrier to obtaining menial jobs in the future*[22] (emphasis added).

If the ghetto labor force is to become more productive, it is probably more important to restructure ghetto industries than to attempt to restructure the work habits of the working poor. It is shown empirically, at least for this one project that "instability of labor force experiences . . . rather than lack of education or skills characterized many ABCD applicants."[23]

EDUCATION AND EARNINGS AMONG THE WORKING CLASS

A key human capital variable in many labor force studies is formal education level. Across the whole range of occupations, formal education appears to explain a great part of the variance in personal income. The manpower development prescription for ameliorating wage poverty has been, to a great extent, based on such empirical find-

---

Weber (ed.) *1969 Research Volume of the Industrial Relations Research Association*, 1969, p. 102.

21 Peter B. Doeringer, ed., "Low-Income Labor Markets and Urban Manpower Programs: A Critical Assessment" (report submitted to the Office of Manpower Research, U.S. Department of Labor, January 1969).

22 *Ibid.*, p. 14.

23 *Ibid.*, p. 12.

ings. However, the results of some preliminary research on the effect of formal education on working class income differentials appears to contravene some of the conclusions drawn from the earlier studies.

Using data from the 1960 Population Census, a crude estimate can be made of the effect of education on mean hourly earnings of working class males.[24] Table 1 correlates an index of hourly earnings by occupation with the median years of education completed by the labor force in that occupation. Clearly, in every occupation but one, education explains some of the variance in wage rates. In fact, the simple regression analysis used here probably underestimates the effect of education on wages for a number of reasons. Median years of education fails to recognize differences in the "quality" of education and is much too gross an estimate of the extent of education in an occupation. Formal education reflects only one source of "human capital" and is therefore an inadequate measure of on-the-job productivity. Furthermore, the absence of other qualifying variables such as race, age, and region tends to cloud the real effect of education on earnings.

Nonetheless, even if the effect of education on earnings were *double* the estimates in Table 1 education would explain less than half of the variance in wages for operatives and kindred workers, service workers, and laborers. For the total sample of 249 occupations, education would account for little more than a *third* of the total variance in earnings. What is evident from these data is that the type of occupation and industry one works in is more important than the amount of formal education one has received. Male service workers, for instance, are, on the average, better educated than either laborers or operatives. Nevertheless, men who become trapped in service trades because of race, lack of job information, or risk engendered by mobility, end up earning, on average, over 25 percent less than operatives and 20 percent less than laborers. A similar situation would probably be found if female employment were investigated.

The return to an added year of education appears to be quite low for most working class occupations. For all operatives and kindred workers, an extra year of high school will add only about $.19 an hour to an average paycheck. For service workers, the addition is less than $ .17, and for all occupations combined, the addition for another year of education is only $ .15 an hour according to the regression analysis used here. Salesmen and salesclerks appear to contradict some of these results. Yet this is the exception that proves the rule. The occupations within the category "salesmen and salesclerks" range from highly skilled wholesale tradesmen who need to understand the intricacies of

24 U.S. Department of Commerce, Bureau of the Census, *U.S. 1960 Census, Series PC (2) 7A, Occupational Characteristics* (Washington: U.S. Government Printing Office, 1969).

TABLE 1: THE EFFECT OF FORMAL EDUCATION ON WORKING CLASS OCCUPATIONAL WAGE DIFFERENTIALS OF MALES. REGRESSION COEFFICIENTS AND MEANS BY OCCUPATIONAL CATEGORY, 1959

Average Hourly Earnings[1] $[W] = a + b$ (Education)[2] $[E]$

Occupation	W	E	a	b	R[2]
Salesmen and sales clerks	$2.37	12.16	−6.0023	.6883 (.1053)	.79
Operatives and kindred workers—specific skills	2.34	9.55	1.4987	.0881 (.0583)	.05
All operatives and kindred workers	2.34	9.50	.5135	.1926 (.0306)	.23
Service workers	1.69	9.59	.0683	.1685 (.0842)	.20
Laborers, excluding farm and mine	2.11	8.79	−.1554	.2582 (.0605)	.18
Total sample	2.22	9.40	.8030	.1505 (.0215)	.17

Source: United States Census of Population, Subject Report PC(2) 7A, Occupational Characteristics; U.S. Department of Commerce, Bureau of the Census, 1960.

[Standard errors are in ( ).]

[1] Average hourly earnings refers to an index of earnings based on median annual earnings in an occupation divided by hours and weeks worked.

[2] Education is measured by median school years completed in an occupation.

their industry in detail, to part-time salesclerks in limited-price variety stores. Here, the range of skill and education is quite broad and we would expect education to explain a significant portion of the total variance in earnings.

No doubt if we were to analyze _all_ occupations from the most menial to the professional, the relationship of education to income would also be extremely significant. The reason for this is self-evident. Yet when we investigate the impact of education on earnings _within_ an occupational class, in this case the traditional working class, we find that beyond the pure statistical decrease in total variance, education explains much less of the remaining variance. This is largely due to the barriers, imperfections, and immobilities which characterize the American labor market and overshadow the human capital elements in wage determination. Concentrating solely on the human capital side of the market through manpower programming will therefore solve only part of the problem.

RESTRUCTURING THE TRIPARTITE ECONOMY

These preliminary studies, the research done by labor economists in the 1950s, and more comprehensive studies now underway indicate that the elimination of poverty in America requires bold efforts on *both* the supply side *and* the demand side of the market. The human capital component of the poor needs augmenting, but of equal importance, existing low-wage jobs must be upgraded to provide adequate income for the workers who fill them. The creation of new jobs at decent wages is also needed if poverty incomes are to be abolished. This requires restructuring America's tripartite economy.

Here, the discussion will be restricted to the demand side or industry side of the wage nexus. This is not so much because the supply side has been dealt with adequately in poverty programs, but because the demand side has not been dealt with at all. The strategies suggested in this section indicate the need for greater social planning of the overall economy. For this reason, such strategies have been rejected in the past and no doubt will face strong opposition from many quarters in the future. Intervening on the supply side has never carried the onus which is historically associated with deliberate intervention on the demand side of the market.

Regardless of official rhetoric, government has never been neutral in the marketplace. Federal, state, and local governments combined are responsible for nearly a third of the annual output of the whole economy, and the distribution of government purchases is heavily weighted toward a small set of goods and services. Government, merely as consumer, exerts a powerful influence on the distribution of profits, wages, and wealth among industries. And as public expenditures increase relative to private consumption, government's distributional impact on the economy will increase as well.

In terms of federal purchases in 1970, $82.2 billion or 78 percent of a budgeted total of $105.6 billion was earmarked for the defense department.[25] This 78 percent was heavily concentrated in a small number of industries, notably aerospace, electronics, ordnance, and transportation equipment. To a great extent, these industries are part of the core economy precisely because of government intervention in the marketplace. The addition to an industry's total product demand, due to government purchases, often makes the difference between that industry rising into the core economy or being left behind in the periphery. None of the peripheral industries are noted for large defense contracts. Within the list of peripheral industries, only hospital services are significantly affected by government expenditures. Low wages in retail trade, personal services, and nondurable manufacturing, as well as in agriculture, are a function, in part, of government purchasing policy.

The federal government has also had an investment policy and a tax policy which are far from neutral. Much of the private core economy

---

[25] *Budget of the U.S. Government,* Special Analysis A, p. 15.

benefited from $45 billion in government-financed capital investment during World War II and shortly thereafter.[26] During the war, the federal government built plants and outfitted them with machinery for private industry. Much of this investment was amortized over a period of five years, thus amounting to a continuing subsidy for certain industries. Again, the beneficiaries were primarily within the core sector. Many industries, in fact, developed the attributes of the core economy specifically because of such direct government grants to private industry. The periphery, on the other hand, gained little.

The application of federal corporate tax policy has also not been neutral. The corporation income tax has been constructed in such a way as to give maximum gain to the core economy. Liberalized depreciation and depletion allowances, investment credits, and other special tax write-offs favor the concentrated, capital-intensive, high profit industries of the core economy. The peripheral firms, when they realize a profit, are often taxed at higher rates than many industrial giants. Such a policy has had a significant and measurable effect on inter-industry wage differentials and wage increases over time.

In the past there has never been an explicit recognition of the public manipulation of wage differentials. The tripartite economy is *de facto* testimony, however, of the strategic role government plays in structuring individual industries and economic markets.

[26] Robert J. Gordon, "45 Billion of United States Private Investment Has Been Mislaid," *American Economic Review*, 59, 3 (June 1969).

VI

Social scientists and the poor

Frances Fox Piven, Professor of Politics at Boston University, is coauthor with Richard Cloward of *Regulating the Poor*. Piven and Cloward's articles in *The Nation* are generally credited with stimulating the welfare rights protest movement and the development of the Welfare Rights Organization. Dr. Piven, an urban planner and political scientist, taught for many years at the Columbia University School of Social Work and has spoken frequently to social scientists, social workers and low-income groups. In the following chapter, originally presented as a talk to the Massachusetts Sociological Society, Piven examines critically the role social scientists have played in the formulation and development of public policies for the poor. She concludes by recommending actions social scientists and others could take to actually reduce poverty and inequality.

c h a p t e r   t w e l v e

Social science and social policy

FRANCES FOX PIVEN

When social scientists convene to discuss "social science and social policy" it is ordinarily with the firm conviction that social science is useful in formulating more benign and effective social policies. We take it for granted that social scientists can provide political lead-

Talk delivered before the Massachusetts Sociological Society, May 5, 1973. Copyright © by Frances Fox Piven, 1973. Reprinted by permission of Frances Fox Piven.

ers with accurate assessments of the current state of social affairs, and with accurate prognoses of the outcomes of alternative government policies. And we also take it for granted that political leaders will use these "scientifically based" assessments in the neutral and objective spirit in which they are presumably given. Whatever might be the potential uses of social science in social policy if there were no such thing as politics, these views ignore the actual uses of social science and social scientists in politics. Bound by the conviction that we play a useful role consistent with our credo, we refuse to pay attention to the ways in which our knowledge and authority are regularly abused by policy makers to serve purposes quite different from those we profess.

The debate over the role of social scientists and professionals in the Great Society programs illustrates how our convictions restrict our understanding. The work of Daniel Patrick Moynihan provides a particularly striking example, for while Moynihan's view of the value of these programs changed over time, his view of the role of social scientists did not. Thus, in 1965, Moynihan wrote an article entitled "Professionalization of Reform" [1] in which he argued that we had arrived at a new era in policy formulation. The outstanding achievements of this new era he credited to professional social scientists. Their ability to observe, measure, and record the state of our society, particularly the state of the poor in our society, had made possible a mode of policy-making that was virtually above politics, that did not depend upon the intrusion of clamorous interest groups. A few years later Moynihan published a book called *Maximum Feasible Misunderstanding*.[2] By this time Moynihan was by no means so sanguine about the Great Society programs. Indeed, he had come to the conclusion that they were all a dreadful mistake. But just as, in 1965, he saw professional social scientists as playing a major role in promoting good policies, in 1969 he saw professional social scientists as playing a major role in promoting the series of mistakes by which "The great Republic had —incredibly, monstrously—been brought to the point of instability."

The assumptions implicit in these judgments, when stated baldly, are startling. We are told that the political system of the United States can be moved by the whim or whimsy of a few social scientists, either wise and well-informed social scientists, or foolish and slovenly social scientists. In other words, the series of major federal programs for the inner cities first begun in 1962 and regularly expanded until 1967 had little to do with major social, economic, and political upheavals in this country associated with the black migrations to the cities; had little

[1] Daniel Patrick Moynihan, "Professionalization of Reform," *The Public Interest*, no. 1 (Fall, 1965): 6–16.

[2] Daniel Patrick Moynihan, *Maximum Feasible Misunderstanding* (New York: The Free Press), 1969.

to do with the resulting electoral problems of the National Democratic Party; had little to do with the rising disturbances of dislocated and unemployed peoples in our impacted urban ghettoes. These developments are put to one side and instead we are told that professional social scientists relying on good data or bad data, on good theory or bad theory, shaped the public policies of the federal government.

Moynihan has, of course, been widely criticized by the social scientists he alternately applauds and condemns. But he has been criticized for the position that he has taken in supporting or opposing particular public programs, and not for the role that he attributes to social scientists. Instead, social scientists in the universities, in the foundations, and in the federal bureaucracies, make claims that are quite consistent with Moynihan's underlying view of the relationship between social science and politics.

For example, one of the programs singled out for criticism by Moynihan was the Mobilization for Youth project established on the Lower East Side of New York City in 1962. The Mobilization project was widely regarded as the prototype of the Community Action Programs, which were to follow some years later. It was also a prototype for the use of social science in the federal social policies of the 1960s. Moynihan attacked the social scientists who were involved for having been irresponsible in their use of social science. But the social scientists themselves made this attack seem plausible by virtue of the claim they also made for the role of social science in the design of the project. They themselves considered the Mobilization project as nothing less than a "scientific demonstration in social policy." Even in the early 1960s, when social scientists had somewhat more of a right to be naïve about government and politics, this claim was clearly not credible, and for several reasons.

First, the Mobilization for Youth planners claimed that a social science theory, in this case, a theory of delinquency, guided the design of both research and action. But to specify a general theory of delinquency in terms sufficiently concrete so as to identify the specific empirical variables that ought to be subject to research, and the specific empirical variables that ought to be addressed by action programs, was, to say the least, no mean feat, and, in fact, one never accomplished. Instead, the researchers satisfied themselves, and the government agencies on which they depended, by conducting community surveys. This resolution of the problem was not surprising, for survey techniques are very popular among social scientists.

Second, for the project to be a "scientific" demonstration in any sense, the substantial research program which was conducted in the community ought to have been conducted *prior* to the design of the action program. That is the very least that a "scientifically" planned program ought to mean. But not surprisingly the several federal and local government agencies which were involved in the project were less interested in the actual conduct of the research prior to the establishment of the action program than they were in the claims that research had been done. Consequently, the research and the design of the action program went on simultaneously, not sequentially. And, of course, whatever research was done was not the basis for the design of the action programs.

Third, a "scientific demonstration in social policy" would have required that the results of each of the specific endeavors undertaken by the Mobilization for Youth project be evaluated scientifically. This in turn would have required first, the clear structuring of each of these endeavors; the components of policy would have had to be clearly specified; and once specified, could not be changed without compromising the research. Second, it would have required that control groups be set up so that those who were exposed to the program could be contrasted with those who were not. And third, it would have required that the desired outcomes anticipated in designing each of these specific endeavors be specified in advance. Whether it is in fact possible to design action programs to suit these minimal requirements of evaluational research is a moot point. At best, it would have been difficult; in the less-than-best real world, it was never actually tried, for the bureaucratic and political imperatives which ultimately shaped the specific programs of the project were far more important than evaluational research requirements—far more important not only to the program administrators, but to the social science researchers themselves.

Finally, it was also claimed that the program was a comprehensive, multifaceted approach to the social problems of the Lower East Side. That is, the knowledge supplied by the social sciences regarding the complex, interrelated etiology of a host of social problems would be reflected in a complex, interrelated series of social programs. Surely this was, even allowing for the enthusiasm of social scientists newly appointed as policymakers, a preposterous sort of claim. Little enough was understood about the etiology of any particular social problem, and any particular form of amelioration, much less of the effects of a "comprehensive and multifaceted" approach. In any case, were the approach indeed to be comprehensive and multifaceted, it would have been all the less likely that the project could have fulfilled its simultaneous claim as a scientific evaluation of particular forms of social intervention.

My object, however, is not to criticize the scientific merit of the work of the social scientists who were involved in the government programs of the 1960s. Rather, I am trying to argue that what they did was very different from what they claimed to be doing and they ought to have known as much and acknowledged as much. Social scientists and social science did not play much of a role at all in the overall design of the programs of the 1960s. But they did play an important role in facilitating and justifying these programs. Rather than providing the scientific basis for the formulation of policies, they provided the scientific authority which political leaders borrowed to justify these policies. Rather than providing knowledge which would make possible scientific precision in policy formulation, they lent to policymakers the obscurantism of their scientific language which facilitated federal policy simply because it dulled the wits of those who might have disagreed. To serve these purposes, it was important only that the social scientists who became involved with federal policy provided a general outlook congenial with the federal approach. In the 1960s that simply meant that social scientists ought to have a theoretical perspective which stressed the importance of local institutional arrangements in the generation of social problems because it was to these local institutions that federal programs in delinquency, manpower, education and poverty were addressed. But aside from this general outlook stressing the importance of local institutions and institutional change in the amelioration of social problems, the relationship of social science theory to the specific programs generated by the federal government remained vague and suggestive.

All of this is only to say that social scientists and social science cannot be given either much of the credit or much of the blame for the federal domestic policies of the 1960s, for they did not formulate those policies. Rather they served in a process which was of course political. As federal policy-makers struggled to contend with the forces unleashed by black migration to the cities, they turned to social scientists to provide some of the justification and protection they required.

The politics and programs of the Kennedy and Johnson administrations are now a thing of the past. The Nixon administration, reflecting its distinctly different political constituencies, has introduced a series of new policy "innovations" of its own, many of which consist in the elimination of programs inaugurated during the Great Society period. Once again, we find social scientists much in evidence.

Those who have now come to the fore emphasize the importance of stability and constraint in maintaining social order, and emphasize the importance of heredity and family in the creation of "social problems." If these perspectives do not represent "scientific" findings, neither did the institutional change theories of the 1960s represent scientific findings. The difference between the one and the other is less one of science than of fundamental political outlook. But whatever the nature of the theories, the social scientists of the Nixon administration are no more shaping or forming the new policies than did the social scientists of the Kennedy-Johnson regime. It is simply that changed directions in federal policy have created opportunities for a different group of social scientists, and indeed may even create new social science fashions.

It follows from this that when President Nixon condemns the programs of the 1960s for having been "ineffective," his accusation is true enough, but largely misleading. It is true in the sense that programs advertised as expert-designed solutions to social problems, were in fact nothing of the sort. It is misleading because the fundamental outlines of government policy are never shaped by social science experts and can never stand the test of scientific effectiveness in terms of ostensible program goals. If we choose to play the game, the wheel will spin, and we will have our turn at hauling similar assaults of "ineffectiveness" at the Nixon administration's alternatives to domestic policies of the 1960s.

As government policies go, the federal programs for the cities in the 1960s were relatively benign. If the uses of social scientists by government were limited to such efforts, there might not be such need for wariness. But, of course, social scientists have managed to make themselves useful to government in many other policies as well. Thus, although social scientists did not create the Cold War, they eagerly served in justifying it. Although social scientists did not create the war in Vietnam, they again eagerly served in justifying it. Social scientists do not create executive concentration in the federal government but, as executive concentration proceeds, whittling away what remains of a pluralist polity in the United States, social scientists readily provide the expert opinions that justify it.

The patterns evident in the federal government are evident in city government as well. Again, social scientists did not create the large-scale, "expert"-manned bureaucracies that regularly service and defer to the business and property groups that dominate city politics. Nor do social scientists need to take credit for periodic "reorganizations" of city government, each of which successively removes the local bureaucracies further and further from the possibility of citizen control. Social scientists have neither the will nor the means to create oligarchy; they are merely the willing handmaidens of those who do have the will and the means. The services that they provide for the powerful are those of justification and obscurification, whether in the heady language of the "science" of international relations or in the dull and plodding jargon of administrative science.

My conclusions are simple. In the American experience, social science has not served as the basis for policy formation, but as one basis for the enhancement of power. Like the priesthoods of old, social scientists today give their blessings, and their mumbo-jumbo justifications, to policies decided by those who really rule. Nor is there much reason to think that the involvement of social scientists with government will follow a different pattern in the future. The temptations that power holds for social scientists are great. They include the temptations of grants, ever more tantalizing as social scientists become more and more committed to elaborate and expensive research undertakings. They include the tantalization of power, or at least the reputation and rituals of power. In any case, whatever the motives of social scientists who become involved with government, the condition of their involvement is their subservience; the relationship will be maintained only so long as the social scientists provide the kinds of "expertise" that are useful to political leaders.

WHAT SHOULD SOCIAL SCIENTISTS DO?

One might ask, what should social scientists do? The answer, of course, is to stay away from government, to stay away from those earnest, self-important endeavors known as social policy formation. True, social scientists would then have to be satisfied with doing independent, small-scale investigations. But much is possible on a small scale. We could do critical evaluations of American public policies, drawing on the vast data resources of government itself, and testing and questioning that data with unyielding criticality. We cannot rely on government, or government-paid social scientists, to do as much. We ought to do comparative studies, so that American public policies can be scrutinized in comparison to the public policies of entirely different societies. And finally, we ought to begin to build a more systemic understanding of the relationship of social problems and social policies in the United States to basic structural features of the American political economy. All of this can be done, and it can be done within the limited resources that are available without government grants, contracts, and consultantships. But it will not be done until at least some social scientists resist and defy the twin temptations of money and power.